DOES LAW MATTER FOR ECONOMIC (

EUROPEAN STUDIES IN LAW AND ECONOMICS SERIES

DOES LAW MATTER FOR ECONOMIC GROWTH?

A Re-examination of the 'Legal Origin' Hypothesis

Guangdong Xu

intersentia

Cambridge – Antwerp – Portland

Intersentia Publishing Ltd.
Sheraton House | Castle Park
Cambridge | CB3 0AX | United Kingdom
Tel.: +44 1223 370 170 | Email: mail@intersentia.co.uk

Distribution for the UK:
NBN International
Airport Business Centre, 10 Thornbury Road
Plymouth, PL6 7 PP
United Kingdom
Tel.: +44 1752 202 301 | Fax: +44 1752 202 331
Email: orders@nbninternational.com

Distribution for the USA and Canada:
International Specialized Book Services
920 NE 58th Ave. Suite 300
Portland, OR 97213
USA
Tel.: +1 800 944 6190 (toll free)
Email: info@isbs.com

Distribution for Austria:
Neuer Wissenschaftlicher Verlag
Argentinierstraße 42/6
1040 Wien
Austria
Tel.: +43 1 535 61 03 24
Email: office@nwv.at

Distribution for other countries:
Intersentia Publishing nv
Groenstraat 31
2640 Mortsel
Belgium
Tel.: +32 3 680 15 50
Email: mail@intersentia.be

Does Law Matter for Economic Growth? A Re-examination of the 'Legal Origin' Hypothesis
Guangdong Xu

© 2014 Intersentia
Cambridge – Antwerp – Portland
www.intersentia.com | www.intersentia.co.uk

ISBN 978-1-78068-246-4
D/2014/7849/94
NUR 820

British Library Cataloguing in Publication Data. A catalogue record for this book is available from the British Library.

ACKNOWLEDGEMENTS

Five years ago, when I was admitted by the Erasmus School of Law (ESL) as a doctoral candidate, it seemed to be an impossible mission to complete a thesis that would meet the basic academic standards and language requirements of ESL in a timely manner, given that I had never written and published academic papers in English. In addition, as an associate professor at the Research Centre for Law and Economics (RCLE) at the China University of Political Science and Law (CUPL), I was occupied with my daily work, such as giving lectures and supervising students, and I faced serious problems with time management. Fortunately, I am blessed with friends, colleagues, and family who have never hesitated to encourage, help, and support me in this fantastic academic adventure. Thanks to their helping hands, I have finally reached the end of this journey, with this book (based on my doctoral thesis) as the landmark.

Prof. Michael Faure, my promoter, is the person that I want to thank first and foremost. It was by accident that Prof. Faure became my promoter; luckily, it turned out to be a happy accident. None of the improvements in my thesis writing would have been possible without his informative guidance, inspiring encouragement, and continuous help. I hope that this book is worthy of the tremendous help that I have received from him over the last five years.

I owe great thanks to Mrs Weichia Tseng, managing director of the Erasmus University China Centre (EUCC), and her assistants, such as Sizhen Rao and Yaxian Wu. Mrs Tseng and her team have provided valuable and indispensable help throughout my doctorate studies, including document preparation, information notification, and accommodation assistance. Their efficient work and generous help have made my studies and my stay in the Netherlands easier and more convenient. Help from Prof. Yuwen Li and her team at the Erasmus China Law Centre was also appreciated.

This book benefited greatly from my experience as a visiting scholar at the Rotterdam Institute of Law and Economics (RILE). I enjoyed my stay at the RILE, where my colleagues not only treated me with friendship and hospitality but also inspired and motivated me with their excellent studies. I am extremely grateful to Marianne Breijer and Wicher Schreuders for their efforts in helping me to prepare for the visit, to fit into the community at RILE, and to facilitate my stay at RILE. I am equally thankful to Prof. Klaus Heine and Prof. Alessio M. Pacces, who have always been willing to provide valuable comments on my thesis and reviewed the thesis as members of the inner committee. Comments and suggestions from another member of the inner committee, Dr Niels Philipsen, are also highly appreciated.

Papers based on different parts of this book have been presented in seminars at CUPL, the University of Bologna Law School, International Institute for Asian Studies (Leiden), and the Royal Netherlands Academy of Arts and Sciences (KNAW). I have benefitted greatly from discussions with and comments by seminar participants, including Prof. Gilberto Antonelli, Dr Julan Du, Prof. Hans-Bernd Schaefer, Prof. Jan Smits, and Prof. Thomas Ulen. Comments from Prof. Jonathan Klick and Dr Rainer Kulms have been helpful and appreciated. I also want to thank Prof. Robert Cooter, who sponsored my visit to the UC Berkeley School of Law, where I first became interested in the connection between legal rules and economic growth.

I want to express my special gratitude to my colleagues at the RCLE, whose spirit of devotion and solidarity make the RCLE a wonderful team. My gratitude goes especially to Prof. Tao Xi, director of the RCLE, who has made every effort to facilitate my research, and to Dr Binwei Gui, who has helped me to reach a deeper understanding of the problems in the empirical literature through his expertise in econometrics. I equally owe thanks to Mrs Liang, the secretary of the RCLE. This book has also benefited from my teaching experience in the RCLE, where I have consistently learned from the intelligent and challenging questions raised by the master's and doctoral students. In particular, I thank Wenming Xu, Liu He, Haixin Gong, and Nan Yu for their excellent research assistance.

I am lucky to have good friends on whom I can always rely, regardless of the situation. Weiqiang Hu helped me immensely during my stay in Rotterdam, Wei Zhang offered valuable comments and suggestions on my thesis, and Zhiyong Sun taught me to pay attention to what was happening in the real world. Fang Wang's continuous encouragement is the power that drives me to march onward and to never give up.

Although my parents may not understand the subject of my work, they do their best to support my studies and are proud of every single achievement that I have made. My wife is a great partner in my life. Her understanding, encouragement, and support are the preconditions without which this book could not have been accomplished.

Finally, I am grateful to the publisher Intersentia for their kind, professional, and efficient support in the publication of this book.

CONTENTS

LIST OF ABBREVIATIONS

ACFTU	All-China Federation of Trade Unions
ADRI	antidirector rights index
BERI	Business Environmental Risk Intelligence
CCP	Chinese Communist Party
CI	coordination index
CMEs	coordinated market economies
CPRs	common property resources
D&O Insurance	directors' and officers' liability insurance
DOJ	US Department of Justice
FD	Fair Disclosure
Fed	US Federal Reserve System
FPPR	formal private property rights
FSA	British Financial Service Authority
GADP	government antidiversion policies
GDP	gross domestic product
ICRG	International Country Risk Guide
IFC	International Finance Corporation
LLSV	La Porta, Lopez-de-Silanes, Shleifer, and Vishny
LMEs	liberal market economies
LSE	London Stock Exchange
NASD	US National Association of Securities Dealers
NPC	National People's Congress of China
NYSE	New York Stock Exchange
OECD	Organization for Economic Co-operation and Development
OLS	ordinary least squares
OTC	over-the-counter
OTCBB	OTC Bulletin Board
ROA	return on assets
RMB	Renminbi
SEC	US Securities and Exchange Commission
SEPA	China's State Environmental Protection Administration
SIB	British Securities and Investment Board
SMEs	small and medium-sized enterprises
SOEs	state-owned enterprises
SPC	Supreme People's Court of China

SROs	self-regulatory organisations
TFP	total factor productivity
TVEs	township and village enterprises
2SLS	two-stage least squares

LIST OF TABLES AND FIGURES

TABLES

FIGURES

CHAPTER 1

INTRODUCTION

"The consequences for human welfare involved in questions like these are simply staggering. Once one starts to think about them, it is hard to think about anything else".

> Lucas (1988)

This study addresses the role of legal institutions in economic growth. The notion that institutions profoundly influence economic performance is, of course, an old idea, which may be dated to the late eighteenth century when Adam Smith wrote his *An Inquiry into the Nature and Causes of the Wealth of Nations*. According to Adam Smith, the security of property rights against expropriation by fellow citizens or the state is an important condition for encouraging individuals to invest and accumulate capital, which in turn would boost economic growth. Smith's wisdom persists and is reflected in contemporary approaches that have used history and theory to make the case that institutions are crucial to economic growth.

Broadly, institutions contribute to economic growth by shaping individual incentives and governing markets. Different institutions lead to different economic environments and hence different incentives: while some "good" institutions create the correct incentives that encourage productive activities, including saving, investment, innovation, and entrepreneurial behaviour, other "bad" institutions open the door for unproductive activities, such as opportunism, rent-seeking, and corruption. It is a basic principle of economics that resources tend to gravitate toward their most valuable uses if a market is permitted to function. However, markets are so fragile that they cannot operate in isolation without institutional support designed to reduce transaction costs, eliminate externalities, and promote competition. Briefly, economic growth will be achieved by "getting the incentives right" and "getting the price right" through a set of rules, institutions, and policies.

Compared to so-called informal institutions such as social norms, culture, and social capital, legal institutions are recognised to exert a more important influence on economic performance in contemporary economies, which are based on complex and large-scale impersonal exchange and hence render informal institutions ineffective. As North (1990: 58–59) clearly states, the emergence and survival of the state as a credible, low-cost, and formal third party with the responsibility for monitoring property rights and enforcing agreements by the threat of coercion is a necessary condition for realising the gains from trade inherent in the technologies of the modern, interdependent world. North's theory has been extensively expanded by subsequent studies, among which the most notable may be the works of La Porta et al. (1997, 1998), which resulted in substantial controversy by stressing the superiority of common law over civil law in economic growth. Contributions of La Porta et al. also inspire this research, which attempts to comprehensively understand the relationship between legal systems and economic performance.

1.1. ECONOMIC GROWTH: THE BIG PICTURE

Economic growth is typically measured by the increase in a country's output of goods and services, or what economists call gross domestic product (GDP). Economic growth is desirable because more rapid growth in output and services in an economy translates into higher incomes for everyone, and high incomes would in turn make it possible for more individuals to live a more enjoyable and satisfying existence. High income is undoubtedly not the only goal of society[1], but it will make other valuable goals such as good health, a clean environment, leisure and entertainment more viable. Possible merits of high national income are reflected in figures 1.1 and 1.2,[2] which document that differences in GDP per capita are strongly associated with differences in consumption and health as measured by life expectancy. Thus wealthy countries not only produce more goods and services than poor countries, but their citizens also consume more and live longer.

---

[1] For an extensive discussion of how income and other economic indicators influence individual happiness, see Frey and Stutzer (2001). They find that factors such as rising income only minimally increase individual happiness, while institutions that facilitate more individual involvement in politics (such as democracy and local autonomy) have a substantial effect.

[2] These figures are called scatter plots. In a scatter plot, each observation (countries in this case) is represented by a single point. One variable (log GDP per capita in figures 1.1 and 1.2) is measured along the horizontal axis, and one variable (log consumption per capita in figure 1.1 and life expectancy in figure 1.2) is measured along the vertical axis. A scatter plot allows us to observe the overall relationship between two variables, particularly the correlation, which describes the degree to which two variables tend to move together. The lines in these figures are known as regression lines, which make the correlation between two variables more apparent.

Figure 1.1. The association between GDP per capita and consumption per capita in 2000

Log consumption per capita, 2000

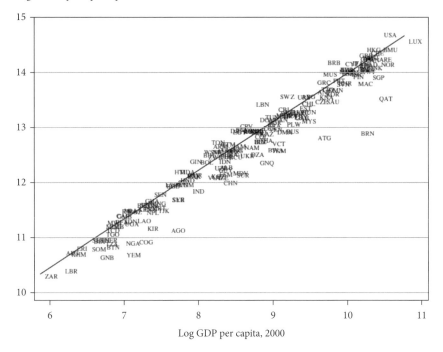

Source: Acemoglu (2009: 7).

Economic growth rates are significant because even small inter-country differences in per capita income growth rates, if sustained over long periods of time, lead to remarkable differences in relative standards of living between nations. A convenient rule of thumb that might be helpful in understanding the consequences of economic growth is the so-called "rule of 70", which states that a country growing at *g* percent annually will double its per capita income every 70/g years (Lucas, 1988; Jones, 1998: 10). For example, any country with per capita income growth of g = 2% will see its living standards double in 70/g = 35 years. In the short term, the economic gains from growth may not be apparent owing to a modest growth rate; however, welfare will improve notably over multiple generations.[3]

---

[3]   For instance, the annual average compound growth rate of GDP per capita in Western Europe from 1820 to 1998 was only 1.51%, which nonetheless improved the level of GDP per capita from 1,232 dollars to 17,921 dollars (both measured in 1990 international dollars) and made Western Europe one of the most wealthy regions in the world (Maddison, 2003: table 1.2).

Figure 1.2. The association between GDP per capita and life expectancy at birth in 2000

Life expectancy, 2000 (years)

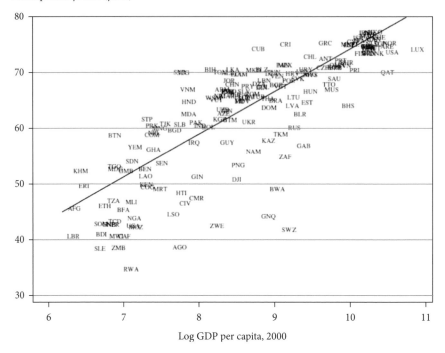

Log GDP per capita, 2000

Source: Acemoglu (2009: 8).

Snowdon and Vane (2005: 590–591) illustrate the striking impact of economic growth on national wealth using an example of five hypothetical countries. As table 1.1 shows, there are five countries labelled A–E, each of which begins with a per capita income of $1000 but will experience different growth rates in the coming years. Over a period of 50 years, variations in growth rates (g) among countries A–E cause a substantial divergence of relative standards of living.

Unfortunately, a review of human history leads us to agree with McCloskey on her judgment that "no previous episode of enrichment approaches modern economic growth – not China or Egypt in their primes, not the glory of Greece or the grandeur of Rome" (McCloskey, 1994). Sustained, long-term economic growth is a fairly recent phenomenon, and no society achieved steady growth before the nineteenth century. According to Maddison (2003), global GDP per capita was no higher in the year 1000 than in the year 1, and only 53% higher in 1820 than in 1000. At some time around 1820, Western Europe experienced a substantial transformation that drove the economies of Western Europe and its offshoots (Australia, Canada, New Zealand, and the United States) onto a path of sustained growth, or what Kuznets (1966) termed "modern economic growth".

Table 1.1. The cumulative impact of differential growth rates

Period in years	A g = 1%	B g = 2%	C g = 3%	D g = 4%	E g = 5%
0	$1 000	$1 000	$1 000	$1 000	$1 000
10	1 100	1 220	1 340	1 480	1 630
20	1 220	1 490	1 800	2 190	2 650
30	1 350	1 810	2 430	3 240	4 320
40	1 490	2 210	3 260	4 800	7 040
50	1 640	2 690	4 380	7 110	11 470

Figure 1.3. The evolution of average GDP per capita in Western offshoots, Western Europe, Latin America, Asia, and Africa, 1820–2000

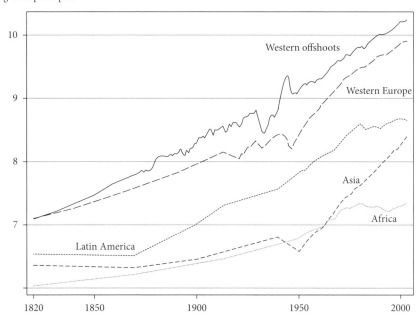

Source: Acemoglu (2009: 13).

Gradually, "modern economic growth" spread from its origins in Western Europe to other parts of the world and resulted in dramatic improvements in standards of living. However, this diffusion has been highly uneven and in some cases negligible. The result of this long period of uneven growth is the nearly unbelievable and substantial differences in incomes per capita between the wealthiest and poorest countries. Figure 1.3 illustrates the difference by depicting the evolution of average income among five groups of countries: Africa, Asia, Latin America, Western Europe, and offshoots of Western Europe.

As figure 1.3 shows, the proportional gap in GDP per capita between the wealthiest countries and the poorest grew from 3 in 1820 to 19 in 1998. In brief, uneven growth led to unprecedented global inequality, or what Pomeranz (2000) calls the "Great Divergence".

What explains this great divergence? To answer this question, it is necessary to delve into the determinants of growth. In other words, we need to identify the specific factors that differ in quantity and quality between countries and play a fundamental role in explaining divergent economic performance. In this study, we attempt to contribute to this issue by focusing on the institutional structures of economies that could explain a majority of the differences in economic growth rates among countries and over time. In particular, we will devote particular attention to the legal system, which provides critical incentives for all members of society to conduct value-creating or value-adding activities instead of unproductive behaviours, such as fraud, theft, and even extortion.

1.2. LAW MATTERS: WHAT WE KNOW AND WHAT WE DO NOT

Over the past several decades, a number of scholars have devoted themselves to exploring the aforementioned problems and provided alternative theories on potential sources of cross-country income differences. Numerous variables, such as capital accumulation, technological progress, productivity, policy choice, political structure, the legal system, and even geography are investigated on both the theoretical and empirical levels. We will survey these studies in the following chapter. The proposition that institutions[4] matter seems to receive the most support from the evidence, across both time and space, and has thereby become the consensus among scholars, advisors, and even international agencies (Acemoglu, 2009; Helpman, 2004; Weil, 2005; World Bank, 2002).

On a theoretical level, North pioneered a theoretical framework for understanding the relationship between institutions and long-run economic success or failure and thereby provided explanations for the emergence of the Industrial Revolution and the rise of the Western world (North and Thomas,

---

[4] Different scholars define institutions in different ways, which leaves some ambiguities and confusion. According to neoclassical economists, institutions should be identified with the rules of the game. For example, North (1990: 3) states that "institutions are the rules of the game in a society or, more formally, are the human devised constraints that shape human interaction. In consequence they structure incentives in human exchange, whether political, social, or economic". Conversely, game theorists regard institutions as equilibrium outcomes of the game rather than the rules of the game. According to this approach, institutions are rules of conduct. However, instead of being given exogenously by the political or legislative process, such rules are assumed to be endogenously created within the economic process as a solution to the game (Schotter, 1981: 11; Aoki, 2001: 7–9). Unfortunately, no clear, measurable and broadly agreed-upon definition has yet emerged.

1973; North, 1981, 1990). Another precursor, Mancur Olson, also argues for the importance of institutions and identifies the conditions necessary for economic development as including "a government that is believed to be both strong enough to last and inhibited from violating individual rights to property and rights to contract enforcement" (Olson, 1993). Consequently, a lack of efficient institutions that encourage productive cooperation hampers poor countries from realising their potential income, as if hundreds of billions or even trillions of dollars were dropped on the sidewalk (Olson, 1996).

Proponents of the proposition that institutions matter are increasingly supporting their case with numerous empirical studies that focus on such institutional factors as democracy (Barro, 1996; Minier, 1998; Durham, 1999), property rights (Knack, Keefer, 1995; Clague et al., 1999; Hall, Jones, 1999; Acemoglu et al., 2001, 2002), inequality, distributive conflict, political instability (Alesina, Rodrik, 1994; Alesina et al., 1996; Alesina, Perotti, 1996; Barro, 2000; Persson, Tabellini, 1994), religion, trust, and social capital (Guiso, Sapienza, Zingales, 2003, 2006; Knack, Keefer, 1997; Zak, Knack, 2001) and concluded that "the quality of institutions is key" (Rodrik, 2003), or "differences in economic institutions are the fundamental cause of differences in economic development" (Acemoglu et al., 2005).

These studies, which may be labeled studies of "institutions and growth" or "institutions and development" and build on pioneering ideas of new institutionalism, such as Coase and North, have substantially deepened our understanding of the relationship between institutions and economic growth. However, one of the most important institutions, laws, seems to have been largely neglected by this theoretical movement. However, law and economics, a discipline that considerably overlaps with new institutional economics[5] and exclusively considers the operation of legal systems, has long shown no interest in topics such as economic growth.

---

[5]   The relationship between new institutional economics and law and economics is somewhat complicated. In Posner's opinion, there is considerable overlap between them, but they are not identical: the subject matter of law and economics overlaps with that of new institutional economics in a number of respects such as vertical integration, corporate governance, and long-term contracts; however, the new institutional economists' preoccupation with transaction costs leads them away from price theory toward theoretical concepts tailor-made, as it were, for transaction-cost problems, while scholars in law and economics are likely to heavily rely on the tools of price theory (Posner, 1995: Chapter 21). Posner goes further and criticises the Coasean version of new institutional economics for its rejection of economic formalism and its scepticism of econometrics and rational utility maximisation. Consequently, the convergence between the two approaches would have been complete short of Coase's influence. Coase (1993) strongly refutes Posner's criticism by reemphasising the importance of realism in economic research. He states that "I do not dislike abstraction … What I object to is mindless abstraction which does not help us to understand the working of the economic system". This controversy reveals a fundamental divergence with respect to assumptions in economics: while the Chicago School approach followed by Posner maintains that the realism of assumptions is irrelevant, as advocated by Friedman (1953), Coase (1937) contends that assumptions should be realistic.

Originating with Coase's seminal article[6] on social cost, which was published in 1960 in the *Journal of Law and Economics*, law and economics, or the economic analysis of law, has become "the single most influential jurisprudential school" in America (Kronman, 1995). It may be defined as "the application of economic theory (primarily microeconomics and the basic concepts of welfare economics) to examine the formation, structure, processes, and economic impact of law and legal institutions" (Mercuro, Medema, 1997: 3). Specifically, law and economics comprises three closely related efforts:[7] predicting what effect particular legal rules will have, explaining why particular legal rules exist, and deciding what legal rules should exist (Friedman, 2001: 15). The first effort helps us to perceive consequences of laws and legal decisions by making extensive use of price theory, while the second, based on public choice theory, attempts to interpret the existence of the legal rules that we observed as the result of complex interactions among politicians, bureaucrats, interests groups, and citizens. Finally, the third effort provides a useful normative standard for evaluating legal institutions through the conceptual framework of welfare economics, especially in terms of Pareto efficiency[8] or Kaldor-Hicks efficiency.[9]

Law and economics has attracted numerous excellent scholars since its inception. For example, Coase (1960) specifies the relationship between efficient resource allocation and the legal assignment of property rights, Calabresi (1961) emphasises the role of tort law in mitigating externalities, Alchian (1965), Demsetz (1967), and Alchian and Demsetz (1973) elaborate the function of property rights institutions in resolving conflicting claims over scarce resources,

---

[6]   Other seminal articles include Calabresi (1961) and Alchian (1965). For a comprehensive survey on the history of law and economics, see Mackaay (1999).

[7]   Parisi and Klick (2003) provide a similar trichotomy by classifying law and economics into three distinct schools: the positive school, normative school, and functional school. The positive school, historically associated with the Chicago School, restricts itself to the descriptive study of the incentives produced by the legal system and recognises the limits of its role in providing normative prescriptions for legal reform. However, the normative school, historically associated with the Yale School, believes that there is greater need for legal intervention to correct pervasive forms of market failure and formulates normative propositions regarding what the law ought to be. The functional school, closely related to public choice theory, is quite sceptical of both the normative and positive alternatives and focuses on the incentives underlying the legal or social structures that generate legal rules.

[8]   The Pareto efficiency welfare criterion was introduced by the great Italian economist Vilfredo Pareto, in 1896. Pareto efficiency refers to a state of affairs in which no one can be made better off without making someone else worse off. The obvious limitation of this criterion is that it is not applicable to most institutional changes because few changes have no losers. The conditions for Pareto efficiency are almost never satisfied in the real world; hence economists have developed another criterion, Kaldor-Hicks efficiency. For a more detailed discussion on Pareto efficiency, see Zerbe (2001: 3–4).

[9]   The Kaldor-Hicks efficiency criterion, or a potential Pareto improvement, allows changes in which there are both winners and losers but requires that the winners gain more than the losers lose. In principle, the winners can compensate the losers while retaining a surplus for themselves, although compensation need not actually be made. For a more detailed discussion on Kaldor-Hicks efficiency, see Zerbe (2001: 4–10).

Becker's article on the economics of crime and punishment (1968) sheds light on deterrence effect of criminal law, and Posner (1973) offers a framework to evaluate legal procedures according to how well they minimise procedural costs.

These contributions triggered a flood of articles that extended law and economics to nearly every aspect of the legal system, not only including the aforementioned property law, tort law, criminal law, and legal procedures but also contract law, corporate law, bankruptcy law, antitrust law, and even constitutional law.[10] These articles allow us to derive a central proposition of law and economics: the primary function of law is to alter incentives[11] (Posner, 2002: 266–267). Law and economics assumes that rational individuals regard legal sanctions as (implicit) prices for certain types of activity and only engage in prohibited activities when their expected benefits from the activities exceed the expected costs. Ceteris paribus, the higher the costs of prohibited activities, the less likely individuals are to commit them. Consequently, legal rules can guide individual behaviours in a social desirable direction by correctly setting the prices of these behaviours.

In brief, the logic underlying law and economics suggests that changing legal rules will ultimately affect economic performance, which may be expressed as: Δ legal rules $\rightarrow$ Δ incentive structure $\rightarrow$ Δ individual behaviour $\rightarrow$ Δ economic performance (Mercuro, Medema, 1997: 22). This line of reasoning directs our attention to the importance of legal rules in an attempt to determine the drivers of economic growth. However, before the 1990s, law and economics scholars were primarily concerned with how legal rules influence individuals' incentives and firms' behaviours at the micro-level, instead of relating different levels of economic growth to the differences in legal rules at the macro-level. This situation has changed dramatically since the end of the 1990s as a result of a series of cross-country econometric analyses conducted by four economists, La Porta, Lopez-de-Silanes, Shleifer, and Vishny (LLSV), concerning what legal rules best contribute to the development of financial markets and therefore economic growth.

The major conclusion of LLSV is that legal origins are central to understanding the divergence in standards of living across regions and countries. Relative to civil law countries, especially those with French civil law

---

[10]   For a comprehensive survey of the contributions of law and economics, see Polinsky and Shavell (2007).

[11]   Analysing legal incentives is identical to an ex ante perspective on the law. For economists, past events are irreversible and represent sunk costs that should not affect rational actors' decisions regarding future behaviours. However, legal decisions based on past cases will influence the future behaviour of individuals engaged in activities that give rise to the type of harm involved in the case. In other words, ex post sanctions are translated into ex ante guidance. Friedman (2001: 11) states this clearly: by allowing the criminal to go unpunished, the court is announcing a legal rule that reduces the risk of punishment confronting other criminals facing similar temptations in the future; executing a murderer will not bring his victim back to life, but the legal rules it establishes may deter future murderers and thereby save those who would have been their victims.

tradition, common law countries have enjoyed superior economic outcomes. The seminal articles by LLSV resulted in an explosion of studies on the relationship between legal institutions and economic growth, some of which confirm LLSV's conclusion regarding the superiority of common law over civil law (Levine, 1998, 1999; Levine et al., 2000; Beck et al., 2003a, 2003b; Mahoney, 2001), while others question each of the premises underlying LLSV's theory[12] (Berkowitz et al., 2003; Coffee, 2007; Dam, 2006; Roe, 2006; Rajan, Zingales, 2003a).

LLSV substantially contribute to our understanding of the economic consequences of legal origins. However, their studies leave a number of questions unresolved. For example, what are the specific mechanisms by which legal origins influence economic growth? What roles do different legal rules, such as property law, contract law, and corporate law, play in guiding individuals to undertake productive activities instead of engaging in rent-seeking behaviour? Is a common law system significantly different from a civil law system in these respects, or are there other differences? If a common-law tradition is so beneficial, why have certain common law countries experienced economic failures and disasters (for example, Nigeria and Zimbabwe), while some civil law countries and regions have enjoyed economic successes and even growth miracles (for example, South Korea and Taiwan)? Finally, what implications do they have for policy reforms in developing and transitional countries; do they imply that implementing common law institutions in less-developed economies is a desirable objective? In brief, the primary contribution of LLSV's work is that it provides an impetus for additional and more in-depth studies on the role legal rules play in economic growth rather than providing convincing evidence of the advantageousness of common law systems.

This study may be regarded as a critical extension of LLSV's proposition concerning the advantages of common law systems. However, it falls outside the scope of the present work to provide a comprehensive theoretical framework for interpreting the relationship between legal institutions and economic growth based on a systematic comparative analysis of common law systems compared to civil law systems. Nevertheless, we can advance the field somewhat by rudimentarily addressing some of the aforementioned problems.

1.3. APPROACH AND STRUCTURE

Our approach in this book is essentially consistent with the methodology of law and economics, rooted in the hard core[13] of neoclassical economics, especially

---

[12]   For a comprehensive survey on LLSV's contribution and related literature, see La Porta et al. (2008) or Beck and Levine (2005).

[13]   Lakatos (1970) divides a research program into two components: the program's invariable hard core and its variable protective belt. Modifying a research program implies readjusting the

the rational choice approach.[14] Therefore, traditional microeconomic analytical tools, such as maximisation approach, cost-benefit analysis, and equilibrium analysis, will be employed in this book. However, we will not confine ourselves to the application of traditional price theory (microeconomic analysis) to legal issues. On the contrary, we will also employ approaches that have recently been developed to generalise price theory by introducing such factors as information and transaction costs while retaining all of the essential elements of price theory, such as new institutional economics, the economics of information, and so on.

We will follow the basic principles of neoclassical economics; nonetheless, our analysis will nearly completely eschew mathematical methods of presentation. It is well known that mathematical formalism has become one of the hallmarks of neoclassical economics given its advantages of clarity and precision.[15] This type of predilection, as Rutherford (1994: 25) argues, has often led neoclassical theory to sacrifice the understanding of real institutional details and historical context to develop highly formal, abstract, and simple models that are difficult to apply to concrete and dynamic institutional events. Whatever their strengths, highly formal methods cannot provide an adequate approach to institutional analysis. Consequently, we will present our analysis in a more literary style of theorising combined with case studies and historical studies, without forgoing the standard economic analysis.

Our analysis in this book undoubtedly belongs to the category of positive analysis rather than normative analysis,[16] as we attempt to explain legal rules

---

protective belt, but an alteration of elements in the core represents a shift to a new research program (paradigm). According to Eggertsson (1990: 5), stable preferences, rational choice, and equilibrium frameworks for interaction constitute the hard core of the microeconomic paradigm. Eggertsson's judgment may be traced back to Becker (1976: 5), when he states that "the combined assumption of maximising behaviour, market equilibrium, and stable preferences, used relentlessly and unflinchingly, form the heart of the economic approach as I see it".

[14]   Under this approach, individuals are assumed to have a set of preferences that are complete, reflexive, and transitive. Given these conditions, consumer preferences can be represented by a utility function that enables individuals to rank all possible outcomes according to their relative desirability, and they will choose to consume the bundle of goods that maximises their utility. The assumption of rational utility maximisation leads to a straightforward result regarding the decision-making process: individuals will engage in additional units of an activity as long as the additional benefit derived from another unit of that activity is greater than the additional cost, that is, as long as the marginal benefit is greater than the marginal cost (Mercuro, Medema, 1997: 57). See also Varian (2005: chapter 3–5) and Hausman and McPherson (2006: chapter 4, 5). The rational choice approach has recently been subject to harsh critique in law and economics, especially by behavioural law and economics (Jolls, Sunstein, Thaler, 1998; Korobkin, Ulen, 2000). See also Posner (1998), who refutes that standpoint from the perspective of Chicago School, and Mitchell (2001), who questions the conclusions of behavioural law and economics from the point of view of psychology.

[15]   As Rutherford (1994: 7) states, mathematical formalism encourages more explicit statements of assumptions, including initial conditions and behavioural hypothesis, and makes the derivation of implications not only more exact, but also much more transparent and open to examination.

[16]   John Neville Keynes clearly distinguishes between positive science and normative science by defining the former as "a body of systematized knowledge concerning what is" and the latter as

and outcomes as they are rather than evaluate them on the basis of subjective criteria or provide some institutional proposals to improve them. We have no intention of underestimating the importance of the normative approach to law and economics, yet we prefer factual issues related to positive analysis to the value judgments associated with normative analysis, which inevitably generates controversy[17] due to its subjectivity. Furthermore, we believe that convincing positive studies may contribute to the clarification of existing normative issues and hence make it more likely that a consensus will be reached. For example, numerous positive studies have indicated the superiority of market economies over planned economies in terms of efficient resource allocation and thus reduce the attractiveness of central-planning-oriented thoughts and advice.

Our interest in the similarities and differences between types of legal origins relates our study to comparison-oriented approaches, such as comparative institutional analysis[18] (Aoki, 2001), new comparative economics[19] (Djankov et al., 2003), and especially, comparative law and economics (Mattei, 1997). We agree with Mattei's complaint that "American law and economics has been remarkably parochial … In the legal context, the mistake is that of accepting the American legal process as an undisputed background and building up models

---

"a body of systematized knowledge discussing criteria of what ought to be" (Friedman, 1953). This distinction may be traced back to David Hume, when he advanced the proposition that "one cannot deduce ought from is", which has been labelled "Hume's guillotine" (Blaug, 1992: 112–113). For extensive discussions on this issue, see Friedman (1953) and Blaug (1992: chapter 5).

[17] For example, Kaplow and Shavell (2002) claim that the welfare-based normative approach, or welfare economics, should be exclusively employed in evaluating legal rules, whereas the notions of fairness or justice should receive no independent weight in the assessment of legal rules. Their viewpoint has come under heavy criticism from scholars both within the law and economics tradition, such as Richard Craswell and Lewis Kornhauser, and without, such as Jules L. Coleman. However, such arguments are of little value, as every criterion used to evaluate legal rules, whether welfare, fairness, or justice, is too vague and ambiguous to serve as a helpful benchmark in social policy making.

[18] The basic research agenda of comparative institutional analysis is to explore two fundamental questions through game theory: the synchronic problem, the goal of which is to understand the complexity and diversity of overall institutional arrangements across the economies considered, and the diachronic problem, the goal of which is to understand the mechanisms of institutional evolution/change (Aoki, 2001: 2–3). Aoki acknowledges that, in isolation, a game-theoretic analysis in the traditional sense cannot provide a systemic study of institutions. It is necessary to rely on comparative and historical information to understand why particular institutional arrangements have evolved in one economy but not in others. Therefore, an institutional analysis must also be comparative and historical.

[19] The traditional field of comparative economics primarily addressed the comparison of socialism and capitalism and studied the circumstances under which either a planned or market economy delivers greater economic efficiency. New comparative economics, as Djankov et al. (2003) argue, focuses on the differences among alternative capitalist models and their consequences for economic performance. Djankov et al. (2003) present an interesting framework in which the basic function of institutions is to guard against the twin dangers of dictatorship and disorder, which are considered the two central dangers faced by any society, and mitigating one must be traded-off by an increase in the other. The efficient institutional choice for a given society lies on the point at which the total social costs of dictatorship and disorder are minimised.

and/or generalizing observations about the efficiency of the law without considering the contingency and relativity of such background … certain generalizations of traditional law and economics simply cannot be used to explain the law – let alone be normative – outside the particular milieu of the American legal system" (Mattei, 1997: 69–70). The introduction of a comparative approach in law and economics will extricate the field from "American-centric provincialism", and increase its explanatory power outside of America, especially in developing and transitional countries.

This book is organised as follows. In chapter 2, we will comprehensively review the works of LLSV. We will first discuss the role of fundamental variables, such as geography, trade, culture, and institutions, in explaining economic growth. Next, we will survey the contributions of LLSV. Finally, we will review the arguments and evidence surrounding LLSV's claim that common law systems are superior to civil law systems with respect to economic growth.

In chapter 3, in a further reflection on LLSV's theory, we will analyse the legal institutions related to the development of financial markets, of which corporate law and securities law will receive the greatest attention. We will first discuss the contribution of stock markets to economic growth. Next, we will explore the role of corporate law in the development of stock markets. Finally, we will examine the role of securities law in the development of stock markets. Overall, we will demonstrate that the relationship between law and stock markets is more complex than implied by LLSV.

In chapter 4, we will explore the effect of a single, basic legal institution, namely property law. We will first discuss the definition and taxonomy of property rights. Next, we will review theoretical arguments and empirical studies on the relationship between property law and economic performance and show that property law fails to have demonstrable, positive effects in many developing countries. Finally, we will offer some explanations for the failure of formal property rights in most developing countries.

In chapter 5, we will analyse China, a seemingly obvious counterexample to the proposition that "law matters". We will first describe China's legal system, which was created from scratch in 1978 and has subsequently experienced substantial changes in every field. Next, we will examine China's economic growth record in detail, examine the nature of this growth, and review various theories that have been proposed to explain China's rapid growth over the last three decades despite its institutional weakness. Finally, we will reveal the true role that legal institutions have played in China's economic miracle, explain whether China is an anomaly that defies the proposition that "law matters", and attempt to predict the prospects for China's economy and the future direction of its legal system.

Based on the research above, we will conclude this book in chapter 6. Ultimately, we arrive at a sceptical perspective regarding LLSV's conclusions in light of their overestimation of the differences between common law and civil law systems, their neglect of the complex interactions between legal institutions and economic growth, and their failure to address other institutional factors, such as political structure and the distribution of power, which play a fundamental role in developing countries. Moreover, we call for further research on the relationship between law and economic growth, which will not only expand the field of study from private law and business law to public law and regulation but also coherently combine the clarity and precision provided by economics with the richness and actuality of jurisprudence.

CHAPTER 2

THE DETERMINANTS OF ECONOMIC GROWTH: FROM HARROD-DOMAR TO LLSV[*]

2.1. INTRODUCTION

This chapter briefly reviews economic growth theory and pays special attention to the role of legal institutions. In reviewing the theory of economic growth, it is useful to begin by distinguishing between proximate and fundamental causes of growth, as suggested by Snowdon and Vane (2005: 596). Proximate causes relate to the accumulation of factor inputs such as capital and labour, and also to variables that influence the productivity of these inputs, such as economies of scale and technological change. However, once we try to explain divergent economic performance with these factors, we are left with a serious question: why do poor countries fail to improve their technologies, invest in physical capital, and accumulate human capital as much as others? It appears therefore that any explanation that simply relies on proximate causes is incomplete; there must be other more fundamental causes that are trapping those poor countries in economic failure.

Compared with other possible fundamental causes, such as geography, trade, and culture, the institutions that shape incentives and determine the distribution of resources, have been increasingly accepted as being the fundamental determinants of economic growth. The importance of institutions may be illustrated by a "natural experiment" in the dramatically divergent growth paths of North and South Korea. After World War II, Korea was split into two independent countries that adopted entirely different sets of institutions: central planning in the North versus free market in the South. After 50 years of development, the South had become a member of the Organization for Economic Co-operation and Development (OECD), with a GDP per capita 16 times higher than that of the North. With a high degree of similarity in many respects at the time of separation – including endowments of natural resources, education

---

[*]   A paper based on this chapter has been published in the *Journal of Economic Surveys* (2011, Vol. 25, No. 5, pp. 833–871). The title of the paper is "The Role of Law in Economic Growth: A Literature Review".

levels, and income per capita, in addition to a common culture and history –
there is only one plausible explanation for the radically different economic
experiences of the two Koreas after 1950: their different institutions led to
divergent economic outcomes (Acemoglu, Johnson, Robinson, 2005).

Nonetheless, we still have one problem to work out: which type of institutions
matter? According to North (1990: 9), there are three dimensions of institutions:
formal rules, informal constraints, and the effectiveness of their enforcement. In
other words, there are two basic types of institutions, i.e., formal institutions in
which the legal system dominates and informal institutions that resolve people's
disputes through private methods. Due to the cost of using the formal legal
institutions, it is reasonable to argue that parties can benefit by resorting to
informal institutions such as the norms of rural residents in California's Shasta
County (Ellickson, 1991), the law merchant system in the early Middle Ages
(Milgrom, North, Weingast, 1990), the collective information-sharing and
punishment mechanism in Maghribi Trades (Greif, 1993, 1994), and even the
mafia in Sicily (Gambetta, 1993).

The major challenge faced by the informal sector is that the conditions under
which extralegal transactions might be undertaken, such as repeated interaction,
sufficient information, and small-sized groups, are so limiting that a great
number of potentially mutually beneficial exchanges among a much larger
network of trading partners must be foregone (Cross, 2002). The long-term
consequences of limiting one's business partners to a small number of
individuals with whom one is familiar and has long transacted include the
shortage of new firms, the dearth of new ideas and entrepreneurship, the
inability to adopt and develop complex technologies, and, as a result, economic
stagnation. In other words, although markets can arise in the absence of a
mandatory legal framework, they neither function optimally nor develop to their
full potential without such an infrastructure (Coffee, 2001). Therefore, we posit
that legal institutions (when compared with informal institutions) exert an
important influence on economic performance in modern economy.

The interaction between law and economic outcomes has been extensively
studied since the 1960s within the discipline of law and economics that
originated with Coase's seminal article on social cost. Coase's contribution
became the seed for a flood of articles that have extended the approach of law
and economics to almost every area of the legal system. However, prior to the
1990s, scholars of law and economics were concerned mostly with how legal
rules influence individuals' incentives and firms' behaviour on a micro-level
instead of relating different levels of economic growth to the differences of legal
rules on a macro-level. This situation was dramatically changed by the end of the
1990s after a series of cross-country econometric studies conducted by LLSV.[20]

---

[20]   It is worth noting that when we talk about the contributions of LLSV, we refer to a series of
articles as products of a team that includes Andrei Shleifer, Rafael La Porta, Florencio Lopez-
de-Silanes at its core, with additional coauthors, such as Robert Vishny, Simeon Djankov, et al.

A wave of research on the relationship between law and economic growth that was initiated by the works of LLSV has greatly deepened our understanding of the sources of economic growth and contributed to shift the attention of scholars of law and economics to macroeconomic outcomes of legal systems. However, the controversies set off by LLSV's proposition about the superiority of common law over civil law indicate that there are a number of important puzzles that are difficult to explain through LLSV's theory and thus call for more comparative analyses of different legal families before a consensus can be reached.

The rest of this chapter is organised as follows. Section 2 discusses the role of proximate causes versus fundamental variables in explaining economic growth. Section 3 surveys the contributions of LLSV. In section 4, we review the arguments and evidence surrounding LLSV's claims about the superiority of common law over civil law on economic growth. Finally, we conclude in section 5.

2.2. FROM PROXIMATE CAUSES TO FUNDAMENTAL CAUSES

2.2.1. PROXIMATE CAUSES: CAPITAL, TECHNOLOGY, AND PRODUCTIVITY

The idea that the accumulation of physical capital[21], such as machines, buildings, and infrastructure would yield growth goes back a long way. In the 1940s, Roy Harrod (1939) and Evsey Domar (1946) independently developed theories that related an economy's rate of growth to its investment and savings. The basic conclusion of the Harrod–Domar model is that the growth rate of GDP is jointly determined by the savings ratio divided by the capital–output ratio; the higher the savings ratio and the lower the capital–output ratio, the faster will an economy grow. By assuming a fixed capital–output ratio, the Harrod–Domar model attaches paramount importance to the accumulation of capital and suggests that the central growth problem is simply increasing the resources that are devoted to investment.

---

[21]   Human capital is another factor that is stressed by economists as one of the secrets to economic growth. Verspoor (1990) summarises that "the education and training of men and – although often neglected – of women contributes directly to economic growth through its effects on productivity, earnings, job mobility, entrepreneurial skills, and technological innovation". On an empirical level, Barro (1991) has found the growth of output to depend positively on initial schooling. However, Pritchett (2001) could find no positive association between growth in education and growth of output per worker. For more extensive discussions, see Easterly (2002: Chapter 4) and Weil (2005: Chapter 6).

The Harrod–Domar model became extremely influential in the development economics literature during the 1950s, and economists involved with international financial institutions still use it today regarding aid, investment, and growth projects (Easterly, 2002: 35). However, the effectiveness of the Harrod–Domar model has long been a subject of contention. After all, one of the basic tenets of economics is that there are diminishing returns associated with the addition of any one factor of production. With a given labour force, adding more and more machines will produce more output, but at a steadily declining rate. Therefore, more investment can raise the level of total output but not its growth rate in the long run.

The weakness inherent in an investment-driven growth pattern was clearly revealed by the famous Solow model. According to Solow (1956), the economy will end up at a steady state that represents the long-term equilibrium regardless of the level of capital with which an economy begins. In the steady state, unfortunately, there is no per capita growth: the output per worker is constant, whereas output itself is growing at the rate of population growth. A higher savings rate does temporarily increase the growth rate during the period of transition to a new steady state and it also permanently increases the level of output per worker. However, an increase in the savings rate raises growth only until the economy reaches the new steady state, which indicates that the savings rate has no effect on the long-term sustainable rate of growth.

This reasoning leads to a serious problem: How can we observe sustained growth of output per worker in those industrial economies for two centuries when such sustained growth is not economically possible? Solow's answer is technological progress. Therefore, to escape from the steady state, an economy must transform its growth style from factor-based growth to technology-based growth, or from "growth by brute force" to "smart growth" (Baumol et al., 2007).

Solow's neoclassical theory of growth thus brought technological progress to prominence as a major explanatory factor in the analysis of economic growth; however, technological progress is exogenous in Solow's theory, i.e., not explained by the model. This leads Barro and Sala-i-Martin (2003: 18) to criticise the model: "the obvious shortcoming, however, is that the long-run per capita growth rate is determined entirely by an element – the rate of technological progress – that is outside of the model ... Thus we end up with a model of growth that explains everything but long-run growth, an obviously unsatisfactory situation". In response to perceived theoretical deficiencies associated with the neoclassical model, Romer (1986) and Lucas (1988) initiate a new wave of endogenous growth theory whose central proposition is that broad capital accumulation (physical and human capital) does not experience diminishing returns. Thus the growth process is driven by the accumulation of broad capital and the production of new knowledge created through research and development (Snowdon and Vane, 2005: 625).

Another contribution of Solow on growth theory is the so called "growth accounting" that divides growth in output into different sources and calculates their relative importance (Solow, 1957). The basic growth accounting equation can be written as $\Delta Y/Y = \Delta A/A + \alpha\Delta K/K + (1-\alpha)\,\Delta L/L$ and shows that the growth of aggregate output ($\Delta Y/Y$) depends on the contribution of changes in total factor productivity (TFP)[22] ($\Delta A/A$), changes in the weighted contribution of capital, $\alpha\Delta K/K$, and changes in the weighted contribution of labour $(1-\alpha)\,\Delta L/L$.[23] Growth accounts have been used extensively within growth theory. For example, Mankiw, Romer, and Weil (1992) find that differences in physical and human capital account for approximately 80% of the observed international variation in income per capita. By contrast, Klenow and Rodríguez-Clare (1997) claim that TFP accounts for 90% of the cross-country variation in growth rates. Recently, Bosworth and Collins (2003) construct growth accounts for 84 countries over a period of 40 years from 1960–2000 and conclude, "both capital (physical and human) accumulation and improvements in economic efficiency are central to the growth process".

2.2.2. FUNDAMENTAL CAUSES: GEOGRAPHY, TRADE, CULTURE, AND INSTITUTIONS

In exploring what accounts for the rise of the Western world, North and Thomas (1973: 2) challenge traditional wisdom by asking the question: "if all that is required for economic growth is investment and innovation, why have some societies missed this desirable outcome?" North and Thomas go further and say that "the factors we have listed (innovation, economies of scale, capital accumulation, etc.) are not causes; *they are growth*" (North, Thomas, 1973: 2, italics in original). Therefore, it is necessary to go beyond these factors and delve into the wider fundamental determinants to understand why certain countries have performed much better than others. Many possible explanations have been offered in the literature, which can be classified into four categories: geography, trade, culture, and institutions.

---

[22] Narrowly speaking, TFP refers to the level of technology. In broad terms, however, TFP is a variable that accounts for effects in total output that are not explained by inputs. Bosworth and Collins (2003) differentiate TFP from technological process by stating that TFP "provides a measure of gains in economic efficiency (the quantity of output that can be produced with a given quantity of inputs), which can be thought of as shifts in the production function. However, such shifts reflect myriad determinants, in addition to technological innovation, that influence growth but that the measured increases in factor inputs do not account for. Examples include the implications of sustained political turmoil, external shocks, changes in government policies, institutional changes, and measurement error. Therefore this residual should not be taken as an indicator of technical change".

[23] In the equation, the exponent on the capital input α measures the elasticity of output with respect to capital and the exponent on the labour input $(1-\alpha)$ measures the elasticity of output with respect to labour. The weights α and $1-\alpha$ are estimated from national income statistics and reflect the income shares of capital and labour, respectively.

2.2.2.1.　Geography

According to Acemoglu et al. (2005), there are at least three versions of the
geography hypothesis, each underlining a different mechanism for how
geography affects prosperity. The first and earliest version of the geography
hypothesis goes back to Montesquieu, who believed that climate – and heat, in
particular – shaped human attitudes and effort, which in turn affected economic
outcomes. The second version of the geography hypothesis stresses the impact of
geography on the technologies available to a society, particularly in agriculture.
For example, Diamond (1997) argues that the fundamental factor behind
Europe's conquest of the Americas was the geographical advantage of Eurasia
(i.e., better biological resources), from which would emerge a settled agriculture
and a complex society with advanced civilisation and technologies. The third
version of the geography hypothesis links poverty in many areas of the world,
particularly tropical areas, to their disease burden (Bloom and Sachs, 1998).

However, Acemoglu (2009: 118–119) makes it clear that the geography
hypothesis is not convincing by arguing that most of the technological
differences emphasised by these authors refer to agriculture, but the origin of
differential economic growth across countries goes back to the age of
industrialisation. Modern economic growth came with industry, and it is the
countries that have failed to industrialise that are poor today. As to the disease
burden version, he notes that the fact that many undeveloped countries have
unhealthy environments is, at least in part, a consequence of their failure to
develop economically.

2.2.2.2.　Trade

Some scholars argue that more open economies grow faster than more closed
economies. For example, in one of the most heavily cited studies on the
relationship between openness and growth, Dollar (1992) constructs two
separate indices relating to "outward orientation", i.e., the "index of real
exchange rate distortion" and the "index of real exchange rate variability", and
demonstrates in a sample of 95 developing countries that these indices were each
negatively correlated with growth over the period 1976–1985. In another
influential paper, Sachs and Warner (1995) classify countries into two categories
– closed economies and open economies – and find a strong correlation between
openness and economic growth.

Rodriguez and Rodrik (2000) question this proposition by surveying recent
empirical studies among which the aforementioned two articles are paid special
attention. They argue that, in many cases, the indicators of "openness" used by
researchers are problematic as measures of trade barriers or are highly correlated
with other sources of poor economic performance. In addition, the empirical
strategies used to ascertain the link between trade policy and growth have

serious shortcomings. In an earlier survey paper, Edwards (1993) expresses similar dissatisfaction.

2.2.2.3. Culture

Some scholars emphasise cultural differences between nations and argue that a nation's cultural attributes are the key determinant of its economy. The most famous link between culture and economic growth is that proposed by Max Weber (1930), who stressed that the origins of industrialisation in Western Europe could be traced to the Protestant reformation and particularly the rise of Calvinism. Recently, Landes upholds Weber's perspective and states further "if we learn anything from the history of economic development, it is that culture makes all the difference" (Landes, 1998: 516). In addition to religion, trust and social capital are also regarded as crucial determinants of economic performance and social governance (Fukuyama, 1995; Putnam, 1993). Finally, the proponents of this view support their arguments with numerous empirical studies and conclude, overall, that cultures are important to fundamental economic issues (Guiso, Sapienza, and Zingales, 2006).

The culture view is criticised for several reasons. First, as Acemoglu (2009: 122–123) notes, it is difficult to measure culture, although there has been some progress in measuring certain cultural characteristics with self-reported beliefs and attitudes in social surveys. Second, there are so many counterexamples. If cultural values are responsible for the successful growth experience of South Korea, why do these same values not spur economic growth in North Korea? If cultural values are essential for China's growth today, why did they not lead to a better economic performance under Chairman Mao's control? Third, the culture view generally treats culture as if it was an immutable and exogenous factor. In reality, culture may represent a response to external conditions and change as those conditions change. Thus, a society's culture may be an endogenous product of societal institutions rather than an exogenous constraint that controls the effects of institutions (Cross, 2002).

2.2.2.4. Institutions

Researchers have increasingly used history and theory to make the case that institutions are crucial to economic growth. This approach is closely associated with the new institutional economics and Douglass North, in particular, who won a Nobel Prize for his efforts and insights in studying the role of institutions. According to North and Thomas (1973: 2) and North (1981: 6), growth will simply not occur unless individuals are lured by incentives to undertake socially productive activities such as investment, innovation, and specialisation. "Good" institutions, such as well-specified and enforced property rights, can thus cause growth by "getting the incentives right", i.e., by bringing private returns and social returns closer to one another. Thus, institutions play a fundamental role in societies: "they are the underlying determinant of the long-run performance of economies" (North, 1990: 107).

North's exploration of human history arrives at the conclusion that institutions are at the heart of economic history: the difference between property rights in hunting and agriculture is crucial to an explanation of the First Economic Revolution (or the Neolithic Revolution), whereas an important step in the development of the Second Economic Revolution (the Industrial Revolution) is the evolution of property rights, and particularly of patent and complementary laws aimed at protecting intellectual property rights; compared with France and Spain, the prosperity associated with representative assembly and the establishment of private property rights helped England to become the economic leader of Europe (North, 1981). A paramount factor contributing to England's success was the Glorious Revolution of 1688, which gave rise to certain fundamental constitutional changes that allowed the government to commit credibly to upholding property rights (North, Weingast, 1989). In subsequent research, Delong and Shleifer (1993) confirm North's judgment by showing that absolutist governments are associated with low economic growth (measured as city growth) during the eight hundred years prior to the Industrial Revolution.

The relationship between institutions and economic growth is supported by many cross-country regression studies. For example, in an influential paper, Knack and Keefer (1995) first provide institutional indicators compiled by two private international investment risk services – the International Country Risk Guide (ICRG) and Business Environmental Risk Intelligence (BERI).[24] Using these indicators, they run regressions on data from 1974 to 1989 and find significant correlations among institutions and economic growth. Similarly, Hall and Jones (1999) offer a term of Social Infrastructure[25] that indicates the institutions and government policies that provide the incentives for individuals and firms in an economy. Across 127 countries, their research presents statistical evidence that indicates that differences in social infrastructure account for much of the difference in long-term economic performance throughout the world, as measured by output per worker. In sum, the empirical evidence is strongly in favour of a positive and important effect from institutions to growth.

---

[24]   ICRG variables include *Expropriation Risk, Rule of Law, Repudiation of Contracts by Government, Corruption in Government*, and *Quality of Bureaucracy*. The BERI measures consist of *Contract Enforceability, Infrastructure Quality, Nationalization Potential*, and *Bureaucratic Delay*.

[25]   Hall and Jones form their measure of social infrastructure by combining two indices. The first is an index of government antidiversion policies (GADP) created from the ICRG indicator. The second index, which is based on the measures of Sachs and Warner (1995), captures the extent to which a country is open to international trade.

2.3. LAW MATTERS: CONTRIBUTIONS OF LLSV

2.3.1. COMMON LAW VERSUS CIVIL LAW[26]

LLSV's starting point is the recognition that laws in different countries are transplanted from a few legal traditions that emerged in Europe in the previous centuries through conquest, colonisation, and imitation. LLSV identify two main legal traditions: common law, which is English in origin; and civil law, which derives from Roman law and can be further classified into French, German, and Scandinavian law. Another special category is the socialist legal family,[27] which originated in the Soviet Union and was spread by the Soviet armies to the former Soviet republics and Eastern Europe. However, after the collapse of the communist regimes in 1989 and 1990, the countries of the former Soviet Union and Eastern Europe reverted to civil law systems.

Figure 2.1. The distribution of legal origin

Legal Origins

- English
- French
- German
- Scandinavian
- Socialist

Source: La Porta et al. (2008).

Following Napoleon's conquest of Italy, Poland, the Low Countries, and the Habsburg Empire, the Napoleonic Code was introduced into these regions. In the colonial era, France extended its legal influence to the Near East and to Northern

---

26 This section is based on LLSV (1998), Beck and Levine (2005), and La Porta et al. (2008).
27 This variable is only used in several studies, such as LLSV (1999), Djankov et al. (2002, 2003), La Porta et al. (2004), and Djankov et al. (2007).

and Sub-Saharan Africa, Indochina, Oceania, and the French Caribbean Islands. In addition, the French Code heavily influenced the Portuguese and Spanish legal systems, which helped spread the French legal tradition to Central and South America. Common law spread exclusively to the British colonies, and forms the basis of law in such countries as Australia, Canada, the United States, India, South Africa, etc. The German legal tradition influenced Austria, the former Czechoslovakia, Greece, Hungary, Switzerland, Yugoslavia, Japan, Korea, China (including Taiwan), and a few countries of the former Soviet Union. The Scandinavian legal system did not spread to any country outside Northern Europe.

Because there are relatively few countries in the German and Scandinavian families, the comparison between common law and civil law is generally narrowed down to common law and French civil law countries. The differences between these two legal systems are attributed to three factors that have been shaped by history. First, judges in common law jurisdictions enjoy great independence from other branches of government and are empowered to review the constitutionality of legislation and administrative acts, whereas in French civil law countries, as a legacy of Napoleon, judges are designed to be bureaucrats employed by and subordinate to the state. Second, common law relies heavily on judicial resolution of private disputes rather than legislation as a solution to social problems. According to Damaška (1986), civil law is "policy implementing" whereas common law is "dispute resolving". Finally, compared with civil law countries, the greater respect for jurisprudence as a source of law in common law countries suggests that judges have broader interpretation powers and courts are more able to mold and create law as circumstances change. In summary, to LLSV, "common law stands for the strategy of social control that seeks to support private market outcomes, whereas civil law seeks to replace such outcomes with state-desired allocations" (La Porta et al., 2008).

2.3.2. WORKS OF LLSV

LLSV's approach in their empirical studies is to first construct indices to measure the quality of specific legal rules in different countries, such as the level of investor protection in corporate and securities laws, and then to show that these legal rules vary systematically across legal origins by running a test of means (or medians). Finally, they use cross-country ordinary least squares (OLS) regressions to estimate the effects of these legal rules on economic outcomes and on financial development, in particular. Legal origin dummy variables that identify the legal origin of the specific legal rules of each country are frequently included in the regression as explanatory variables.

The methodology of LLSV can be summarised in the following simple regression model:

$$E_i = \beta_0 + \beta_1 LR + \beta_2 LO + \beta_3 CV + \varepsilon_i$$

where E_i is a measure of economic performance for country i (stock or bond market capitalisation to GDP, private credit to GDP, etc.), LR measures the attributes of specific legal rules (the strength of legal protection of outside investors' interests in commercial laws, for example), LO is the legal origin dummy variable, CV is a set of control variables (GDP per capita, inflation, etc.), and ε_i is the error term. The coefficient β_1 is of most interest for LLSV, who interpret a positive and significant coefficient as evidence for a positive correlation between law and economic performance.

Only in a few LLSV studies are legal origins used as instruments for legal rules in a two-stage least squares (2SLS) regression, where the second stage explains economic outcomes, such as stock market development. Despite the advantage of using legal origins as instruments in solving endogeneity problems, this technique is not recommended by LLSV because "legal origins influence a broad range of rules and regulations and we cannot guarantee that the relevant ones are not omitted in the first stage" (La Porta et al., 2008).

In the appendix, we list fifteen LLSV articles that will be discussed in this chapter, seventeen additional articles applying the LLSV methodology and supporting their conclusions, and sixteen articles and one book doubting their theories. For each article (and book), the appendix describes the methodology, data, dependent and independent variables, and the article's main findings.

The first and most notable finding by LLSV is that common law countries protect investors (shareholders and creditors) better than civil law countries (particularly the French civil law); free of expropriation by corporate insiders, investors are more willing to finance firms and financial markets flourish in common law countries. In their first collaborative work, LLSV (1997) construct an antidirector rights index (ADRI),[28] which measures how strongly the corporate law favours minority shareholders against managers or dominant shareholders in the corporate decision-making process, and a creditor index,[29]

---

[28] The index is created by adding 1 when: (1) the country allows shareholders to mail their proxy vote; (2) shareholders are not required to deposit their shares prior to the General Shareholders Meeting; (3) cumulative voting is allowed; (4) an oppressed minorities mechanism is in place; and (5) the minimum percentage of share capital that entitles a shareholder to call for an Extraordinary Shareholders Meeting is less than or equal to 10%. Higher values indicate greater minority shareholder rights. In a later article, LLSV (1998) add another element to the ADRI, a shareholder's preemptive right to buy new issues of stock that can be waived only by a shareholder vote.

[29] The index is formed by adding 1 when: (1) the country imposes restrictions, such as creditor's consent or minimum dividends, to file for reorganisation; (2) secured creditors are able to gain possession of their security once the reorganisation petition has been approved (no automatic stay); (3) the debtor does not retain the administration of its property pending the resolution of the reorganisation; and (4) secured creditors are ranked first in the distribution of the proceeds that result from the disposition of the assets of a bankruptcy firm. Higher values indicate greater creditor rights.

which addresses how creditors, particularly those secured by collateral, are treated in the process of bankruptcy. Using a sample of 49 countries, they find that common law countries protect both shareholders and creditors most, French civil law countries protect shareholders and creditors the least, and German and Scandinavian civil law countries are in the middle. Furthermore, the regression results show that high levels of shareholder protection in common law countries are associated with flourishing equity markets, whereas the worse shareholder legal protections provided by French civil law countries are correlated with underdeveloped stock markets.

Subsequent studies based on the ADRI indicate that shareholder protection is also related to ownership structure of large corporations, dividend policies, and corporate valuation (La Porta et al., 1999; LLSV, 2000, 2002). First, a comparison of countries with different types of shareholder protection shows that widely held firms are more common in countries with good protection, whereas countries with poor protection have more of most other types of firms (family-controlled or state-controlled firms). Second, firms in common law countries in which investor protection is typically better make higher dividend payouts than firms in civil law countries. Third, corporations with controlling shareholders have higher valuations in common law countries than in civil law countries, which is consistent with the theory that poor shareholder protection is penalised with lower valuations.

As Black (2001) argues, a strong securities market depends on a complex network of legal and market institutions, of which securities law regarding information disclosure and insider liability deserves special attention because of its role in deterring fraud, self-dealing, and other opportunistic behaviours. La Porta et al. (2006) examine the effect of securities law on stock market development in 49 countries, with a focus on mandatory disclosure, liability standards, and public enforcement. Their regression results show that both disclosure requirements and liability standards are positively correlated with larger stock markets; however, public enforcement plays a modest role at best in the development of stock markets. Furthermore, they show that common law and civil law countries differ significantly in disclosure and liability standards, according to which the superiority of common law is confirmed again.

La Porta et al. (2006) find that the ADRI is less important in explaining the difference in financial development than disclosure and liability standards, which leads Djankov et al. (2008) to construct a new measure of legal protection of minority shareholders against expropriation by corporate insiders: the anti-self-dealing index.[30] Djankov et al. (2008) show that the anti-self-dealing index

---

[30]   The index is created by averaging the indices of ex ante and ex post private control with respect to self-dealing. Ex ante private control with respect to self-dealing is made up of four components: (1) approval by disinterested shareholders; (2) disclosure by buyer; (3) disclosure by the controlling shareholder of the buyer; and (4) independent review. Ex post private control with respect to self-dealing is made up of six components: (1) disclose in periodic filings; (2) standing to sue; (3) ease in rescinding the transaction; (4) ease of holding the

is sharply higher in common law countries than in civil law countries and that the anti-self-dealing index is associated with a variety of measures of stock market development. Finally, interesting comparative analyses among the anti-self-dealing index, the ADRI, and the two variables used in La Porta et al. (2006) (disclosure and liability standards) are conducted to show that the anti-self-dealing index is a more robust predictor of the development of stock markets than the ADRI, yet a less robust predictor than disclosure and liability standards.

A disconcerting conclusion of LLSV (1997) is that their measure of creditor rights is not so effective in explaining the different level of indebtedness among legal origins. Djankov et al. (2007) thereupon undertake a study that expands the available data set to cover 129 countries and 25 years of data but remains based on the method of measuring the legal rights of creditors used in LLSV (1997). Djankov et al. (2007) also collect data on the public and private registries in different countries during the same period that collect information on credit histories and current indebtedness of various borrowers and share it with lenders. They find that common law countries have higher creditor rights scores than French civil law countries; the latter, by contrast, have a much higher incidence of public credit registries than do the former; finally, both better creditor rights and the presence of credit registries are associated with a higher ratio of private credit to GDP.[31]

The second strand of their studies addresses the consequences of government regulation and ownership. In an analysis of the regulation of market entry in 85 countries, Djankov et al. (2002) find that stricter regulation of market entry is associated with higher levels of corruption and a greater relative size of the unofficial economy instead of better quality of public or private goods. Moreover, countries with more limited and representative government and countries of English legal origin (and of Scandinavian origin) have fewer regulations. Botero et al. (2004) support the conclusion of Djankov et al. (2002) by arguing that legal traditions are a strikingly important determinant of the variation in the regulation of labour markets, with common law countries being less protective of workers and less generous in social security expenditures than civil law countries. Far from improving efficiency, heavier regulation of labour has adverse consequences for labour force participation and unemployment. In addition, government ownership of banks, according to La Porta et al. (2002), is particularly common in civil law countries, which is in turn associated with slower financial development, lower per capita income growth, and lower

---

controlling shareholder civilly liable; (5) ease of holding the approving body civilly liable; and (6) access to evidence.

[31] This finding leads to the acknowledgement that widespread public credit registries in French legal origin countries "highlight a successful civil law response to financial underdevelopment" and "suggest that the choice between common and civil law approaches to solving economic problems is a matter of comparative advantage of alternative strategies of social control and not just of the absolute advantage of common law solutions".

productivity growth. In general, relative to common law countries, French civil law countries are more interventionist and thus have inferior overall governmental performance (LLSV, 1999).

The third aspect of their research concerns the effect of legal origins on the characteristics of the judiciary and the effect of such judiciary characteristics on the security of property rights and contract enforcement. For example, La Porta et al. (2004) construct empirical measures of judicial independence and constitutional review and examine the impact of such measures on economic freedom and political freedom across countries. They find that judicial independence appears to be particularly important for economic freedom, whereas constitutional review is particularly important for political freedom. Again, compared with French legal origin countries, common law countries have higher levels of economic freedom,[32] although the differences in political freedom among them are insignificant. Djankov, La Porta, Lopez-de-Silanes, and Shleifer (2003) construct an index of procedural formalism related to dispute resolution to study the effectiveness of courts in simple disputes, such as evicting a tenant for nonpayment and collecting a bounced check. They find that such formalism is systematically greater in civil law than in common law countries and is associated with higher expected duration of judicial proceedings, less consistency, less honesty, less fairness in judicial decisions, and more corruption.

Finally, LLSV attempt to use a historical narrative to provide a theoretical foundation for the superiority of common law. Glaeser and Shleifer (2002) trace the differences between common law and civil law back to the twelfth and thirteenth centuries and present a theoretical model to capture the origin of the differences. They argue that a central requirement in the design of a legal system is the protection of law enforcers from coercion by litigants through either violence or bribes; the higher the risk of coercion, the greater the need for protection and control of law enforcers by the state. In the twelfth and thirteenth centuries, England was a relatively peaceful country with weak local feudal lords who were not capable of subverting local justice, and then a decentralised legal system based on independent juries materialised. Conversely, France was a less peaceful country, in which local magnates were so powerful that there was no possibility of effective local justice when the interests of these magnates were involved. Therefore, a much more centralised system that was organised, maintained, and protected by the sovereign was more efficient. In subsequent years, the conditions in England and France reinforced the initial divergence in the legal system.[33]

---

[32] This conclusion corresponds with conclusions from several other studies, such as Mahoney (2001), Berkowitz and Clay (2006).

[33] A substitute (or perhaps complementary) theory is presented by Mahoney (2001) and Klerman and Mahoney (2007). They argue that the fundamental divergence between English and French legal institutions occurred during the seventeenth through nineteenth centuries.

In summary, La Porta et al. (2008) generalise their findings into four propositions: "First, legal rules and regulations differ systematically across countries, and these differences can be measured and quantified; second, these differences in legal rules and regulations are accounted for to a significant extent by legal origins; third, the basic historical divergence in the styles of legal traditions (the policy-implementing focus of civil law versus the market-supporting focus of common law) explains well why legal rules differ; fourth, the measured differences in legal rules matter for economic and social outcomes". Consequently, "legal origins are central to understanding the varieties of capitalism".

2.4. IS COMMON LAW BETTER? SUPPORTING EVIDENCE AND DISSENTING OPINIONS

LLSV's seminal articles have resulted in an explosion of studies on the relationship between legal institutions and economic growth, some of which confirm their conclusions about the superiority of common law over civil law, although others question LLSV's theory on various grounds from the conceptual ambiguity of LLSV's variables to oversimplification and bias in comparing different legal traditions. Numerous institutional details and historical evidence are presented to cast doubt on LLSV's propositions. We will first review the supporting studies and then the countervailing views.

2.4.1. SUPPORTING EVIDENCE

LLSV's propositions are supported by a number of financial economists who continue the studies of the relationship between the legal system and corporate finance and aggregate financial development based on the indicators compiled by LLSV. On the macro-level, Levine (1998) applies the index of creditor rights to explore the determinants of banking development and finds that both creditor rights and legal origins have a profound impact on bank development. As an extension of Levine (1998), Levine, Loayza, and Beck (2000) examine the relationship between the development of financial intermediaries and creditor rights, contract enforcement, and accounting standards and find that financial intermediaries are better developed in countries with legal and regulatory systems that (1) provide high priority to creditors in bankruptcy, (2) enforce contracts effectively, and (3) promote comprehensive and accurate financial reporting by corporations.

Using instrumental variables to extract that part of overall financial development (including both stock markets and financial intermediaries) determined by (1) legal codes that support shareholders, (2) legal codes that support creditors, and (3) the efficiency with which laws are enforced, Levine (2002) finds that this component of overall financial development is strongly and positively linked with long-run growth. Demirgüç-Kunt and Maksimovic (2002) report that firms' access to external finance is affected by the development of both the securities markets and the banking system and that this effect is closely tied to the level of development of the country's legal environment. Moreover, Beck and Levine (2002) demonstrate that the overall level of financial development and an effective legal enforcement mechanism help externally dependent industries grow faster, foster the establishment of new ventures, and facilitate more efficient capital allocation.

On the micro-level, first, some studies suggest that investor legal protections influence the valuation of firms and the private benefits of corporate control. For example, Klapper and Love (2004) find significant correlations between firm-level corporate governance scores and a firm's operating performance, as measured by return on assets (ROA), and valuation, as measured by Tobin's Q, which are stronger in countries with weaker legal systems (which is measured by three indicators including ADRI). This conclusion is confirmed by Durnev and Kim (2005). In addition, Caprio, Laeven, and Levine (2007) find that stronger investor protection, as measured by higher ADRI values, tends to enhance bank valuation. By interpreting block premia as indicative of the private benefits of control, Dyck and Zingales (2004) estimate the private benefits of control in 39 countries and find that better legal protection of minority shareholders is associated with a lower level of private benefits of control. Similarly, Nenova (2003) measures the private benefits of control by the value of corporate voting rights – specifically, the value of the control block of votes – and shows that control-block votes are significantly less valuable in a stricter legal environment.

Second, empirical analysis also finds strong connections between legal enforcement (the level of legal formalism used by Djankov et al. (2003)) and firm size and financial contracting. In an analysis of 210 developing-country private equity investments, Lerner and Schoar (2005) find that investments in countries with a common law tradition and with better legal enforcement are more likely to use convertible preferred stock[34] and to have more contractual protections for private equity investors, such as supermajority voting rights and antidilution provisions. By contrast, investors in countries with civil law or socialist legal backgrounds and in which legal enforcement is difficult rely more heavily on common stock (or even debt) and control the firm via majority ownership and board dominance. Using the same indicator that Lerner and Schoar (2005) used

---

[34]   Generally speaking, these securities allocate control to the entrepreneurs when things are going well, but allow the investors to assert control when the firm is doing poorly. These securities will give stronger incentives to entrepreneurs than majority control based on common stock contracts because they prevent the holdup of entrepreneurs by investors when the entrepreneurs are running the firm well.

to measure the efficiency of the legal system, Beck, Demirgüç-Kunt, and Maksimovic (2006) find a positive association between the efficiency of legal systems and firm size.

Third, the creditor rights index is demonstrated to act on a firm's ability to obtain credit, the ownership and terms of bank loans, collateral requirements of banks, and the use of bankruptcy proceedings in case of default. Giannetti (2003) shows that protecting creditor rights is important for guaranteeing access to credit for companies investing in intangible assets and lengthening debt maturity[35] for companies with highly volatile returns. Qian and Strahan (2007) find that, in countries with strong creditor protection, bank loans are associated with more concentrated ownership,[36] longer maturities, and lower interest rates. Davydenko and Franks (2008) study the bankruptcy codes in France, Germany, and the United Kingdom and show that large differences in creditors' rights across these countries lead banks to adjust their lending and reorganisation practices to mitigate their losses in default. For example, in response to the French bankruptcy code, which limits creditor control rights and dilutes the value of collateral, French banks demand higher levels of collateral per dollar of debt.

Finally, researchers are beginning to examine the channels through which legal origin matters. For example, Beck, Demirgüç-Kunt, and Levine (2003b) empirically assess two channels through which legal origin may influence financial development. The political channel stresses that legal traditions differ in the priority that they give to the rights of individual investors relative to the power of the state, whereas the adaptability channel holds that legal traditions differ in their responsiveness to changing socioeconomic conditions.[37] The results provide support for the adaptability channel but not for the political channel. In other words, legal origin matters because legal traditions differ in

---

[35] If the law does not sufficiently guarantee creditor rights, lenders may prefer short-term debt to control entrepreneurs' opportunistic behaviour by using the threat of not renewing the loan. Better protection of creditor rights makes the use of debt maturity to control borrowers unnecessary.

[36] In other words, diffuse loan ownership provides banks a tool to mitigate risk when their legal rights are weak.

[37] The political channel argues that civil law tends to emphasise the power of the state, rather than private property rights, with adverse implications for financial development. By contrast, the common law historically stood on the side of private property owners against the state. The common law's comparative emphasis on private property rights relative to the state tends to support financial development to a greater degree than the civil law. According to the adaptability channel, legal systems that embrace case law and judicial discretion tend to be more responsive to changing economic conditions than legal systems that rely more strictly on judgments based purely on statutory law. Legal systems that reject jurisprudence necessarily rely more on statutory law changes to modernise and adapt the law. However, statutory law is slow and costly to change, and the absence of jurisprudence tends to hinder the efficiency with which laws adapt to changing conditions. Consequently, the adaptability channel predicts that countries with their legal origins in French civil law have a lower probability of having an efficiently flexible legal system than German civil law and particularly common law countries.

their ability to adapt efficiently to evolving economic circumstances and legal systems that adapt quickly will foster financial development more effectively. Using the same methodology, Beck, Demirgüç-Kunt, and Levine (2005) examine how legal origins influence firms' access to financing and support the conclusion of Beck, Demirgüç-Kunt, and Levine (2003b) by showing that the adaptability of a country's legal system is more important for explaining the obstacles that firms face in accessing external financing than the political channel, such as the independence of the judiciary.

2.4.2. DISSENTING OPINIONS

LLSV's conclusions have drawn criticism on various grounds, particularly in view of the existence of abundant anomaly countries, some of which have developed rapidly from civil law origin and others have stagnated, notwithstanding their legal origin in common law. For an obvious example, although French civil law is assumed to be inefficient, France in fact experienced greater economic growth than the United Kingdom over most of the period from 1820 to 1998. French civil law seems to have worked adequately, at least for France (Dam, 2006: 38–39). In addition to these apparent counterexamples, LLSV are also criticised on other grounds, such as oversimplification or even bias in choosing indices and classifying legal families, inconsistency with historical evidence, and losing explanatory power when other factors are included.

2.4.2.1. *Methodological Weaknesses*

LLSV's studies are criticised for their methodology in relying on ordinary least squares (OLS) regression to estimate the relationship between law and economic performance because OLS can fail to yield reliable estimates of causal effects for many reasons, two of which are particularly salient. First, there might be reverse causality. For example, when one observes the correlation between laws protecting investors and financial development, it is plausible to argue that countries must improve their corporate law and securities law to protect investors because of political pressure from these very investors, who thrive as a result of financial development. In other words, the causal chain is from financial development to (specific) legal rules, rather than from (specific) legal rules to financial development. The relationships among legal origin, legal rules, and financial development may thus be summarised as "legal origin → financial development → legal rules", instead of "legal origin → legal rules → financial development" as suggested by LLSV. This inference is partially supported by Coffee (2001), who finds that common law countries such as the UK and the US, were able to develop active stock markets without strong legal protection of investors (see section 2.4.2.3 below), and Pistor (2009), who argues that better investor protections tend to be a response to market development and the crises associated with such development. The reverse causality problem is difficult to address because a two-stage least squares regression in which legal rules protecting investors are instrumented by legal origins in the first stage is not appropriate (because the legal origin influences finance through channels other than these rules).

Another doubt cast upon LLSV's research concerns omitted variable bias, which can arise if explanatory variables that should be included in regression equations are not included whereas these variables are correlated with the included explanatory variables. A potential candidate for omitted variable is the initial conditions in the colonies suggested by Acemoglu, Johnson, and Robinson[38] (2001, 2002). The basic logic is that, in realms suitable for forced work in agriculture or mining because of high local population density, or in which Europeans could not easily survive because of local disease, European colonisers set up "extractive states" to transfer as much of the resources of the colony to the coloniser instead of protecting private property rights and limiting the power of the government; by contrast, in other regions, such as New England, where the natives were not easy to enslave, where it was difficult to organise massive exploitative activities, and where the local (disease) environment was hospitable to colonisers, many Europeans settled down and attempted to replicate European institutions with strong emphasis on private property and checks against governmental power.

In a recent study, Acemoglu and Johnson (2005) conduct an interesting "horse race" between property rights institutions – as instrumented by mortality rate of European settlers (or the indigenous population density in 1500) – and contracting institutions that use legal origin dummy as instrumental variable. They report that after property rights institutions are controlled for, contracting institutions seem to have no impact on income per capita, the investment to GDP ratio, and the private credit to GDP ratio, except for stock market development. In addition, they examine the semi-reduced-form specification in which property rights institutions are instrumented but English legal origin enters the second-stage regression directly and show no evidence that English legal origin has a positive effect on the economic outcomes aforementioned.

Instead of focusing on the conditions in the colonies, Berkowitz, Pistor, and Richard (2003) pay more attention to the pattern of transplanting legal institutions from the original countries to the receiving countries during their legal formation period. These authors argue that receiving countries that had developed legal systems internally, adapted the transplanted law to local conditions, or had a population that was already familiar with basic principles of

---

[38] Engerman and Sokoloff (1997) and Sokoloff and Engerman (2000) emphasise the importance of initial colonisation conditions from another perspective.

the transplanted law have more effective legality[39] than countries that received foreign law without any similar pre-dispositions. Using data from the same 49 countries used by LLSV, they show that both the transplanting process and legal origins have a significant impact on legality. However, compared with the transplanting process, which has a strong indirect (rather than direct) effect on economic development via its impact on legality, the overall impact (indirect plus direct) of legal origins on economic development is negligible.

Some scholars claim that culture might be a potential explanation of the evidence about legal origins. For example, Stulz and Williamson (2003) examine the relationship between culture (proxied by religion and language) and investor protection and find that there is no correlation between the LLSV shareholder rights index and culture when legal origin is controlled for, whereas the LLSV creditor rights index is strongly correlated with their measurement of religion. In addition, after controlling for legal origin and openness, they find that stock market development is correlated with a country's legal origin, whereas debt markets and banking development are correlated with culture.

Finally, political institutions are argued to be a more fundamental cause of divergent economic performance; thus, if politics were appropriately controlled for in the regressions, legal origin would not matter. In the context of democracy, Pagano and Volpin (2005) show that electoral systems fundamentally influence the level of investor protection. In particular, a proportional electoral system pushes political parties to cater more to the preferences of social groups with homogeneous preferences, such as controlling shareholders and employees. Under a majoritarian system, by contrast, there is keen competition for the votes of pivotal districts in which no focused interest group is dominant. Therefore, dispersed investors may be pivotal in choosing elected politicians in a majoritarian system. These authors also provide empirical evidence of a negative correlation between investor protection and a proportional system in a panel of 45 of 49 countries studied by LLSV (1997, 1998), and positive correlation between labour protection and a proportional system in a panel of 21 OECD countries. Moreover, the results of a panel regression on the determinants of shareholder protection indicate that the coefficients of all the legal origin dummies are no longer significantly different from zero when political variables and legal origins are introduced jointly. The significance of politics is also emphasised by Bordo and Rousseau (2006), who find that the effects of legal origins on financial development are not stable over time when compared with political variables, such as proportional representation election system, number of revolutions or coups, etc., and by Roe (2006), who claims that certain national experiences during the first half of the twentieth century (such as involvement in the world wars) predict financial development as well as, or better than, legal origins.

---

[39]   Legality is a weighted average of five components: judicial efficiency, rule of law, corruption, risk of expropriation, and risk of contract repudiation.

2.4.2.2. Problems of Coding and Classifying

From the beginning, legal commentators have questioned whether LLSV's indices capture the most important aspects of corporate law. For example, Dam (2006) systematically examines – and criticises – the famous ADRI used by LLSV. First, he finds that certain variables, such as preemptive rights, are not a good measurement of investor protection; second, the adoption of ADRI is not systematic within legal families; third, LLSV have scored certain continental countries too low partly by focusing on statutory law instead of what courts actually do and partly by ignoring functional substitutes; finally, even if the variables are roughly correct, the variance among countries within any legal family is remarkably high, which casts doubt on the decisive role of legal origin. As for the creditor rights index, Dam also finds wide dispersion within each of the four legal families and some oddities.

The ADRI is further examined by Spamann (2008), who finds high levels of ambiguity in the definitions of the variables and thus inconsistency in value assignment across countries. For example, the first component of ADRI, "Proxy by Mail Allowed", makes no sense if read literally because shareholders can always "mail their proxy vote to the firm". Another component, the "Oppressed Minority Mechanism" is defined so broadly that only two countries in the sample do not have this mechanism, whereas LLSV find that only half of the countries in the sample provide it. A particularly clear case of inconsistency is Australia, which is given the value 1 for the variable of "Preemptive Rights to New Issues", although its preemptive rights provision is almost literally identical to the German provision which is assigned the value 0 for this variable. Spamann collects legal data with the help of lawyers in the respective jurisdictions to correct the ADRI value in a more consistent manner and finds that accurate ADRI values are neither distributed with significant differences between common law and civil law countries nor correlated with stock market size and ownership dispersion.

LLSV relate their classification to the mainstream comparative law literature, such as that of Zweigert and Kötz (1998), whereas modern comparative law scholarship barely recognises such global classifications and generalisations as that proposed by LLSV. On a general level, three degrees of criticism can be distinguished (Armour, Deakin, Mollica, and Siems, 2009). First, some legal scholars doubt whether the distinction between "common law" and "civil law" can be justified from a historical perspective. Second, others argue that, despite their historical differences in legal origins, legal systems are becoming international, transnational, and even global at the end of the twentieth century, such that the idea of a strict common law-civil law divide is an anachronism. Finally, even those comparative law theorists who continue to use the notion of legal families emphasise the limits of this concept and posit that it is really no more than a didactic device.

The difficulties of classifying countries according to such a loose and problematic criterion as legal origin help explain why some divisions made by LLSV in their studies seem questionable. For example, LLSV treat Lithuania as being of French legal origin and Latvia as German origin. However, legal traditions beyond the German and French influenced Latvian and Lithuanian law (Siems, 2007). In recent years, both legal systems have been influenced by legal advice from the Nordic countries and the United States, in addition to the implementation of European Union directives. Moreover, historical similarities among the Baltic States are reflected in their legal rules and practices that cannot be placed in separate categories. The categorisation problem can be further illustrated by the case of China and Japan, whose company laws are a mixture of various legal influences, some African countries in which transplanted Western laws are of almost no practical significance compared with customary law and Islamic law, and Latin American countries whose commercial laws are influenced to a large extent by the United States. To some extent, the categorisation undertaken by LLSV is arbitrary and thus makes their conclusions less convincing.

Finally, even if clear distinctions might be drawn among countries by reference to their legal origins, and even if the superiority of commercial laws in common law jurisdictions over those in civil law jurisdictions is confirmed without controversy, it does not suggest that common law is better than civil law in nature. The heart of the differences between common law and civil law systems lies in the area of private law, such as property, contracts, and torts, to which LLSV pay little attention. Instead, they focus on commercial laws and regulations and neglect the fact that both commercial laws and regulations are legal areas in which most countries, common law and civil law countries alike, rely on statutory law. Consequently, even if their conclusion that commercial laws and regulations in common law countries are better for economic development holds, it does not mean that the common law method of judge-made law is superior to legislative enactment[40] (Dam, 2006: 33).

2.4.2.3.   Contrary Historical Evidence

As La Porta et al. (2008) admit, perhaps the most difficult challenge to the hypothesis that legal origins cause outcomes has been posed by historical

---

[40]   Schauer (2004) posits that, developed as a concept in a smaller and simpler society and out of a desire to settle disputes, common law loses its comparative advantage in a more complex society whose primary function is to guide people's behaviour instead of resolve their disputes. Thus "even in common law countries, the civil law model seems so much in the ascendancy, and the common law model seems so much in decline". In reality, even Shleifer himself argues that the rise of the regulatory state in the US was a response to the dissatisfaction with common law as a mechanism of addressing market failure (Glaeser, Shleifer, 2003).

arguments. It is difficult for legal origin, with its time invariant nature, to explain financial change over time. For example, Rajan and Zingales (2003a) examine the financial development of developed countries during the twentieth century and find that the state of development of the financial sector does not change monotonically over time. In contrast to the findings of LLSV, these authors present evidence showing that French civil law countries in 1913 had more developed financial markets than common law countries. However, compared with common law countries, the financial markets in civil law countries declined more between 1913 and the early 1990s. This type of "great reversal" is hard to explain using the theory of LLSV, which implies the invariable influence of legal origins over financial development. Musacchio (2008) also finds that most French civil law countries had strong creditor rights in 1910; however, creditor protection declined in the following years and resulted in prodebtor laws by 1995.

Based on the finding of the "great reversal", Rajan and Zingales (2003a) present an interest group theory to explain the rise and fall of financial markets in developed countries. They argue that incumbents, both in the financial sector and in industry, have a vested interest in preventing financial development because a more efficient financial system facilitates entry and encourages competition, which leads to lower profits for incumbent firms and financial institutions. However, when a country's borders are open to both trade and capital flows, the incentives and abilities of incumbents to oppose financial development are muted and financial development will flourish. In addition, Rajan and Zingales (2003a) argue that it is easier for a small group representing private interests to influence policy implementation in civil law countries because the governance system is so centralised that it is easier to capture. By contrast, the judiciary in common law countries is less easy to capture because it is dispersed and subject to local influences.

Perotti and von Thadden (2006) provide another political explanation for the "great reversal". They present a model to show that the preference of the median class depends on the distribution of financial wealth relative to human capital. When financial wealth is concentrated, a political majority has more at stake in the form of firm-specific human capital instead of financial holdings, and therefore supports a financial system dominated by banks that reduces risk exposure for labour income. By contrast, if the median voter has sufficient financial stake, he will prefer dispersed equity ownership, which results in riskier but more profitable investment. Thus, the inflation shock after the First World War had a different effect on the financial holdings of the middle class in different countries. Those countries with an impoverished middle class turned to a more corporatist system with suppressed financial markets, whereas other countries escaped high inflation and maintained market friendly institutions, although some in this latter group, such as the Netherlands and Switzerland, have the "wrong" legal origin.

Recently, more empirical studies based on time series data have emerged to address the obvious weakness in LLSV's works, i.e., they rely heavily on cross-sectional analysis. Thanks to Armour et al., four new data sets[41] have been produced to date: three are five-country (France, Germany, the United Kingdom, the United States, and India) data sets for the period 1970–2005, which cover the fields of shareholder protection, creditor protection, and labour regulation; the last covers only shareholder protection for a wider range of countries over a shorter period of time (20 countries over the period 1995–2005). Based on the last data set, Armour et al. (2009) find that common law systems had stronger shareholder protection over the period 1995–2005, but civil law systems were catching up with their common law counterparts over that same period. Moreover, these authors find that there is no significant positive relationship between their shareholder protection index and the various stock market development indicators, even after controlling for legal origin.

Some historical evidence about legal and financial development in their early stages has also been presented to challenge LLSV's conclusions. A logical inference from LLSV's studies is that legal rules providing investors with sufficient protection against insider opportunism must be in place for dispersed share ownership and strong securities markets to develop. However, this is not supported by the experience of the United Kingdom, where the common law originated. Cheffins (2001) explores how a widely dispersed pattern of ownership emerged in the United Kingdom and finds that, compared with private forces such as reputation-valued financial intermediaries (which undertook the function of "quality control" over public companies) and the London Stock Exchange (LSE, which acted as an effective private regulator by establishing a wide range of listing rules to address preemptive rights, insider trading, information disclosure, etc.), statutory provisions and judicial relief played a trivial role until the 1980s.

Similarly, Coffee (2001) examines the early development of the New York and London Stock Exchanges and contrasts their experiences with the development of securities markets in France and Germany over the same period. He finds that, even in the absence of strong legal protections for minority shareholders, vigorous stock markets emerged and dispersed ownership rose in both the UK and the US. The key point is that common law countries such as the UK and the US were more hospitable than civil law countries to private self-regulatory institutions that were enforced by private bodies (most notably, by private stock exchanges) to convince minority shareholders that they would not be exploited.

---

[41]   For more details on these data sets, see www.cbr.cam.ac.uk/research/programme2/project2-2output.htm (homepage of the "Law, Finance and Development" project on the Cambridge Centre for Business Research website).

Conversely, in more centralised economies such as France and Germany, the government intervened in the securities markets aggressively and ultimately stunted their potential for growth.

In their research, LLSV choose bankruptcy laws as a representative creditor's rights institution, and conclude that common law countries protect creditor rights better than civil law countries. However, based on an original database of 51 bankruptcy laws ranging over 15 European countries and more than a hundred years (1808–1914), Sgard (2006) shows that all legal traditions strongly protected creditor rights over the entire period, except for English law, which was shown to be *prima facie* less protective. The evidence also suggests that the evolution of these laws was influenced less by legal origins than by economic factors, such as the emergence of large publicly traded firms, development of the financial and capital markets, and reduced informational problems.

A significant advantage of common law over civil law, as argued by LLSV, is the flexibility through which private contracting is facilitated. A comparison of the law governing business organisational forms in France and the United States during the nineteenth century indicates that the contracting environment in the US was neither freer nor more flexible than that in France (Lamoreaux, Rosenthal, 2005). US businesses had a more limited menu of organisational choices and also much less ability to adapt the basic forms to meet their needs. Moreover, American law did not evolve more readily in response to economic change than French law.

2.5. CONCLUSION

Over the past several decades, a great number of scholars have devoted themselves to exploring the determinants of economic growth and have provided alternative theories about potential sources of cross-country income differences. Numerous variables, such as capital accumulation, technological progress, productivity, policy choices, political structures, legal systems, and even geography have been investigated at both the theoretical and empirical levels. The proposition that institutions matter seems to receive most support from the evidence across both time and space and has become a consensus among scholars, advisors, and even international agencies.

Compared with other institutions, legal institutions exert a more important influence on economic performance in modern economies. The interaction between law and economic outcomes has been extensively studied since the 1960s within the discipline of law and economics. Before the 1990s, scholars of law and economics were concerned mostly about how legal rules influence individuals' incentives at the micro-level, instead of relating different levels of economic growth to the differences in legal rules at the macro-level. This situation has dramatically changed since the end of the 1990s after the series of cross-country econometric studies conducted by LLSV.

LLSV's theory, or the legal origins hypothesis, is regarded as "one of the most important and influential ideas to emerge in the social sciences in the past decade" (Armour, Deakin, Mollica, and Siems, 2009). It has greatly changed the research paradigm in several fields, including comparative law, comparative economics, and law and economics, by demonstrating the possibilities and power of quantitative legal study. From a practical perspective, some of the policy prescriptions presented by LLSV still hold despite all the critiques we have reviewed in this chapter. For example, the claim that the development of financial markets relies on the protection of outside investors by formal laws is perhaps the least controversial in light of the extensive supporting evidence from both theoretical and empirical studies. To some extent, this claim may be argued to provide theoretical underpinning for the worldwide legal reforms over the past decade that have aimed to strengthen shareholder rights, improve corporate governance standards, and enhance creditors' rights. Another proposition that heavy regulation of entry has adverse impacts on markets is compatible with the conventional wisdom of mainstream economics and "has encouraged regulatory reforms in dozens of countries", particularly "in the reductions of entry regulation" (La Porta et al., 2008) through the ongoing series of the IFC (International Finance Corporation, a member of World Bank Group) reports on *Doing Business*, which borrow their methodology from LLSV and attempt to measure the efficiency of the legal environments of different countries by establishing the rank of these countries according to certain variables and providing policy recommendations accordingly.

LLSV did substantially contribute to the understanding of the economic consequences of legal origins. However, plenty of unsolved problems remain from their studies. In future studies, a deeper understanding of the relationship between legal origins and economic performance is in prospect if more academic efforts are directed to resolving the unanswered questions left by LLSV. For example, it is necessary to clarify the mechanisms through which legal origins influence economic outcomes, to compare the explanatory power of legal origins versus other variables such as initial colonial conditions more broadly, to measure and codify targeted legal rules and classify countries with further caution, and to encourage more historical studies (including both time-series econometric research and case studies) before a coherent and convincing theory can finally emerge. In this process, lawyers who are more adept in distinguishing "law in action" from "law in books" should play a more important role than before.

APPENDIX: LEGAL ORIGINS AND ECONOMIC PERFORMANCE: LITERATURE REVIEW

(Articles are listed in the order they appear in this chapter).

Articles	Dependent Variables	Main Explanatory Variables	Methodology	Data	Key Results
LLSV (1997)	1) External cap/GNP[1] 2) Domestic firms/Pop[2] 3) IPOs/Pop[3] 4) Debt/GNP[4]	1) ADRI 2) Creditor rights 3) Legal origin	1) Tests of means 2) Ordinary least squares regression (OLS)	49 countries in 1994	Part of the differences in stock market development across countries is captured by the differences in ADRI, although the effects of legal origin are also significant.
LLSV (1998)	Ownership concentration[5]	1) ADRI 2) Creditor rights 3) Legal origin	1) Tests of means 2) OLS	49 countries in 1994	Common law countries provide the best legal protection to investors, and thus have the lowest concentration of ownership.
La Porta et al. (1999)	Ownership structure of large corporations (widely held or not)	ADRI	Tests of means	27 countries in 1995	Widely held firms are more common in countries with good shareholder protection.
LLSV (2000)	Dividend payout	1) ADRI 2) Legal origin	1) Tests of means 2) OLS	33 countries in 1994	Firms in common law countries make higher dividend payouts than firms in civil law countries.
LLSV (2002)	Tobin's q[6]	1) ADRI 2) Legal origin	1) Tests of means 2) OLS	27 countries in 1995	Better shareholder protection is associated with higher valuation of corporate assets.
La Porta et al. (2006)	1) External cap/GNP 2) Domestic firms/Pop 3) IPOs[7] 4) Block premia[8] 5) Access to equity[9] 6) Ownership concentration 7) Liquidity[10]	1) Disclosure requirements index[11] 2) Liability standard index[12] 3) Public enforcement index[13] 4) Legal origin	1) Tests of means 2) OLS 3) Two-stage least squares regression (2SLS) (with legal origin as an instrumental variable)	49 countries over the period 1996–2000	Common law countries have both more extensive mandatory disclosure requirements and stricter liability standards, which in turn are positively correlated with larger stock markets.

Articles	Dependent Variables	Main Explanatory Variables	Methodology	Data	Key Results
Djankov et al. (2008)	1) Ratio of stock market capitalisation to GDP 2) Control premium (block premia) 3) Domestic firms/Pop 4) IPOs 5) Ownership concentration	1) Anti-self-dealing index 2) Legal origin	1) Tests of means 2) OLS 3) 2SLS (with legal origin as an instrumental variable)	72 countries in 2003	The anti-self-dealing index is sharply higher in common law countries than in civil law countries and is associated with a variety of measures of stock market development.
Djankov et al. (2007)	Ratio of private credit to GDP[14]	1) Creditor rights 2) Presence of public and private registries 3) Legal origin	1) OLS 2) Panel regression	129 countries over the period 1978 to 2003	1) Both creditor rights and credit registries are associated with higher ratios of private credit to GDP. 2) Common law countries have higher creditor rights scores, whereas French civil law countries have a higher incidence of public credit registries.
Djankov et al. (2002)	1) Procedures[15] 2) Time[16] 3) Cost[17]	1) Political variables 2) Legal origin	1) Tests of means 2) OLS	85 countries in 1999	Countries of English (and Scandinavian) legal origin have lighter regulation of entry and therefore lower levels of corruption and a smaller unofficial economy.
Botero et al. (2004)	1) Employment laws index[18] 2) Social security laws index[19] 3) Collective relations laws index[20]	1) Political variables 2) Legal origin	OLS	85 countries in 1997	Socialist, French, and Scandinavian legal origin countries have higher levels of labour regulation than common law countries. Heavier regulation of labour is associated with lower labour force participation and higher unemployment.
La Porta et al. (2002)	Government ownership of banks	1) Characteristics of countries 2) Legal origin	1) Tests of means 2) OLS	92 countries in 1970 and 1995	Government ownership of banks is particularly common in civil law countries and is associated with worse economic and financial performance.

Articles	Dependent Variables	Main Explanatory Variables	Methodology	Data	Key Results
LLSV (1999)	1) Government intervention[21] 2) Public sector efficiency[22] 3) Output of public goods[23] 4) Size of public sector[24] 5) Political freedom[25]	1) Ethnolinguistic fractionalisation 2) Legal origin 3) Religion	OLS	152 countries in 1990s	Compared with common law countries, French civil law and socialist law countries are more interventionist and less efficient.
La Porta et al. (2004)	1) Economic freedom[26] 2) Political freedom[27]	1) Judicial independence[28] 2) Constitutional review[29] 3) Legal origin	OLS	71 countries in 1990s	Compared with French legal origin countries, common law countries have higher levels of economic freedom, which can be partly explained by their higher levels of judicial independence.
Djankov et al. (2003)	1) Duration of legal enforcement[30] 2) Other judicial quality measures[31]	1) Procedural formalism[32] 2) Legal origin	1) Tests of means 2) OLS 3) 2SLS (legal origin dummies as instruments)	109 countries	Procedural formalism is systematically greater in civil than in common law countries and is associated with higher expected duration of judicial proceedings and lower judicial quality.
Glaeser and Shleifer (2002)			Theoretical and historical studies		The differences between common law and civil law can be traced back to the twelfth and thirteenth centuries and explained by the different distribution of power between feudal lords and kings in England and France.
Levine (1998)	1) Banking development[33] 2) Per capita GDP growth 3) Physical capital accumulation 4) Productivity growth	1) Creditor rights 2) Efficiency of legal systems[34] 3) Legal origin	1) OLS 2) General method of moments (GMM) estimation (legal origin dummies as instruments)	42 countries over the period 1976–1993	1) Creditor rights, legal efficiency, and legal origins all have profound impact on banking development. 2) There is a strong and positive relationship between the growth indicators and banking development (instrumented by creditor rights and legal efficiency or legal origins).

Articles	Dependent Variables	Main Explanatory Variables	Methodology	Data	Key Results
Levine et al. (2000)	1) Financial intermediary development[35] 2) Per capita GDP growth	1) Creditor rights 2) Efficiency of legal systems 3) Level of corporate accounting standards 4) Legal origin	1) Cross-sectional GMM estimation (legal origin dummies as instruments) 2) Dynamic panel GMM estimation	Panel data for 74 countries over the period from 1961–1995[36]	1) Creditor rights, legal efficiency, and accounting standards explain a significant amount of the cross-country variation in the three financial intermediary indicators. 2) The exogenous component of financial intermediary development exerts a large, positive impact on economic growth.
Levine (2002)	Per capita GDP growth	1) Financial structure (bank or market based) 2) Activity, size, and efficiency of overall financial sector	1) OLS 2) 2SLS (using ADRI, creditor rights, and legal efficiency as instruments)	48 countries over the period 1980–1995	The component of overall financial development explained by the legal rights of outside investors and the efficiency of the legal system in enforcing these rights is strongly and positively linked with long-run growth.
Demirgüç-Kunt and Maksimovic (2002)	Firm growth	1) Bank/GDP[37] 2) Turnover[38]	2SLS (using ADRI, creditor rights, legal efficiency, and legal origin as instruments)	40 countries over the period 1989–1996	In those countries in which the legal environment predicts a larger banking sector and more active stock market, a larger proportion of firms obtain outside financing and grow at rates that could not have been self-financed.
Beck and Levine (2002)	1) Industry growth 2) New establishment formation 3) Capital allocation	1) Financial structure (bank or market based) 2) Overall financial development 3) Judicial efficiency[39]	1) OLS 2) 2SLS with panel data (using legal origin and religion as instruments)	Panel data for 42 countries over the period 1980–1990[40]	The overall level of financial development along with effective legal environment helps externally dependent industries grow faster, fosters new establishment formation in these industries, and improve efficiency in capital allocation.
Klapper and Love (2004)	1) Corporate performance (ROA and Tobin's q) 2) Corporate governance index[41]	1) Judicial efficiency 2) Legality 3) ADRI 4) Firm-level characteristics	OLS	14 countries in 2000	Better governance is positively correlated with better market valuation and operating performance, and this relationship is stronger in countries with weaker legal systems.

Articles	Dependent Variables	Main Explanatory Variables	Methodology	Data	Key Results
Durnev and Kim (2005)	1) Corporate governance index[41] 2) Firm valuation (Tobin's q)	1) Legal variable[42] 2) Firm-level characteristics	OLS	27 countries in 2000	The quality of corporate governance is positively related to firm valuation, whereas this relationship is weaker in more investor-friendly countries.
Caprio et al. (2007)	1) Bank valuation (Tobin's q and market value of equity/ book value of equity) 2) Bank ownership concentration	1) ADRI 2) Supervision and regulatory policies 3) Cash-flow rights of controlling shareholders	1) Tests of means 2) OLS 3) 2SLS (ADRI is instrumented by legal origin)	44 countries in 2001	1) Except in a few countries with strong shareholder protection laws, banks are not widely held. 2) Strong legal protection of shareholders increases bank valuations.
Dyck and Zingales (2004)	1) Private benefits of control (block premia) 2) Ownership concentration 3) External cap/GNP 4) Domestic firms/Pop 5) IPOs/Pop	1) ADRI 2) Accounting standards 3) Rule of law (legal enforcement) 4) Extra-legal institutions	1) OLS 2) 2SLS (block premia are instrumented by legal origin)	39 countries over the period 1990 to 2000	1) Taken in isolation, many institutional variables including better shareholder protection and law enforcement are associated with a low level of private benefits of control. 2) In countries in which private benefits of control are large, ownership is more concentrated and capital markets are less developed.
Nenova (2003)	1) Private benefits of control (value of control-block votes)	1) ADRI 2) Rule of law 3) Takeover regulations 4) Corporate charter provisions	1) Tests of medians 2) OLS	18 countries in 1997	Law enforcement, investor protection, takeover regulations and corporate charter provisions together explain 68% of the systematic differences in the value of control-block votes.
Lerner and Schoar (2005)	1) Security structure[43] 2) Allocation of equity[44] 3) Structure of the board 4) Contract protections[45]	1) Legal origin 2) Contract enforcement[46]	OLS	30 countries over the period 1987–2003	Investments in high enforcement and common law nations frequently use convertible preferred stock with contractual protections. In low enforcement and civil law nations, investments tend to use common stock and debt, relying on equity and board dominance.

Articles	Dependent Variables	Main Explanatory Variables	Methodology	Data	Key Results
Beck et al. (2006)	Firm size (total sales of a firm)	1) Private credit/GDP 2) Contract enforcement 3) Property rights protection	1) OLS 2) 2SLS (using legal origin dummies as instruments)	44 countries over the period 1988–2002	Firm size is positively related to financial intermediary development, the efficiency of the legal system and property rights protection.
Giannetti (2003)	1) Leverage of firms[47] 2) Debt maturity of firms[48]	1) Financial development[49] 2) Creditor rights	OLS	8 countries in 1997	Good creditor protection favours access to credit for firms investing in intangible assets and helps lengthen debt maturity for firms with volatile returns, particularly for unlisted companies.
Qian and Strahan (2007)	1) Concentration of loan ownership 2) Contract terms (collateral requirement, maturity, and interest rate)	1) Credit rights 2) Firm, loan, and country characteristics	OLS	43 countries over the period 1994–2003	Strong protection of creditor rights is associated with greater concentration of loan ownership (lower number of lenders), longer-term lending, and lower interest rates.
Davydenko and Franks (2008)	1) Bank's recovery rate 2) Amount and composition of collateral required by banks 3) Interest spreads	1) Bankruptcy code 2) Industry, firm, and loan characteristics	1) Logit regression 2) OLS 3) Heckman two-step estimation	3 countries over the period 1984–2003	French banks require more collateral than lenders elsewhere, and rely on special collateral forms. However, recovery rates for banks in France remain significantly below those in the United Kingdom and Germany.
Beck et al. (2003)	Financial development[50]	1) Political channel[51] 2) Adaptability channel[52] 3) Legal origin	1) OLS 2) 2SLS (with legal origin dummies as instruments)	115 countries over the period 1990–1995	The exogenous component of legal system adaptability rather than that of political channel explains cross-country differences in financial development.
Beck et al. (2005)	Firm's financing obstacles[53]	1) Political channel 2) Adaptability channel 3) Legal origin	Ordered probit model	38 countries in 1999	Cross-country variation in legal system adaptability instead of that of judicial independence helps explain variation in the obstacles that firms face in accessing external finance.

Articles	Dependent Variables	Main Explanatory Variables	Methodology	Data	Key Results
Acemoglu and Johnson (2005)	1) GDP per capita 2) Investment/GDP 3) Private credit/GDP 4) Stock market capitalisation/GDP	1) Property rights institutions[54] 2) Contracting institutions[55]	1) OLS 2) 2SLS[56]	71 countries in the 1990s	Property rights institutions have a first-order effect on income per capita, the ratio of investment to GDP, the level of credit, and stock market development. Contracting institutions appear to have an impact only on stock market development.
Berkowitz et al. (2003)	1) Legality 2) GDP per capita	1) Transplanting process (receptive vs. unreceptive) 2) Legal origin	OLS	49 countries over the period 1980–1995	The transplanting process has a strong indirect effect on economic development via its impact on legality, although the impact of particular legal families is weaker and not robust.
Stulz and Williamson (2003)	1) ADRI 2) Creditor rights 3) Stock market development 4) Debt markets and banking development	1) Legal origin 2) Culture (proxied by language and religion) 3) Openness	OLS	49 countries over the period 1985–1995	Catholic countries have significantly weaker creditor rights than other countries, which holds when the origin of the country's legal system is controlled for.
Pagano and Volpin (2005)	1) ADRI 2) Employment protection[57]	1) Proportional electoral system 2) Legal origin	1) OLS 2) Panel regression	Panel data for 45 countries over the period 1993–2001[58]	The proportionality of the voting system is significantly and negatively correlated with shareholder protection in a panel of 45 countries and positively correlated with employment protection in a panel of 21 OECD countries. Legal origin has some additional explanatory power only for employment protection.
Bordo and Rousseau (2006)	1) Financial development (Broad money/GDP) 2) Growth in per capita GDP	1) Legal origin 2) Political variables[59]	1) OLS 2) 2SLS (with legal origin and political variables as instruments)	17 countries over the period 1880–1997	Both legal origin and political environment matter for financial development, but only the effects of the latter are stable over time.

Articles	Dependent Variables	Main Explanatory Variables	Methodology	Data	Key Results
Roe (2006)	Ownership structure of large corporations and other financial development variables	1) Legal origin 2) Occupation or revolution in OECD countries during the twentieth century	OLS	Part or all of the OECD countries in 1990s	Historical factors do approximately as well as legal origin in explaining differences in national financial outcomes statistically for the OECD countries.
Dam (2006)			Survey of literature		The LLSV choice of indicators and their interpretations of those indicators are problematic, which may invalidate their regression results.
Spamann (2008)	1) External cap/GNP 2) Domestic firms/Pop 3) IPOs/Pop 4) Ownership concentration	Corrected ADRI	OLS	46 countries in 1994	For 33 out of 46 countries, the ADRI value from LLSV must be corrected. Accurate index values are neither distributed with significant differences between common and civil law countries nor correlated with stock market size and ownership dispersion.
Siems (2007)			Comparative legal analysis		LLSV's categorisation of legal families, which aims to cover most countries of the world, is to a large extent just arbitrary.
Rajan and Zingales (2003)	Financial development[60]	1) Trade openness 2) Openness to capital flows	1) OLS 2) 2SLS 3) Panel regression	24 countries over the period 1913 to 1999	Trade openness is correlated with financial market development, particularly when cross-border capital flows are free. This phenomenon can be explained by an interest group theory.
Musacchio (2008)			Historical studies	11 countries in 1910 and 1995	The ranking of legal families according to the protection they accord creditors is not constant over time.

Articles	Dependent Variables	Main Explanatory Variables	Methodology	Data	Key Results
Perotti and von Thadden (2006)			Theoretical analysis		A financially weakened middle class in the countries previously ravaged by inflation preferred a more corporatist financial system.
Armour et al. (2009)	1) Stock market capitalisation/GDP 2) Value of stock trading/GDP 3) Stock market turnover ratio 4) Domestic firms/Pop	Shareholder protection index[61]	Panel regression	20 countries over the period 1995–2005	There is no evidence of a positive impact of the changes in shareholder protection law on stock market development.
Cheffins (2001)			Historical studies		The development of stock markets in Britain suggests that alternative institutions can perform the role that the legal system plays.
Coffee (2001)			Historical studies		In the early stage of the development of stock markets, self-regulation could act as a partial functional substitute for formal legal rules, at least in common law countries.
Sgard (2006)			Historical studies	15 countries over the period 1808–1914	Over the entire period, all legal traditions strongly protected creditor rights, except for English law coming out prima facie as less protective.
Lamoreaux and Rosenthal (2005)			Historical studies		US businesses had a more limited menu of organisational choices and also much less ability to adapt the basic forms to meet their needs.

Notes:
1. The ratio of the stock market capitalisation held by minorities to gross national product.
2. The ratio of the number of domestic firms listed in a given country to its population (in millions).
3. The ratio of the number of initial public offerings of equity in a given country to its population (in millions).
4. The ratio of the sum of bank debt of the private sector and outstanding non-financial bonds to GNP.
5. The average percentage of common shares owned by the three largest shareholders in the ten largest nonfinancial, privately owned domestic firms in a given country.
6. The ratio of the market value of assets to their replacement value at the end of the most recent fiscal year.
7. The average ratio of the equity issued by newly listed firms in a given country (in thousands) to its GDP (in millions).
8. The block premia are computed as the difference between the price per share paid for the control block and the price on the Exchange two days after the announcement of the control transaction, divided by the price on the Exchange and multiplied by the proportion of cash flow rights represented in the controlling block.
9. Index of the extent to which business executives in a country agree with the statement "Stock markets are open to new firms and medium-sized firms".
10. The average total value of stocks traded as a percentage of GDP.
11. Disclosure requirements index is calculated as the average of the following six proxies: (1) prospectus, (2) compensation, (3) shareholders, (4) inside ownership, (5) contracts irregular, and (6) transactions.
12. Liability Standard index is calculated as the average of the following four proxies: (1) liability standard for the issuer and its directors, (2) liability standard for distributors, and (3) liability standard for accountants.
13. The index of public enforcement equals the arithmetic mean of (1) supervisor characteristics index, (2) rule-making power index, (3) investigative powers index, (4) orders index, and (5) criminal index.
14. Ratio of credit from deposit-taking institutions to the private sector to GDP.
15. The number of different procedures that a start-up must comply with to obtain legal status.
16. The time it takes to obtain legal status to operate a firm, in business days.
17. The cost of obtaining legal status to operate a firm, as a share of per capita GDP.
18. The index measures the protection of employment laws as the average of (1) the existence and cost of alternatives to the standard employment contract, (2) the cost of increasing the number of hours worked, (3) the cost of firing workers, and (4) dismissal procedures.
19. The index measures social security benefits as the average of (1) old-age, disability, and death benefits, (2) sickness and health benefits, and (3) unemployment benefits.
20. The index measures the protection of collective relations laws as the average of (1) labour union power and (2) protection of workers during collective disputes.
21. Government intervention is measured by an index of property rights protection, an index of quality of business regulation, and the top marginal tax rate.
22. Public sector efficiency is measured by survey scores on corruption, bureaucratic delay, tax compliance, and a measure of the relative wages of government officials.
23. The output of public goods is measured by infant mortality, school attainment, illiteracy, and an index of infrastructure quality.
24. The size of the public sector is measured by government transfers and subsidies, government consumption, an index of the size of the state enterprise sector, and a measure of the relative size of public sector employment.
25. Political freedom is measured by a democracy index and a political rights index.
26. Four measures of economic freedom are used. The first is a subjective index of the security of property rights against infringement by the government. The second is the number of different steps that a start-up business must comply with to begin operating as a legal entity. The third measure is the intensity of regulation of the employment contracts. The fourth is an estimate of government ownership of commercial banks.

27. Three measures of political freedom are used, including a democracy score, an index of political rights, and an index of human rights.
28. The measure of judicial independence is the average of the measures of tenure of Supreme Court judges, tenure of administrative court judges, and judicial decisions as a source of law.
29. The index of constitutional review is the average of measures of the rigidity of the constitution and judicial review.
30. Duration is measured as the number of calendar days counted from the moment the plaintiff files the lawsuit in court, until the moment when his claims are enforced.
31. Other judicial quality measures include measures of enforceability of contracts, corruption, integrity of the legal system, and confidence in the legal system.
32. The index measures substantive and procedural statutory intervention in judicial cases at lower-level civil trial courts and is formed by adding seven indices together.
33. The measure of banking development equals the value of loans made by commercial banks and other deposit-taking banks to the private sector divided by GDP.
34. This index equals the average of two variables constructed by ICRG, namely *rule of law*, which is an assessment of the law-and-order tradition of the country, and *country risk*, which is an assessment of the risk that a government will modify a contract after it has been signed.
35. Three indicators of financial intermediary development are used: (1) liquid liabilities equals liquid liabilities of the financial system (currency plus demand and interest-bearing liabilities of banks and nonbank financial intermediaries) divided by GDP, (2) commercial–central bank equals the ratio of commercial bank assets divided by commercial bank plus central bank assets, and (3) private credit equals the value of credit from financial intermediaries to the private sector divided by GDP.
36. Cross-sectional data cover 71 countries over the period 1960–1995.
37. Bank/GDP is total assets of deposit money banks divided by GDP.
38. Turnover is total value of shares traded divided by market capitalisation.
39. Judicial efficiency is an assessment of the efficiency and integrity of the legal environment produced by the country risk-rating agency Business International Corporation.
40. Cross-sectional data cover 39 countries over the period 1980–1995.
41. This index is based on the governance rankings produced by Credit Lyonnais Securities Asia (CLSA) in a corporate governance report.
42. The legal variable is calculated by multiplying ADRI and the *rule of law* index.
43. This variable is used to denote whether common stock, straight debt, or convertible preferred stock was employed in private equity investments.
44. This variable is used to denote whether private equity investors have control of the firm's equity when it has its minimum contractually specified share of the equity.
45. This variable is used to denote whether private equity investors can be protected by antidilution provisions, automatic conversion provisions, and supermajority provisions.
46. This index is measured as the "time-to-contract-dispute-resolution" constructed by Djankov et al. (2003).
47. Leverage is defined as the ratio of financial debt to the book value of shareholder's funds plus financial debt.
48. Maturity structure is defined as the ratio of short-term debt to financial liabilities.
49. Financial development is measured by the ratios of stock market capitalisation to GDP and bond market capitalisation to GDP.
50. Indicators of financial intermediary development, stock market development and the protection of property rights are used to measure financial development.
51. Political channel through which legal origin may influence financial development is proxied by the following two variables: tenure of Supreme Court judges and Supreme Court power.
52. Adaptability channel through legal origin may influence financial development is proxied by two variables, namely case law that indicates whether judicial decisions are a source of law and legal justification that indicates whether judgments are based on statutory law rather than on principles of equity.
53. Four measures of financing obstacles are used: (1) the general financing obstacles firms face in raising capital, (2) the degree to which collateral requirements impede firms' access to finance,

(3) the extent to which bank bureaucracy and paperwork represents an important barrier to obtaining external finance, and (4) the difficulty in having access to long-term loans.

54. Three measures are used to proxy for property rights institutions: (1) constraints on executive from the Polity IV data set, (2) protection against expropriation from Political Risk Services, and (3) Heritage Foundation's private property index.

55. Three measures are used to proxy for contracting institutions: (1) index of legal formalism developed in Djankov et al. (2003), (2) index of procedural complexity of resolving a court case involving nonpayment of a large commercial debt from World Bank's report on *Doing Business in 2004*, and (3) the number of distinct procedures involved in the same process.

56. Property rights institutions are instrumented by settler mortality in countries that were colonised by European nations between 1500 and 1900 or by the density of indigenous population per square kilometre in 1500. Contracting institutions are instrumented by legal origin.

57. The measure of employment protection is the 1990 average of the OECD Employment Protection Legislation indicator for regular contracts and short-term contracts.

58. For "employment protection" only, the panel spans the period 1990–1998 and is limited to the 21 OECD countries. Cross-sectional data also cover only the OECD countries.

59. Political variables include indicators for whether (1) a government is based on a parliamentary system, (2) the electoral system is based upon the principle of proportional representation, (3) decisions are made primarily by a single political party that holds a majority of offices, and (4) there is universal female suffrage. Additional measures include the number of elections held each year and the number of revolutions or coups.

60. Four indicators are used to measure financial development: (1) the ratio of deposits (commercial banks plus savings banks) to GDP, (2) the ratio of equity issues by domestic corporations to gross fixed capital formation, (3) total stock market capitalisation, and (4) the number of publicly traded domestic companies per million population.

61. This index focuses exclusively on the law relating to listed companies and contains 10 variables: (1) powers of the general meeting for de facto changes, (2) agenda setting power, (3) anticipation of shareholder decision facilitated, (4) prohibition of multiple voting rights, (5) independent board members, (6) feasibility of director's dismissal, (7) private enforcement of director duties (derivative suit), (8) shareholder action against resolutions of the general meeting, (9) mandatory bid, and (10) disclosure of major share ownership.

CHAPTER 3

LAW, STOCK MARKETS, AND ECONOMIC GROWTH

3.1. INTRODUCTION

The significance of finance is too obvious to ignore when exploring the determinants of economic growth. Historically, economic growth is always accompanied by financial development. For example, when the per capita income of the United States (measured in 1960 US dollars) increased from $413 in 1870 to $1,087 in 1910 and to $3,641 in 1970, its ratio of broad money (M3)[42] to GDP rose from 30.1% to 60.3% and then to 70.4%, respectively (Rousseau and Sylla, 2003). The ratio of stock market capitalisation to GDP in the United States similarly increased from 0.39 in 1913 to 0.66 in 1970 (Rajan and Zingales, 2003a). Comparatively, there are substantial differences in financial systems across countries. Based on a newly constructed data set, Demirgüç-Kunt and Levine (2001) examine the financial structure for a cross-section of up to 150 countries and find that financial sector development – measured as the size, activity, and efficiency of banks, non-bank financial intermediaries, and equity markets – tends to be greater in richer countries.

The relationship between financial development and economic growth, however, is a topic that has been debated in economics since the beginning of the 20th century. In *The Theory of Economic Development*, Schumpeter (1961) argues that well-functioning banks encourage technological innovation by identifying and funding entrepreneurs that have the best chances of successful innovation. Hicks (1969) contends that the industrial revolution would not have been possible in the absence of financial markets that provided liquidity; according to Bencivenga et al. (1996), the industrial revolution had to wait for the financial revolution before it could occur. By contrast, Robinson (1952: 86) argues that

---

[42] The narrowest measure of money that the Federal Reserve System (the Fed) reports is M1, which includes currency, checking account deposits, and traveller's checks. M2 adds to M1 other assets that have check-writing features (money market deposit accounts and money market mutual fund shares) and other assets (savings deposits, small-denomination time deposits and repurchase agreements) that are extremely liquid because they can be turned into cash quickly at very little cost. M3 adds to M2 somewhat less liquid assets such as large-denomination time deposits and repurchase agreements, Eurodollars, and institutional money market mutual fund shares. See Mishkin (2004: 52–53).

"where enterprise leads finance follows". According to this view, financial institutions and markets arise whenever there is economic demand for them. Lucas (1988) goes further to assert that "the importance of financial matters is very badly over-stressed" and therefore dismisses the role of finance in economic growth.

Neither of these theories can be said to have won the argument before the 1990s because of the lack of strong empirical evidence on the importance of the financial system. Fortunately, a growing body of empirical work has emerged in the past two decades,[43] as a result of the advances in computational capacity and the availability of large cross-country data sets with relatively long time dimension. Using country-level, industry-level, and firm-level data, the so-called finance and growth literature provides deeper insights into the finance and growth nexus, and "suggests a positive, first-order relationship between financial development and economic growth" (Levine, 1997). Taken as a whole, the bulk of existing research indicates that countries with better functioning banks and markets grow faster, and a fundamental mechanism through which financial development matters for growth is that better functioning financial systems ease the external financing constraints that impede firm and industrial expansion (Levine, 2005). As Sylla (2006) has succinctly phrased it, "where finance leads, enterprise follows".

The finding that financial development influences economic growth will inevitably lead us to a deeper question, i.e., why do some countries have well-developed growth-enhancing financial systems, while others do not? More specifically, do laws and regulations designed to protect investors against expropriation by corporate insiders determine the emergence and expansion of the financial sector, and can the differences in financial development across countries and time thus be explained by the differences in legal provisions and their enforcement characteristics? As we have shown in chapter 2, such questions have been tentatively addressed by LLSV and their followers who demonstrate a close connection between legal protection of investors and the prosperity of financial markets. However, there are still plenty of unsolved problems left by their studies. For example, can the correlation between law and finance revealed by LLSV be taken as evidence for a causal relationship running from law to finance and not vice versa? What are the different roles played by particular laws,

---

[43] There were sporadic empirical studies on the finance and growth nexus before the 1990s; of these, Goldsmith (1969) stands out. Using data on 35 countries from 1860 to 1963, Goldsmith (1969: 48) finds that "a rough parallelism can be observed between economic and financial development if periods of several decades are considered" and "there are even indications in the few countries for which the data are available that periods of more rapid economic growth have been accompanied, although not without exception, by an above-average rate of financial development". Goldsmith's work, however, is criticised for its weaknesses, including limited observations (only 35 countries), not systematically controlling for other factors associated with economic growth, and failing to identify the direction of causality, etc. (Levine, 1997; Beck, 2008).

such as corporate law, securities law, bankruptcy law, etc. and their enforcement characteristics, in sustaining the operation of financial markets? Can we simply transplant the legal provisions that have been shown to be efficient in developed countries to developing and transitional countries and wait for the boom of the financial sector?

The remainder of this chapter addresses such questions. Before continuing, I want to acknowledge that – because of the wide range of fields covered by the financial system – the focus will have to be narrowed to the relationship between *law and stock markets* rather than the relationship between *law and finance as a whole*, so as not to burden this chapter too much. This strategy can be further justified by the fact that it is the stock markets, instead of the other parts of the financial system, such as banks or bond markets, that have attracted the most attention from scholars who are involved in the LLSV debate. This chapter will therefore concentrate on the institutional preconditions for a strong equity market, with special attention to corporate law and corporate governance, the dynamic relationship between law and the market, and the complicated interaction between political and social factors and law. Thus, some important issues remain outside the scope of this chapter. For example, the effects of law – particularly law that is intended to safeguard the interests of creditors – on banking development and credit expansion will be omitted, regardless of their theoretical attractiveness and practical importance.[44]

3.2. FINANCE, STOCK MARKETS AND ECONOMIC GROWTH: A BRIEF OVERVIEW

The financial system is esteemed as "the brain of the economy" (Mishkin, 2006: 25), in view of its essential role in channelling funds from households and firms whose revenues exceed their expenditures to those who lack resources to fund their good investment opportunities. Without a financial system, it is hard or even impossible to transfer idle funds to more efficient uses; new ideas, innovative products, and productive investments will therefore be abandoned, and society will in turn be trapped in the status quo. According to Rajan and Zingales (2003b: 5), "healthy and competitive financial markets are an extraordinarily effective tool in spreading opportunity and fighting poverty. Because of their role in financing new ideas, financial markets keep alive the process of 'creative destruction' – where old ideas and organisations are constantly challenged and replaced by new, better ones. Without vibrant, innovative financial markets, economies would invariably ossify and decline".

---

[44]   For some recent studies on this issue, see, among others, Qian and Strahan (2007) and Davydenko and Franks (2008) on the influence of bankruptcy law, and Haselmann et al. (2009) on the effects of collateral law.

More specifically, the financial system[45] is expected to influence the allocation of resources across space and time by providing five basic functions:[46] producing information about possible investments and allocating capital; monitoring investments and exerting corporate governance; facilitating the trading, diversification, and management of risk; mobilising and pooling savings; and easing the exchange of goods and services (Levine, 1997, 2005). Although it may be argued that all financial systems exercise these functions, there are great differences in their performance, and the differences in turn contribute to different economic growth records through the channels of capital accumulation and technological innovation.

Stock markets can stimulate the production of information about investments. As markets become larger and more liquid, agents may have greater incentives to expend resources in researching firms because it is easier to profit from this information by trading in large and liquid markets (Grossman and Stiglitz, 1980; Holmstrom and Tirole, 1993). As Rajan and Zingales (2003b: 55) argue, information generated in underdeveloped markets is less useful, more based on aggregate economy-wide indicators or the moods of the stock market than on hard, company-specific information, and stock prices of individual firms would therefore tend to move together. By contrast, more developed markets produce more varied, firm-specific information, and stock prices of individual firms would reflect this variety by substantially diverging from one another.[47]

In addition to collecting information about firms and investments, financial markets can be used to ensure that the recipients of the financing use the funds efficiently and create value for investors by monitoring the recipients' activity and exerting corporate control. Stock markets have been identified as playing an important role in helping address agency problems inherent in financial contracts. In an efficient stock market, share prices will reveal the true value of firms; therefore, stock prices can be used to align the interests of managers with those of owners by linking stock performance to manager compensation (Stewart, 1990; Jensen, 1993).[48] In addition, an active stock market can facilitate

---

[45]   We will only focus on the role of stock markets in this chapter, and therefore must ignore the effects of financial intermediaries.

[46]   See also Bodie and Merton (1999: 24–32), World Bank (2001: 33), and Rousseau and Sylla (2006) on different categorisations of financial functions.

[47]   This argument is empirically confirmed by Morck et al. (2000), who find that less developed stock markets have a higher fraction of stocks that move in the same direction: for example, in emerging markets like China, Malaysia, and Poland, over 80% of stocks frequently move in the same direction in a given week.

[48]   During the 1990s, academics and practitioners alike argued in favour of equity-based compensation (particularly stock options) as a mechanism for aligning the incentives of mangers and shareholders. However, recent studies indicate that there may be "a dark side to incentive compensation" (Denis, et al., 2006). After controlling for other elements of compensation and possible determinants of fraud, Denis et al. find a positive association between option use and the likelihood of allegations of fraud. See also Burns and Kedia

takeovers of poorly managed firms; thus, according to Jensen (1986), a stock market can serve as a "court of last resort" by exerting external discipline upon managers when internal control mechanisms are relatively weak or ineffective.[49]

One of the most important functions of a financial system is to achieve an optimal allocation of risk. The most salient type of risk is liquidity risk, which arises from the fact that assets cannot be expected to be converted into a medium of exchange without any uncertainty because of information asymmetries and transaction costs. Intuitively, the most productive investments often require the commitment of large amounts of funds for substantial periods, but investors are unlikely to devote their funds to such investments unless they are guaranteed to be able to access their savings quickly and easily whenever they need. Financial markets and institutions can be relied on to increase investment in high-return illiquid assets and accelerate economic growth; for example, stock markets can help agents cope with liquidity risk by allowing those investors receiving liquidity shocks to sell their equity claims before the firms in which they invested create new technologies, sell goods, and distribute profits, without disrupting the productive processes occurring within firms (Levine, 1991). In addition to addressing liquidity risk, financial systems may also mitigate the risks associated with individual projects, firms, industries, regions, countries, etc. A developed financial system enables investors to diversify their risk across many investments and thereby to substantially limit (though not completely eliminate) their exposure to any single investment, which reduces the risk premium demanded by investors to part with their funds. As a result, valuable but risky projects get financed (Saint-Paul, 1992; Obstfeld, 1994).

Mobilisation, or pooling, involves the agglomeration of capital from disparate savers for investment. The demands for pooling arise both from producers who seek capital to run their firms and from investors who seek

---

(2006), Johnson et al. (2009), and Peng and Röell (2008) on the association between option-based compensation and the propensity of firms to restate earnings, commit fraud, or be subject to class action lawsuits. Therefore, some features of pay arrangements seem to reflect managerial rent-seeking rather than the provision of efficient incentives, and executive compensation should be viewed not only as a potential instrument for addressing the agency problem but also as part of the agency problem itself (Bebchuk and Fried, 2003).

[49] Market prices of shares generally reflect the value of assets as deployed by the incumbent managers. When a firm is not managed well, its share price declines, and the firm then becomes a potential target of a hostile takeover. The more the share price declines, the more profitable it is for a raider to obtain enough stock, take control of the firm, and revamp the target's structure or management. Finally, thanks to the restructuring, the mismanaged enterprise will become competitive and profitable again, which will not only reward the raider (and shareholders of the enterprise) in terms of appreciation in the price of the shares but also benefit all of society by replacing a value-destroying enterprise with a value-adding business. In addition, investors benefit even if their corporation never becomes the subject of a hostile takeover because even the threat of takeover will motivate managers to improve the firm's performance, thereby increasing the price of the shares and reducing the chance of takeover. For a more extensive theoretical analysis of corporate takeover, see Easterbrook and Fischel (1991: Chapter 7). See also Becht et al. (2007) for some empirical studies.

liquidity and superior risk-bearing opportunities. A world without pooling may be characterised by autarky, in which firm size is limited by household wealth and production processes will thus be constrained to an economically inefficient scale; in addition, households with modest wealth will be forced to invest in one, or at most a few enterprises, exposing themselves to significant nonsystematic risk (Sirri and Tufano, 1995). A financial system may thus emerge to bridge a firm's capital needs and households' investing needs, relieve society of large deadweight costs, and profoundly affect economic development.

Finally, financial arrangements can promote specialisation (and thereby assist economic growth) by facilitating the exchange of goods and services. This idea may be traced back to Adam Smith's *Wealth of Nations*, which made a celebrated argument that division of labour–specialisation is the principal factor underlying productivity improvements. Greater specialisation can be achieved with the benefit of a more effective financial system because more specialisation requires more transactions, and financial development and innovation will continually contribute to reduced transaction and informational costs (Greenwood and Smith, 1997). The most notable and often-cited example is money, which arises to lower transaction and information costs and ease exchange by overcoming the "double coincidence of wants problem" as an easily recognisable medium of exchange (King and Plosser, 1986; Ostroy and Starr, 1990).

The idea that financial development plays a central role in economic growth has been firmly established by a wide variety of articles in the literature[50] that employ cross-country regressions, within-country studies exploiting variance across industries and firms, country-specific case studies, etc. On the country level, a growing body of research demonstrates a strong, positive link between stock market development and economic growth. For example, using data on 47 countries from 1976 to 1993, Levine and Zervos (1998) find that the initial level of stock market liquidity (rather than other stock market indicators, such as volatility, market size, and international integration) has significant relationships with the future values of output growth, capital stock growth, and productivity growth; these authors conclude that stock market liquidity is a robust predictor of future economic growth. This OLS-based conclusion is supported by subsequent research that utilises time-series methods (Arestis et al., 2001) and studies using dynamic panel methodology (Rousseau and Wachtel, 2000; Beck and Levine, 2004).

To address some of the problems associated with the cross-country models, such as omitted variables, reverse causality, and multicollinearity, researchers have turned to a more micro perspective by using industry-level and firm-level data. In a highly influential study, Rajan and Zingales (1998) argue that better

---

[50]   For more extensive reviews of the empirical literature on the finance-growth nexus, see Levine (1997, 2005) and Beck (2008).

developed financial markets and institutions help reduce firms' cost of raising money from outsiders, and industries that are naturally heavy users of external finance should therefore benefit disproportionately from greater financial development than other industries. Thus, the effect of financial development should vary by industry according to its financing needs. Using data on 36 manufacturing industries across 41 countries, Rajan and Zingales (1998) find strong evidence to support their hypothesis that financial development affects relative growth rate of industries.

Following a similar approach as Rajan and Zingales, Beck et al. (2008) examine whether financial development enhances economic growth by easing constraints on industries that are technologically more dependent on small firms. The results indicate that small-firm industries grow disproportionately faster in economies with well-developed financial systems. Fisman and Love (2007) suggest a modification to the method employed by Rajan and Zingales by shifting the emphasis from technological industry differences in financial dependence to a broader notion of growth opportunities, and find that industries with good growth opportunities grow more rapidly in countries with well-developed financial systems. Similarly, Wurgler (2000) also employs industry-level data to examine the effect of financial markets on industries with different growth prospects. Using data from across 65 countries for the period 1963–1985, he constructs country-level estimates of the elasticities of industry investment to industry value added to gauge the extent to which a country increases investment in its growing industries and decreases investment in its declining industries. His main finding is that developed financial markets, as measured by the size of the domestic stock and credit markets relative to GDP, are associated with a better allocation of capital (high investment-value-added elasticities). In other words, financially developed countries increase investment more in their growing industries and decrease investment more in their declining industries.

Rather than relating industry-level growth to financial development, some studies use firm level data to assess the impact of access to financial services on firm growth. For example, Demirgüç-Kunt and Maksimovic (1998) investigate how differences in financial (and legal) systems affect firms' use of external financing to fund growth. These authors first calculate the maximum growth rate that each firm in their 30-country sample could attain without access to long-term financing and then compare these predicted growth rates to growth rates realised by firms in countries with differing degrees of development in their financial (and legal) systems. The empirical results suggest that the proportion of firms growing beyond the rate allowed by internal resources is higher in countries with better developed banking systems and more liquid stock markets (and in countries whose legal systems score high on an efficiency index).[51]

---

[51] Demirgüç-Kunt and Maksimovic (2002) extend their earlier work by using a larger sample (40 instead of 30 countries) and adopting an instrumental variable approach to extract the

Therefore, the existence of active financial markets and a large intermediary sector should make it easier for firms to obtain external funds and grow rapidly.

Finally, a body of country-specific case studies attempts to confirm the nexus between finance and economic growth by referring to historical evidence. For example, Haber (1991) compares industrial and capital market development in Brazil, Mexico, and the United States between 1830 and 1930 and finds that capital market development substantially affected industrial structure and industrial expansion. Wright (2002) examines the integration and expansion in American financial markets between 1780 and 1850, and concludes that "the U.S. financial systems created the conditions necessary for the sustained domestic economic growth (increased real per capita output) that scholars know occurred in the nineteenth century". Rousseau and Sylla (2005) employ a set of multivariate time-series models that relate measures of banking and equity market activity to investment and business incorporation from 1790 to 1850 in the US and find that the financial variables Granger-cause measures of real activity.

In general, the current evidence supports the claim that the financial system, and the stock markets, in particular, plays an essential role in economic growth. As generalised by Honohan (2004), "the causal link between finance and growth is one of the most striking empirical macroeconomic relationships uncovered in the past decade". Well-functioning capital markets ease the external financing constraints that impede firm and industry expansion, encourage capital accumulation and technological innovation, and therefore sustain long-term economic prosperity. Because of the importance of capital markets in promoting economic growth, it is theoretically necessary and practically significant to explore the determinants of their development, which is the task of the rest of this chapter.

3.3. LAW AND STOCK MARKETS: DOES CORPORATE LAW MATTER?

3.3.1. WHY AND HOW DOES CORPORATE LAW MATTER?

It seems like a miracle that stock markets function effectively because buying stock means exchanging a sum of funds today for a promise to return more

---

exogenous component of financial development. These authors find that the use of external financing by firms is positively related to the development of both the predicted banking system and the securities markets in each country and further show that securities markets and bank development have different effects on the type of external financing firms obtain, particularly at relatively low levels of financial development. More specifically, the development of securities markets is more related to long-term financing, whereas the development of the banking sector is more related to the availability of short-term financing.

funds in the future, which is difficult to value ex ante and more difficult to be honoured ex post. Outside investors, who typically have little access to information on the value of the corporation, can hardly tell the difference between good firms (with high expected profits and low risk) and bad firms (with low expected profits and high risk). In addition, outside investors are less likely to be motivated to make the promise enforceable by monitoring the performance of firms in which they have invested, if each of such outside investors owns just a small fraction of the corporation, which indicates that there is a free-rider problem. By contrast, insider controlling shareholders and/or managers of the corporation are typically well informed about and in control of the corporation's affairs, and can thus easily divert benefits to themselves to the detriment of outsider investors. For example, managers may arrange for the corporation to pay them excessively high salaries (Bebchuk and Fried, 2004; Murphy, 1999; and Core et al., 2003) or sell the firm's assets at an artificially low price to their own companies (Johnson et al., 2000).

The problem of misaligned incentives in corporations led Adam Smith ([1776] 1976, Vol. 2, 264–265) to worry about the viability of the corporate form of organisation and to state that "the directors of such [joint-stock] companies, however, being the managers rather of other people's money than of their own, it cannot well be expected, that they should watch over it with the same anxious vigilance with which the partners in a private copartnery frequently watch over their own ... Negligence and profusion, therefore, must always prevail, more or less, in the management of the affairs of such a company". A similar concern about the conflict of interests within corporations was expressed by Berle and Means (1932), who showed that shareholders of large American corporations had surrendered control of the firm to professional managers, and that there was thus a separation of ownership and control that departs from the principle of economic efficiency.[52]

Given the vulnerability of outsider investors to expropriation by insiders, why do people still willingly invest their money in corporations? Obviously, if the corporate form of organisation can only serve as a tool through which insiders enrich themselves at investors' expense, it would have succumbed to alternative forms of organisation long ago in the competitive market place. However, the corporation has gone on to become the dominant means of organising production worldwide. The main reason, according to Fama and

---

[52]   As agency theory claims, when there is a separation of ownership and control, or in other words, when the decision makers (managers) who initiate and implement important decisions are not the residual claimants (shareholders) and therefore do not bear a major share of the wealth effects of their decisions, such decision makers are more likely to take actions that deviate from the interests of residual claimants. A controlling shareholder also has an incentive to appropriate the corporate resources, since he bears only a fraction of costs resulting from his appropriation. See, among others, Jensen and Meckling (1976), Fama and Jensen (1983).

Jensen (1983), lies in the fact that, the modern corporation, with its separation of ownership from control, will benefit society by facilitating the specialisation of management and risk bearing;[53] moreover, the agency problems[54] between outside investors and insider decision makers can be addressed through a combination of market, organisational, and legal methods. Thus, according to Easterbrook and Fischel (1989), "[t]he corporation will flourish when the gains from the division of labour exceed the augmentation of the agency costs".

In general, the key to the success of stock markets where corporations go to raise funds to run and grow their business and where investors can participate in ownership of these firms, is to solve the agency problems inherent in these corporations. Certainly, law is not the only solution, and market forces and non-legal mechanisms can also be relied upon by investors to protect their interests. First, for example, firms with good quality may "signal" their quality through voluntary disclosure of information about the true value of the firm without any mandatory requirements because they want to distinguish themselves from firms with bad quality and raise capital under more favourable terms (Romano, 2001). Indeed, Durnev and Kim (2005) find that in countries with weak legal investor protection, corporations will be motivated by the desire for high market valuation to adopt better corporate governance measures, such as timely and accurate disclosure. Similarly, Klapper and Love (2004) show that firm-level governance provisions matter for firm performance, particularly in countries with weak shareholder protection, and Dahya, Dimitrov and McConnell (2008) find that corporations in countries with weak legal protection for shareholders can raise their value by appointing independent boards. In the early nineteenth century when law offered relatively few rights or protections to investors, many corporations in the United States configured their voting rights in a way that enhanced the relative influence of small shareholders: they used what might be called "graduated voting rights" schemes in which the votes per share to which

---

53 According to Alchian (1987), "the ability to specialize in managerial decisions and talent (control) without also having to bear the risk of all the value consequences, enables achievement of beneficial specialization in production and coordination of cooperative productivity". Although managers specialise in making decisions about the use of resources, shareholders are responsible for bearing the consequent market or exchange values. To the contrary, unifying ownership and control, or restricting residual claims to decision makers, will impose efficiency losses on decision processes, because decision agents must be chosen on the basis of wealth and willingness to bear risk, in addition to decision-making skills. In addition, shareholders must forgo optimal risk reduction through portfolio diversification to ensure that residual claims and decision making can be combined in a small number of agents. Finally, when residual claims are restricted to decision agents, it is generally rational for the residual claimant-decision maker to assign lower value to uncertain cash flows, and the consequent decisions, such as less investment in risky but highly profitable projects, will penalise the organisation in the competition for survival (Fama, Jensen, 1983).

54 See Jensen and Meckling (1976), who present the first theoretical framework on agency problems. See also Armour, Hansmann, and Kraakman (2009) for a general discussion on this issue.

an investor was entitled was a decreasing function of the number of shares held (Hilt, 2008). Campbell and Turner (2011) also find that decisions made at the corporate level in Victorian Britain – such as those regarding dividends, board size, and directorial ownership – may have played an important role in protecting the interests of outside shareholders: high dividend payout ratio, large boards (relative to firm size), and requirements that directors own shares were positively related to corporate value.

The so-called "gatekeepers", such as auditors, attorneys, stockbrokers, stock analysts, etc., are also believed to be capable of shielding the interests of outside investors without much help from legal intervention. Thus, according to Coffee (2006: 2), a gatekeeper acts as a "private policeman, who has been structured into the process to prevent wrongdoing". The gatekeepers can provide a certification or verification service to investors, and therefore assure investors about the quality of the securities issued by corporations. In essence, as repeat players who have served many clients over many years, gatekeepers have accumulated significant reputational capital, which can be lent to corporations who try to raise capital from the market but fail to convince investors that they are trustworthy. As long as the gatekeepers have reputational capital at risk that exceeds the one-time gain from acquiescence in fraud, such gatekeepers can be trusted as such "private policemen".

Other mechanisms matter as well. For example, Franks et al. (2009) show that informal relations of trust[55] rather than formal investor protection promoted the development of capital markets and the dispersion of ownership in the United Kingdom over the twentieth century. Stock exchanges also play important roles. For example, Coffee (2001) describes the New York Stock Exchange (NYSE) as "guardian of the public investor". The NYSE not only rejected the application to list by corporations that lacked an adequate track record or operated in a high-risk industry but also (and more importantly) sought to maintain its reputation by improving standards of corporate disclosure. The London Stock Exchange (LSE) engaged in similar quality control (Cheffins, 2003; Campbell and Turner, 2011).

However, market forces and non-legal mechanisms have been shown to be only partial and inadequate solutions to agency problems; moreover, they will hardly function well without the help and support of the legal framework that underpins them. Firms may adopt investor-friendly governance structures, but the extent to which this strategy is feasible is heavily influenced or even directly determined by the legal environment in which these firms incorporate and operate. Klapper and Love (2004) find that the overall level of firm-level

---

[55]   By trust, they mean "conformity with accepted norms of behaviour in the absence of explicit incentives or penalties to do so". More specifically, the local nature of stock exchanges played an important role in the development of trust between directors and investors. Ordinary shareholders lived close to the company's city of incorporation and its board of directors, and relations of trust flourished as a consequence of this close proximity of investors to firms.

governance is strongly positively related to country-level measures of investor protection; that is, average governance is higher in countries with stronger legal protection. These authors therefore conclude that "firms have limited flexibility to affect their governance, which implies that improving the country-level efficiency of the legal system is likely to lead to an increase in the average firm-level governance". Similarly, Doidge et al. (2007) show that country-level characteristics, such as legal protection granted to investors, stage of economic development, and level of financial development, are more important determinants of a firms' governance quality than firm-level characteristics, such as sales growth, ownership concentration, etc.

Gatekeepers may also fail to perform their desired functions because of conflicts of interest.[56] For example, as the primary gatekeepers for investors in public companies, auditors have failed to provide an adequate answer for corporate insider opportunism. The most serious problem is that accounting firms have traded audits for consulting business. Given the financial importance to accounting firms of the consulting services they were providing,[57] many of their audit clients' managers could use a reduction in the purchase of non-audit services as a disciplining device, pushing auditors to take a pro-management perspective (Choi and Fisch, 2003). Empirical evidence has shown that firms that bought more consulting services from their auditor were more likely to engage in earnings management (Frankel et al., 2002). Indeed, Coffee (2006: 28) argues that the rise of consulting at Arthur Andersen may have caused the internal organisational change that directly contributed to its demise (and the Enron collapse). In addition, attorneys, stockbrokers, securities analysts, investment banks, mutual funds, and rating agencies have all been revealed to suffer from similar conflict of interest problems (Cross and Prentice, 2006; Prentice, 2006). Prentice (2006: 779) therefore concludes that "the short-term self-interest of actors in the securities markets subverts the reputational constraint, rendering it unlikely that capital markets can prosper without stringent regulation".

Stock exchanges have their own weakness. After an examination of the history of self-regulation at 10 exchanges (including NYSE), Pirrong (1995) concludes that prior to the passage of laws that proscribed manipulation, these

---

[56] Gatekeepers may also fail for other reasons, such as the lack of ex post sanctions to offending corporate officers, undersupply of information that is necessary for an efficiently functioning market, etc. For more detailed discussions, see Cross and Prentice (2006, 2007). After studying all reported fraud cases in large US companies between 1996 and 2004 (including all of the high-profile cases such as Enron, HealthSouth, and WorldCom), Dyck et al. (2010) find that the SEC and auditor involvement in the revelation of the fraud is very limited (the SEC accounts for only 7% of the cases and auditors for 10%), whereas actors who are often not considered important players in the corporate governance arena, such as employees, non-financial-market regulators, and the media, play a key role in fraud detection (employees account for 17% of the cases, regulators for 13%, and the media for 13%).

[57] Prentice (2006) reports that consulting fees rose from 17% of audit fees in 1990 to 67% in 1999.

exchanges "took few, if any, measures to curb manipulation". Exchanges have little incentive to retard stock manipulation because such activity increases trading volume and profits (Pritchard, 1999). Exchanges may also have an incentive to hide fraud because fraud means that their rules have been violated and their public image may therefore be damaged (Kahan, 1997). Indeed, many historical studies reveal that before the Securities and Exchange Commission (SEC) was empowered to oversee the exchanges, these exchanges were rife with fraud (Prentice, 2006). It can therefore be argued that there is a fundamental misalignment between the profit maximisation objective of exchanges and their promise to protect the interests of investors (by, for example, fighting against market manipulation and policing fraud).

The weakness of private mechanisms in sustaining stock markets has led Cross and Prentice (2007: 65) to conclude that "while there is obvious truth in recognizing the value of private choice, such choice does not necessarily yield perfect results, and a government regulation system can still offer additional economic benefits … Government action can enhance trust, can reduce transaction costs, and can contribute to valuable network externalities that promote the development of financial markets". After examining the historical development of capital markets, Coffee (2001) similarly argues that although markets can arise in the absence of a mandatory legal framework, they neither function optimally nor develop to their full potential without that infrastructure. In summary, while private mechanisms can affect the quality of corporate management to a large extent, they are in turn deeply influenced and even directly shaped by the legal environment from which they arise and in which they operate, particularly by certain branches of commercial law, such as corporate law and securities law.

According to Armour, Hansmann, and Kraakman (2009), there are two types of strategies used by the law to address agency problems: regulatory strategies and governance strategies. Regulatory strategies attempt to directly safeguard the interests of shareholders by stipulating the content of the agent-principal relationship or by stipulating the formation or dissolution of that relationship. The most common regulatory strategy is to command the agents not to make decisions or undertake transactions that would harm the interests of their principals. By contrast, governance strategies attempt to protect principals indirectly mostly by enhancing their power (to select or remove directors or other managers, for instance).

It seems that corporate law relies mainly on governance strategies to address agency problems, whereas securities law primarily employs regulatory strategies to tackle corporate insiders' opportunism.[58] As Cross and Prentice (2007: 13)

---

[58] The classification here is undoubtedly somewhat crude and arbitrary. While corporate law can be argued to influence agency problems indirectly by shaping the distribution of powers inside the firm, it can also be used to protect shareholders directly through the application of

posit, "the key aspect of corporate law is the allocation of power in the company among the shareholders, the board of directors, and corporate officers". Shareholders (who are deemed the owners of the corporation) are empowered by corporate law to elect or remove directors and make (or approve) certain fundamental decisions for the corporation, such as mergers and dissolutions. In turn, the directors then hire and supervise the officers who generally manage the company on a day-to-day basis.

Theoretically, shareholders have the power to influence company policies through the enforcement of a combination of control rights. Among other things, the right to vote for the board of directors is regarded as "the principal right that equity holders typically get" (Shleifer and Vishny, 1997) or "a core strategy not only for addressing the agency problems of shareholders in relation to managers but also, in some jurisdictions, for addressing agency problems of minority shareholders in relation to controlling shareholders, and of employees in relationship to the shareholder class as a whole" (Armour, Hansmann, and Kraakman, 2009). The obvious utility of this right is to help assure that the board remains responsive to the interests of the firm's owners. Directors' knowledge that they are being monitored by shareholders, and the further knowledge that claims might be aggregated and votes exercised at any time, tends to cause directors to act in shareholders' interests to advance their own careers and to avoid being ousted. Easterbrook and Fischel (1983) therefore conclude that "votes are important despite the collective action problem, and the voting process enables firms to operate more efficiently".

Empirically, shareholders' power, particularly as exercised through their voting rights, has been shown to be economically valuable. For example, Zingales (1995) finds that when a company in the US (where differential voting rights are not particularly prevalent) has two classes of common stock outstanding that differ only in their voting rights,[59] superior voting shares enjoy significantly higher market premia. Furthermore, the value of corporate voting rights is proven to vary widely across countries, depending on the extent to which the corporate controller's private benefits can be constrained by the law (Nenova,

---

fiduciary duties. In addition, it is more difficult to put the legal provisions related to takeover, mandatory disclosure, and anti-fraud in either pole of the dichotomy without controversies. Fortunately, this classification is for the convenience of discussion only and does not influence the basic conclusion.

[59] In his sample, the majority of companies (57) attribute ten votes to the superior voting class and one to the inferior voting class. Based on a bigger sample (the sample size varies between a minimum of 362 firms in 2002 and a maximum of 504 firms in 1998), Gompers et al. (2010) confirm that the 10:1 structure is the most common arrangement used by dual-class firms in the US to create a significant wedge between corporate insiders' voting and cash-flow rights. In many cases, this wedge is sufficient to provide insiders with a majority of the votes despite their claims to only a minority of the economic value (on average, insiders have approximately 60% of the voting rights and 40% of the cash-flow rights in dual-class firms). Unfortunately, the higher the wedge, the lower value of the firm.

2003). Lastly, several studies show that there is a significant relation between firm-level governance indices, in which shareholders' voting rights are an important constituent, and firm performance measured by stock returns, Tobin's Q, etc.[60] (Gompers et al., 2003; Bebchuk et al., 2009)

The board of directors plays a pivotal role in modern corporations. For example, §141(a) of the Delaware General Corporation Law stipulates that "[t]he business and affairs of every corporation organized under this chapter shall be managed by or under the direction of a board of directors, except as may be otherwise provided in this chapter or in its certificate of incorporation". The governance structure of modern corporations can therefore be described as "delegated management with a board structure" (Armour, Hansmann, and Kraakman, 2009). More specifically, in business corporations, all but the most fundamental decisions are delegated by shareholders to a board of directors that has four basic features: (1) the board is (at least as a formal matter) separated from the operational managers of the corporation; (2) the board of a corporation is elected (at least in substantial part) by the firm's shareholders; (3) though largely or entirely chosen by the firm's shareholders, the board is formally distinct from them; and (4) the board typically has multiple members.

When it is well designed and effectively incentivised, the board of directors can be entrusted to safeguard the interests of shareholders, particularly when shareholders are too dispersed to monitor managers effectively.[61] The significance of the board of directors has long been recognised by economists. In an early, but still influential paper, Fama (1980) describes the board as "the ultimate internal monitor" of a firm, whose most important role is "to scrutinize the highest decision makers within the firm", and further argues that the role of the board is to "provide a relatively low-cost mechanism for replacing or reordering top managers". Similarly, Hermalin and Weisbach (2003) define the board as "a market solution to an organizational design problem, an endogenously determined institution that helps to ameliorate the agency problems that plague any large organization".

---

[60] But see Bhagat et al. (2008), who highlight methodological shortcomings of such studies, and argue that there is no consistent relationship between governance indices and measures of corporate performance. That is, there is no one "best" measure of corporate governance. The most effective governance system depends on its context and on firms' specific circumstances.

[61] It is difficult, if not impossible, to organise dispersed shareholders because the classic collective action problem emerges as soon as there is more than one owner (Rock, 1991). Disciplining management is necessary to ensure that managers manage the corporation effectively and in the interests of shareholders. However, discipline is a typical collective good: if it prevents managers from diverting profits from shareholders, all the shareholders benefit in the form of higher earnings and share prices, whether or not they contribute to the discipline. In brief, rational shareholders prefer to free ride on the efforts of others than to subscribe to their pro rata share of the costs of corporate monitoring, and there will thus be undersupply of monitoring in equilibrium. As a result, managers may take advantage of such situations to enrich themselves instead of serving shareholders' interests.

In addition to addressing agency problems by allocating power among shareholders, directors, and managers, corporate law can also protect shareholders' interests by imposing obligations on directors, such as the obligation to comply with fiduciary duties[62] in common law countries. As Pistor and Xu (2003) posit, fiduciary duties are "a core concept in Anglo-American corporate law for delineating the rights and responsibilities of directors and managers, as well as dominant shareholders vis-à-vis minority shareholders". Corporate directors and managers are deemed to be fiduciaries of the corporation they serve and of the shareholders who delegate control rights to them and are expected to run the corporation for the benefit of shareholders.

Fiduciary duties fall into two broad categories: the duty of care and the duty of loyalty. Under the duty of care, "directors of a corporation in managing the corporate affairs are bound to use that amount of care which ordinarily careful and prudent men would use in similar circumstance".[63] More specifically, the duty of care requires fiduciaries to (1) gather pertinent information; (2) focus – pay attention – and deliberate before making a decision; and (3) use their skills in the decision-making process (Frankel, 1998). By imposing the duty of care on fiduciaries in performing their services, corporate law vests in shareholders the legal right to receive quality fiduciary services.[64]

The core of the duty of loyalty, according to Anabtawi and Stout (2008), is a requirement that a corporate fiduciary (an officer or director) should act only in the best interests of the fiduciary's beneficiary (the firm and its shareholders). Thus, the duty of loyalty asks managers to place the interests of the corporation and its shareholders above their own interests. The most easily conceivable way to ensure that fiduciaries act only in their beneficiaries' interests is to eliminate any possibility that fiduciaries can use their powers to benefit themselves, such as by forbidding any type of transaction between managers and their firms that may involve a conflict of interest. However, because such transactions might benefit both parties in some cases, corporate law does not ban them altogether. Instead, corporate law allows corporate officers and directors to use their powers to pursue business transactions that benefit themselves, provided that the

---

[62]   For a detailed overview of fiduciary duties, see Xu and Zhou (2013).

[63]   Graham v. Allis-Chalmers Mfg. Co., 188 A.2d 125, 130 (Del. 1963).

[64]   In practice, however, it is difficult for a director or an officer to be found to have breached the duty of care because the business judgment rule insulates directors and officers from much of their potential liability. The business judgment rule is typically described as a legal presumption that the directors and officers of the corporation have exercised due care by acting on an informed basis, in good faith, and in the honest belief that their actions are in the best interest of the corporation (see Smith v. Van Gorkom, 488 A.2d 858 (Del. 1985)). Unless a plaintiff can produce persuasive evidence rebutting one of these three components – generally a difficult if not impossible task – corporate directors and officers are effectively immune from liability for breach of the duty of care. See, for example, Anabtawi and Stout (2008).

transactions are sanitised by the approval of either fully informed and disinterested directors or shareholders ex ante or by the courts ex post (Velasco, 2010).

As Clark (1986: 141) states, the "general fiduciary duty of loyalty is a residual concept that can include factual situations that no one has foreseen and categorized". In other words, the principles of fiduciary duties can hardly be codified,[65] and the meaning of such principles must be specified by courts in developing a large volume of case law over time. Courts are therefore vested with great discretion in determining the boundaries of managers' obligations to shareholders.[66] Compared with the civil-law approach that relies on statutory rules to govern conflict-of-interest transactions – and may thus invite insiders to structure unfair transactions creatively to conform to the letter of law – the concept of fiduciary duties allows courts in common law countries to assess the substantive terms of the entire transaction, depending on whether these terms are fair to outside shareholders, rather than on whether they conform to a statute (Johnson et al., 2000). Courts in civil law countries may therefore be argued to accommodate more "tunnelling"[67] style problems than courts in common law countries.

The scope and strength of shareholders' power, the relationship between shareholders and the board, and the effectiveness of the board in defending shareholders' interests have therefore become the focus of studies that explore the role of corporate law in the development of stock markets. As we have discussed, in their series of empirical studies on the determinants of stock market development, LLSV construct an anti-director index that measures how strongly the corporate law empowers (minority) shareholders against managers (or dominant shareholders) in the corporate decision-making process and find that high levels of shareholder power are associated with more flourishing equity markets. Numerous subsequent studies that use anti-director indexes confirm the importance of shareholder power in determining the development of stock markets (see chapter 2).

---

[65]   See Pistor and Xu (2003), who argue that attempts to codify fiduciary duties "will either leave out many actions or factual situations that 'no one has foreseen or categorized' (Clark, 1986), or will be phrased so broadly that the meaning can be understood only in the context of specific cases". Hamermesh (2006: 1777) also argues that "[b]y their nature equitable and fact-bound, fiduciary duties resist, and may even suffer from, codification".

[66]   See Fisch (2000), who shows that in the United States, particularly in Delaware, which has been the dominant choice as state of incorporation for the largest US companies (almost half of the companies listed on the New York Stock Exchange and 60% of Fortune 500 companies have chosen to incorporate in Delaware), the statute provides almost no guidance regarding fiduciary principles, and both the interpretation and application of these fiduciary principles rely mainly on judicial decisions.

[67]   The term "tunnelling" is used by Johnson et al. (2000) to refer to transferring resources out of a company to its controlling shareholder (who is typically also a top manager).

3.3.2. QUESTIONING THE ROLE OF CORPORATE LAW

3.3.2.1. Dissenting Voices from Legal Scholars

However, attempting to attribute the prosperity of stock markets to the scope and strength of shareholder power in particular and to corporate law in general has long been doubted by corporate law scholars.[68] For example, Roe (2002) shows the limit of corporate law in addressing agency problems by dividing agency problems into two components, namely stealing and shirking. Whereas the former, which is defined to include the machinations that transfer value to controlling shareholders or managers, is the type of behaviour that corporate law can control, the latter, which refers to bad decision making that inflicts losses on shareholders, such as overexpansion, overinvestment, and reluctance to take on profitable but uncomfortable risks, is beyond the reach of corporate law. Other institutions, such as product market competition, incentive compensation, takeovers, shareholder primacy norms, etc., must be relied upon to control the costs of mismanagement. For these other institutions, corporate law is typically just a supporting prop, not the central institution. Rock and Wachter (2001: 1622) also argue that "the raison d'être of firms is to replace legal governance of relations with non-legally enforceable governance mechanisms (what are sometimes called 'norms')", and corporate law may thus be better understood as playing a secondary role in corporate governance by simply "protecting and perfecting this choice".[69]

The validity of the conventional corporate law theory that enshrines the principle of shareholder primacy is also challenged by the so called "director primacists", who argue in favour of vesting primary decision-making authority in a firm's board of directors rather than in its shareholders. The board of directors is argued to be better understood as "a sort of Platonic guardian serving as the nexus of the various contracts making up the corporation" (Bainbridge, 2002), or "mediating hierarchs" that can tie the hands of shareholders (Blair and Stout, 1999; Stout, 2003) instead of as a mere agent of

---

[68] For a more recent contribution to this debate, see Pacces (2012).

[69] To Rock and Wachter (2001), these norms, or in their terms, "nonlegally enforceable rules and standards (NLERS)", form a great part of what is sometimes referred as the firm's "corporate culture". Within a firm, NLERS operate at many different levels. For example, "discharge only for cause" in a world of employment-at-will is one of the prime NLERS that protects employees. NLERS may also exist in the corporate boardroom: board composition itself is an NLERS. Corporate law facilitates the establishment and maintenance of NLERS by, for example, creating a centralised management dominated by directors, who in turn choose the NLERS in the same manner as they choose the set of physical and intangible assets. When the gains of stealing from the firm are large enough, however, the sanctions related to NLERS may not sufficiently deter such opportunistic activities, and legal remedies, such as the duty of loyalty, are required to complement NLERS. In general, "law plays the role of sheep dog, but does not intervene more than necessary" (Rock, Wachter, 2001: 1662).

shareholders. To Bainbridge (2002), the modern public corporation precisely fits Kenneth Arrow's model of an authority-based decision-making structure that is characterised by the existence of a central agency to which all relevant information is transmitted and which is empowered to make decisions binding the whole. The board of directors and the senior management team then function as the central agency, whose authority should not be challenged by shareholders to prevent disrupting the mechanism of centralised decision-making.[70] Based on a "team production theory of corporate law", Blair and Stout (1999) and Stout (2003) argue that corporate production frequently requires a number of groups in addition to shareholders to make sunk-cost investments that cannot be adequately protected by formal contract or market mechanisms. If shareholders were given unalloyed control of the firm, they might extract wealth from other team members by threatening to destroy or expropriate their specific investments. To address this problem, team members prefer to cede control over the firm to an outside party – the board of directors – that is not itself a residual claimant and thus lacks any direct incentive to take advantage of team members.

Emasculation of shareholder power can also be justified from other perspectives. For example, Anabtawi (2006) argues that shareholders are not a homogenous group; on the contrary, they have significantly divergent and frequently conflicting interests,[71] and consequently may use any incremental power conferred upon them to pursue their private interests to the detriment of shareholders as a class. In that case, vesting primary decision-making authority in the board of directors is necessary to mediate the various and frequently conflicting interests of shareholders. From a stakeholder perspective, Fisch (2006) argues that if the interests of fixed claimants (creditors, employees, suppliers, etc.) are not fully protected by contract, shareholders may benefit by transferring value from fixed claimants to themselves.[72] Increasing shareholder power will therefore damage economic efficiency.

---

[70] In that sense, the corporation is regarded as "a vehicle by which the board of directors hire capital by selling equity and debt securities to risk bearers with varying tastes for risk", while ownership of the residual claim "differs little from ownership of debt claims" (Bainbridge, 2006: 605). For a more detailed discussion, see Bainbridge (2008).

[71] For example, heterogeneity among shareholders with respect to their expected holding periods can lead to differences in shareholder preferences over corporate decision making. In other words, shareholders will disagree with one another about whether managers should make decisions for long-term or immediate profits. Similarly, diversified shareholders and undiversified shareholders are likely to conflict in risk preferences.

[72] For example, shareholders may prefer excessive levels of risk in a corporation. Even when the corporation is financially sound, great risk may reduce the creditworthiness of the firm and thus the value of its debt or may reduce job security, which thereby reduces the value of the firm to its employees.

3.3.2.2. Challenges from Legal Practices in the United States

The hypothesis that corporate law contributes to the prosperity of stock markets by strengthening the power of shareholders versus directors and managers also contradicts the reality of the United States, which has the most developed capital markets in the world. According to the Delaware General Corporation Law, which applies to the majority of US publicly traded companies,[73] shareholders are granted the right to elect directors, approve charter and bylaw amendments, and approve fundamental corporate changes, such as mergers, sales of all or substantially all of the firm's assets, dissolutions, etc. However, in practice, such rights give shareholders little power over corporate decision-making.

To begin with, the right of shareholders to nominate and elect directors is substantially weakened by legal and non-legal factors. The board can be reshuffled by two methods under American corporate law. The first is by proxy fight (or proxy contest), in which an outsider challenges existing management by proposing an alternative slate of directors and attempts to win support from shareholders. The second method is a tender offer, in which a bidder (typically another company or consortium of investors) gives public notice that it will buy shares of stock at a certain price. The price is typically set well above the current market price to encourage shareholders to tender their shares. If the offer is accepted, the bidder acquires control of the target firm and can thus replace, or at least control, management. In both cases, efficient teams are supposed to replace inefficient managers.

Although empirical studies consistently find that proxy fights are associated with accompanying increases in shareholder wealth (Dodd and Warner, 1983; Borstad and Zwirlein, 1992; DeAngelo and DeAngelo, 1989; and Mulherin and Poulsen, 1998), for directors of public companies, the threat of replacement by a rival slate seeking to manage the firm is negligible (Bebchuk, 2007). Bebchuk (2007) reports that during the proxy seasons of the decade from 1996 through 2005, incumbents faced challenges from rival slates seeking to manage the firm in only 118 cases, or roughly twelve per year. When only companies with a market capitalisation that exceeds $200 million are considered, the number diminishes to only 24 cases or less than three per year. Furthermore, among targets with a market capitalisation that exceeds $200 million, challengers won in only eight cases, which is less than one per year. As a result, "[t]he shareholder franchise is largely a myth. Shareholders commonly do not have a viable power to replace the directors of public companies" (Bebchuk, 2007).[74]

---

[73] See Bebchuk and Cohen (2003), who report that Delaware has been the dominant choice as the state of incorporation for the largest US companies: 58% of all public companies and 59% of Fortune 500 companies have chosen to incorporate in Delaware.

[74] But see Veasey (2007), who argues that "the stockholder franchise is not a myth", and "the stockholder power to hold boards accountable and to effect meaningful change has strengthened incrementally since the mid-1980s and into the twenty-first century", and Stout

A plausible interpretation of the low incidence of challenges is that challengers face considerable economic and legal impediments to replace boards. A rival team seeking to replace incumbents will bear significant costs, including the costs of identifying and searching for shareholders who hold shares in street names, mailing proxy cards to individual shareholders and receiving them back, and persuading shareholders that the rival team offers a superior alternative. The problem of cost is exacerbated by the free-rider problem, which means that although challengers must bear their full costs, they will capture only a fraction of the benefits that the contest confers on shareholders collectively. Finally, it may be difficult to convince shareholders that rival directors would perform better, particularly in view of an externality problem faced by shareholders: a shareholder would have to bear the full costs of an investment in assessing which slate of directors would be better but would have to share the benefits from an improved decision with fellow shareholders.

Legal rules matter too. After examining the legal environment faced by shareholders in the United States, Black (1990) argues that "[l]egal obstacles are especially great for shareholder efforts to nominate and elect directors, even to a minority of board seats". For example, shareholders cannot call special shareholder meetings and therefore must wait until the next regular annual meeting to present and vote on a proposal to replace the company's existing board of directors, by which time damage caused by directors' wrong decisions may have been irreversible (Anabtawi, 2006). Various state statutes also permit corporations to adopt so-called shark repellent measures[75] that make it more difficult for a challenger to gain control of the board of directors through a proxy contest. In addition, as the basic rules governing proxy contests, the Proxy Rules under the Securities and Exchange Act of 1934 (the 1934 Act), impose substantial costs, delays, and legal risks on the efforts of shareholders to communicate with one another.[76] A shareholder who nominates and elects directors also faces other legal risks under the 1934 Act, such as disclosure obligations under section 13(d), insider trading risk under section 10(b), control person liability under section 20(a), etc. In addition, under existing legal arrangements, although challengers

---

(2007), who challenges Bebchuk's opinion from both theoretical and empirical perspectives, and states that "we should demand strong empirical evidence indeed before concluding that giving shareholders greater control over corporate directors would be a good idea".

[75] For example, an important and common measure is the classified or staggered board, in which only a fraction (often one third) of the members of the board of directors is elected at each shareholder meeting instead of en masse. When a board is staggered, a challenger must win more than one proxy fight at successive shareholder meetings in order to exercise control of the target firm. For a more detailed discussion of the staggered board, see Bebchuk et al. (2002).

[76] Black (1990) complains that the SEC defines "proxy" and "solicitation" so expansively that a communication that doesn't solicit anything can still be a solicitation. Shareholders who want to find out whether other shareholders are dissatisfied and might be willing to support certain challenges to management will be deemed to be engaging in a proxy solicitation and required to meet all of the associated public notice and advance filing requirements.

receive no reimbursement in the event that they lose, incumbents can charge the full expenses of their defence to the company regardless of the outcome. In general, Manne (1965: 114) describes proxy contests as "the most expensive, the most uncertain, and the least used of the various techniques".

Takeover through tender offer (hostile takeover),[77] or the market for corporate control, is identified as an important corporate governance mechanism, or "a court of last resort" for assets that are not being utilised to their full potential (Jensen, 1986).[78] This perspective can be traced back to Manne (1965), who argues that as the market price of the shares of a poorly managed existing company decline relative to the shares of other companies in the same industry or relative to the market as a whole, an opportunity will then be created for a more skilled management team who can take control of the company by offering an attractive (higher-than-market) price to shareholders, remove the poorly performing management, and finally capture the gains from improved management through higher stock prices. Shareholders will benefit from the tender offer both directly and indirectly: the target's shareholders gain directly by receiving a premium over the market price; and shareholders of non-target firms will benefit indirectly because the managers of such non-target firms will be motivated by the threat of takeover to work hard to improve firm performance and reduce the takeover risk, which leads to higher share prices (Easterbrook and Fischel, 1991: 173).

There are numerous empirical studies on the financial effects of takeover. All studies, whatever the time period or acquisitive form, find statistically significant positive abnormal returns to target shareholders on the announcement of a bid (Jensen and Ruback, 1983; Jarrell et al., 1988; Burkart, 1999; Andrade et al., 2001; Schwert, 2000; Tirole, 2006: 49). By contrast, studies show mixed results for bidder gains. Depending on the time period and the firm sample, acquiring firm shareholders experience positive, negative, or statistically insignificant abnormal returns.[79] The combined abnormal returns to a target and acquiring firm pair are relatively small, but significantly positive, which suggests that takeovers do

---

[77] Hostility is defined as bids pursued without the acquiescence of target management. By contrast, before a bidder makes an offer for another company in a friendly takeover, it typically first informs the company's board of directors. The board then decides whether or not to recommend that the offer be accepted by shareholders.

[78] To some scholars, however, takeover has been deemed as a symptom of, rather than a remedy for, agency problems. For example, managers of acquiring firms may overestimate their ability to improve the target firm's performance, and thus pay too much for the target (Roll, 1986). Takeovers may also be a manifestation of managers' ability to pursue their own interests, such as diversification of the managers' human capital risk at the expense of shareholders (Amihud and Lev, 1981). In addition, a takeover may provide substantial gains to a raider without producing any improvements in efficiency by virtue of reneging on existing contracts, particularly implicit contracts, and by expropriating rents from target stakeholders, such as employees, creditors, etc. (Shleifer and Summers, 1988).

[79] See, among others, Bradley et al. (1988) on positive gains, Travlos (1987) on negative returns, and Stulz et al. (1990) on insignificant results.

create shareholder value on average.[80] In addition, the notion that takeover disciplines inefficient management is supported by empirical evidence, which shows that poorly performing firms are more likely to be targets of takeover attempts (Mitchell and Lehn, 1990; Berger and Ofek, 1996) and that the managers of poorly performing firms are more likely to be fired (Mikkelson and Partch, 1997; Kini et al., 2004).

Whereas hostile takeovers showed its power in disciplining managers in the 1980s, the situation was reversed in the 1990s. For example, Andrade et al. (2001) show that only 4% of takeover transactions in the 1990s involved a hostile bid at any point, compared to 14% in the 1980s. In addition, a hostile bidder acquired less than 3% of targets in the 1990s, while the comparable ratio from the 1980s is 7%. Holmstrom and Kaplan (2001) and Schwert (2000) report a similar decline in hostile takeovers in the 1990s. In summary, hostile takeovers "died out" in the 1990s (Tirole, 2006: 44).

Several factors, such as the collapse of the junk bond market,[81] which was the main source of financing for hostile takeovers, have been identified as contributing to the decline of hostile takeovers. Anti-takeover laws enacted in numerous states[82] are also blamed for that decline by giving boards excessive latitude to fend off unwelcome takeover offers. State anti-takeover laws consists of two categories of rules, i.e., rules restricting bidders and rules governing the use of defensive tactics (Bebchuk and Ferrell, 1999). One method of deterring unwanted takeovers is to restrict what bidders are able to do. For example, "control share acquisition" statutes requires a hostile bidder to put its offer to a vote of the shareholders of the target firm before proceeding with it;[83] "fair price" statutes require a bidder who succeeds in gaining control and then

---

[80] For example, Andrade et al. (2001) find that the average announcement period abnormal returns over the three-day event window for the target and acquirer combined are fairly similar across decades, ranging from 1.4% to 2.6% and averaging 1.8%.

[81] The junk bond market is a type of market that buys and sells "junk" or high-yield bonds. This market is also termed as a speculative grade bond market, non-investment grade bond market, or high-yield bond market. A junk bond has a below investment grade rating at the time when it is bought and carries a greater risk of default and other financial adversities. Because of the higher risk level, junk bonds offer/yield greater interest rates to draw in investors. See http://en.wikipedia.org/wiki/High-yield_debt.

[82] The Williams Act, a federal law regulating takeovers, has also been criticised. According to the Williams Act, anyone acquiring more than 5% of the stock of a publicly traded firm must file a report disclosing his position and intentions. Bidders must file more elaborate reports concerning their financing and plans, and tender offers must remain open for approximately a month. Bidders may not buy stock in the market during their offers and must purchase shares in oversubscribed offers pro rata and at the highest price offered to anyone. Easterbrook and Fischel (1991: 165) argue that "these rules eliminate any advantage to making early tenders", and the act "gives targets both time to maneuver … and legal grounds for objecting, while depriving bidders of strategies that would facilitate acquisitions".

[83] If a bidder does not do so and purchases a large block of shares, it runs a very serious risk of not being able to vote these shares at all and thus will not be able to gain control despite its large holdings.

proceeds with a second-step freeze-out (a transaction removing the remaining shareholders) to pay the remaining minority shareholders the same price it paid for shares acquired through its bid; and "business combination" statutes prevent a bidder that gains control of a target from merging the target with its own assets for a specified period of time (Bebchuk and Cohen, 2003). In addition, "constituency statutes", which allow managers to take into account the interests of nonshareholders (such as employees and creditors) when addressing takeovers, provides managers with additional reasons for opposing a takeover and makes it more difficult for courts to scrutinise such decisions. Another important impediment to takeovers is the wide latitude given to managers to engage in defensive tactics, such as the "poison pill endorsement" statute that explicitly authorises the use of "poison pill" defences[84] against hostile takeovers. All these rules, both statutory and judge-made,[85] as Bebchuk and Ferrell (1999) summarise, "make takeovers more difficult".

Anti-takeover statutes were widely adopted in the mid-1980s. Altogether, control share acquisitions statutes were passed in 27 states, fair price statutes in 27 states, business combination statutes in 33 states, poison pill endorsement statutes in 25 states, and constituency statutes in 31 states (Bebchuk and Cohen, 2003). Anti-takeover statutes can be used as powerful entrenchment tools by managers, and there is evidence that the existence of managers who are insulated from replacement via a hostile takeover leads to some inefficient economic outcomes, such as increases in managerial slack, poorer operating performances, increased consumption of private benefits by executives, and lower firm values (Borokhovich et al., 1997; Bertrand and Mullainathan, 1999; Gompers et al., 2003; and Bebchuk et al., 2009).[86] According to Easterbrook and Fischel (1991: 204), "[e]very device giving managers the power to delay or prevent an acquisition makes shareholders worse off".

Therefore, in the United States, shareholders seeking to exercise their theoretical power to replace directors face substantial legal impediments.[87]

---

[84] Poison pill stock gives shareholders specific rights that mature once any person owns more than a specified bloc (commonly 20%) and entitles their owners (except for the bloc holder) to purchase additional shares at a discount. A poison pill thus can be used to dilute the bloc owner's interest, making each share worth less and requiring the bidder to buy more to gain control. In addition to the poison pill, there are numerous other defensive strategies that can be relied upon to ward off a potential bidder, such as differential voting rights, scorched earth policies, classified or staggered boards, etc. For details of these strategies, see Milgrom and Roberts (1992: 516).

[85] In Delaware, the law on defensive tactics consists almost entirely of judge-made law, while in other states statutory law plays a more important role.

[86] However, after surveying two types of empirical studies of takeover defences (poison pill event studies and poison pill premium studies), Coates (2000) concludes that prior studies of takeover defences do not support the belief that defences either increase or decrease firm value on average.

[87] Blair and Stout (1999: 310–311) even claim that shareholders' voting rights (at least in publicly traded companies) "are so weak as to be virtually meaningless". The result is that

Furthermore, shareholders' power to adopt changes in the company's basic governance arrangements or to make major business decisions is also restricted by corporate law (Bebchuk, 2005). US shareholders must ratify fundamental corporate decisions such as mergers and charter amendments but are powerless to initiate them. All major corporate decisions must be initiated by the board, in addition to routine matters of corporate policy falling within the exclusive province of the board's authority to manage the corporation. The only way in which shareholders can attempt to introduce a new corporate decision is by replacing incumbent directors with a new team that is expected to make such a change, and the reliability of this method should be questioned in view of the evidence discussed above.

American corporate law is silent regarding board composition, insider trading, and mandatory disclosure (Bebchuk and Hamdani, 2006). For example, although independent directors are widely recognised as a key component of good corporate governance,[88] state corporate laws generally grant companies the freedom to choose the composition of their boards and does not require them to appoint independent directors. Thompson and Sale (2003) therefore conclude that "Delaware law is distinctive for its emphasis on directors and its preference for allowing the markets and private ordering, as opposed to law, to regulate (or nor regulate) how directors use that power … under Delaware corporate law, corporations are free to adopt any or all of these requirements if their directors believe those devices might benefit the corporation. The power of shareholders to respond to such director decisions is relatively limited".

The importance of fiduciary duties in protecting the interests of shareholders is also limited. Directors can be held personally liable for failure to comply with their fiduciary duties and may have to pay compensatory (or even punitive damages) to the shareholders. For example, WorldCom's twelve outside directors personally paid $24.75 million as part of a settlement with a plaintiff class led by the New York State Common Retirement Fund (NYSCRF), and Enron's ten outside directors paid $13 million out of their own pockets to settle claims against them (Black et al., 2006). Thus, litigation may be understood to align managers' incentives with shareholders' interests by imposing personal liability on corporate officers and directors for breaching fiduciary duties. This type of hypothesis, however, is not fully supported by the empirical evidence.

"shareholders in public corporations do not in any realistic sense elect boards. Rather, *boards elect themselves*" (italics in original). Bainbridge (2006: 616) argues similarly that in US corporate law, "shareholder control rights in fact are so weak that they scarcely qualify as part of corporate governance".

88   See, for example, Millstein and MacAvoy (1998), who argue that independent directors enhance corporate governance. However, other studies fail to confirm the relationship between board composition (independence) and corporate performance (Hermalin and Weisbach, 1991; Bhagat and Black, 2002). See Hermalin and Weisbach (2003) for a survey of the literature.

For example, Black et al. (2006) analyse the degree to which outside directors of public companies are exposed to out-of-pocket liability risk,[89] and show that this risk is very low. These authors find that during the period from 1980–2005, there were only 17 cases involving corporate law fiduciary duty claims for damages against outside directors (five derivative suits[90] and twelve direct suits). The plaintiffs were successful in six cases, but only in one case was there an out-of-pocket payment made by outside directors; in addition, their empirical investigation unearthed twelve settlements in which outside directors made out-of-pocket payments during the same period, but only three of these cases involved fiduciary duty claims. These authors therefore conclude that "despite the litigious environment in which public companies function, outside director liability is and will in all likelihood remain, a rare occurrence" (Black et al., 2006). This conclusion corresponds with findings from previous studies, such as Romano (1991), who similarly shows that directors of public corporations face a very low risk of liability and is further supported by Armour, Black, Cheffins, and Nolan (2009), who find that lawsuits under corporate law are hardly effective as devices of deterrence.

The infrequency of out-of-pocket liability reflects the fact that corporate charters[91] and the availability of indemnification[92] and D&O (Directors and Officers) liability insurance[93] provide considerable protection for directors against lawsuits (Black et al., 2006). The result is a sharp distinction between nominal liability and the risk of an actual out-of-pocket payment. Thus, although directors of publicly traded US companies are much more likely to be sued for breaching their fiduciary duties than their counterparts in other countries,

---

[89]   Out-of-pocket liability risk refers to the risk of paying legal expenses or damages pursuant to a judgment or settlement agreement that are not fully paid by the company, by another source, or that are covered by directors' and officers' (D&O) liability insurance.

[90]   A shareholder derivative suit is a lawsuit brought by a shareholder on behalf of a corporation against a third party. Frequently, the third party is an insider of the corporation, such as an executive officer or director.

[91]   Virtually every public company incorporated in Delaware has in its charter an exculpatory provision, authorised by section 102(b)(7) of the Delaware General Corporation Law, that in effect requires a court to dismiss a suit seeking damages from directors based on breach of the duty of care unless the plaintiff alleges facts showing that the defendant engaged in intentional misconduct or failed to act in good faith. Companies incorporated elsewhere typically have similar provisions under similar and sometimes broader statutory authorisation.

[92]   Under Delaware corporate law, a corporation may indemnify a director for damages, amounts paid in settlement, and legal expenses so long as the director acted in good faith and in a manner that the director reasonably believed to be in (or not opposed to) the best interests of the corporation. Almost all public companies have indemnification agreements with directors.

[93]   Virtually all public companies purchase D&O insurance for their officers and directors. D&O insurance covers directors' legal expenses, damages paid pursuant to judgment, and amounts paid in settlement. In addition, neither corporate law nor securities law places limitations on the permissible scope of D&O coverage.

lawsuits under corporate law are hardly an everyday occurrence and out-of-pocket liability is scarcely a serious threat. The role of breach of fiduciary duties suits should therefore not be overestimated in the deterrence of manager misconduct because it is merely one of a number of mechanisms that can be relied upon by investors to ensure their investments are being managed appropriately and cannot be resorted to as the sole remedy; therefore, the threat of breach of fiduciary lawsuits is "potentially useful, but not essential" (Armour, Black, Cheffins, Nolan, 2009).

American corporate law is therefore described to be "board-centric", and the "least shareholder-friendly governance law" (Enriques et al., 2009). According to Cross and Prentice (2006: 362), American corporate law is "relatively toothless at punishing directors or otherwise facilitating the monitoring of managers of public companies". If the key to the development of stock markets is a shareholder-friendly corporate law, as suggested by the studies of LLSV, then the experience of the US is a very important anomaly.

LLSV's hypothesis is further challenged when we turn our attention to continental Europe, where capital markets are less developed than in the US but bodies of corporate law are more shareholder-friendly. For example, Enriques et al. (2009) report that major continental European countries, such as Italy, Germany,[94] and France, accord shareholders significant rights that Delaware does not, such as the right "to initiate a shareholder meeting, to initiate a resolution to amend the corporate charter, to place board nominees on the agenda of shareholders' meeting and to remove directors without cause by a qualified majority vote"; in addition, the law in continental European jurisdictions (such as Germany) appears to offer negligent directors less protection from liability than US law.

More specifically, the difference in the distribution of legal powers between US and continental European corporations can be identified along three dimensions, namely the allocation of decision-making power, the allocation of agenda-setting power, and election and removal of directors (Cools, 2005). Under Delaware law, shareholders have the right to initiate and adopt bylaw amendments, but the charter can be amended only upon the board's proposition and with approval of the shareholders at a shareholders' meeting, which means that the board effectively has a veto over any change to provisions in the charter. By contrast, in Europe, charter and bylaws typically are found in one single

---

[94] However, these authors claim that Germany also has shareholder-unfriendly corporate law, because in Germany, codetermination law provides for substantial worker participation in corporate governance by stipulating that all corporations with two thousand employees or more must reserve 50% of the seats on their supervisory board for employee representatives whose interests are (on the surface at least) opposed to those of the shareholder class. German corporate law requires a two-tier board structure for open companies. The two boards are organised vertically with an elected supervisory board that in turn appoints a managing board whose members are the principal managers of the firm.

document, and a shareholders' vote is required for any change in any of its provisions; the board does not even need to agree with an amendment, let alone propose the amendment. In addition, a shareholders' meeting in continental Europe can make more decisions than its counterpart in Delaware. For example, a typical power of shareholders' meetings in Europe is to approve dividends, which in Delaware is the exclusive authority of the board.

Another aspect of the difference between the United States and continental Europe is the allocation of agenda-setting power, i.e., how easy or difficult it is for shareholders in the United States to have their proposals included in the company's proxy, or how smoothly shareholders in continental European countries can put their proposals on the agenda of the shareholder meeting. In the United States, while qualified shareholders[95] are entitled to include certain proposals in the company's proxy materials, the board has a broad variety of permissible grounds for excluding proposals from the company's proxy materials. Conversely, shareholders in Europe can easily include a proposal in the agenda of a shareholder meeting, and it is only in exceptional circumstances that the board can modify a shareholder proposal.

Lastly, compared with their counterparts in the United States, shareholders in Europe can more easily elect and remove directors. Directors in European countries can generally be removed from office at will (*ad nutum*), which means at any time and at the mere discretion of the majority of the shareholders. Combined with strong shareholder agenda-setting rights, this susceptibility to removal means in practice that in most continental European countries, "a shareholder or group of shareholders can convene a meeting and then dismiss all directors by a mere majority vote" (Cools, 2005: 750).

3.3.2.3. *Negative Empirical Evidence*

The significance of shareholder protection offered by corporate law in underpinning the efficient functioning of stock markets is also questioned by recent empirical studies that use new approaches to measure shareholder protection across countries. For example, Spamann (2010) constructs a corrected "antidirector index" by recollecting the legal data for 46 of the 49 countries covered by the original "antidirector index" with a substantially improved method (such as getting help from local lawyers and offering a detailed coding protocol that serves to convert the raw data into replicable index values), and shows that his new index is more accurate, more consistent, and therefore more reliable. It is surprising to find that the US score goes from the sample maximum of 5 in the original index used by LLSV to the sample minimum of 2 in the

---

[95]   Holders of at least $2,000 in market value or of 1% of the company's securities for at least one year by the date the proposal is submitted.

corrected index.[96] In addition, Spamann shows that the alleged connection between legal origin and shareholder protection, and the correlation between investor protection and ownership concentration, in addition to size of the capital market, breaks up with the corrected index.

The conclusion reached by Spamann (2010) is further confirmed by empirical studies that rely on new datasets[97] constructed by a group of scholars (economists and lawyers) affiliated with a project called "Law, Finance and Development", which is sponsored by the University of Cambridge. For example, Lele and Siems (2007: 43) examine shareholder protection across five countries (France, Germany, India, the UK, and the US) and conclude that "law on shareholder protection in the US is weaker than the law of the other four countries". Similarly, Siems and Deakin (2010) show that compared with France, Germany, and the UK, shareholder protection in the US is much weaker. Sarkar and Singh (2010) use a longitudinal dataset on legal protection of shareholders over the period 1970–2005 for France, Germany, the UK, and the US to examine whether shareholder protection matters in the development of the stock market. These authors use the VAR Granger causality test to show that shareholder protection does not influence stock market development. Based on the data set that covers shareholder protection for 25 countries over the period 1995–2005, Armour, Deakin, Sarkar, Siems, and Singh (2009) demonstrate that there is no significant relationship between the shareholder protection index and various indicators of stock market development, including stock market capitalisation, the value of stock traded, stock market turnover ratio, and the number of listed companies.[98]

In general, it is fair to say that the importance of corporate law in assisting the development of stock markets has been overestimated by LLSV and their followers. Certainly, corporate law matters for economic development: for example, by making the legal form of corporation widely available and user-friendly, corporate law "enables entrepreneurs to transact easily through the medium of the corporate entity, and thus lowers the costs of conducting business" (Armour, Hansmann, and Kraakman, 2009: 2). However, the alleged

---

[96]   The score of France, Germany, Italy, Japan and the United Kingdom, is 5, 4, 2, 5, and 4, respectively.

[97]   Five new data sets have been produced to date: three of these are five-country (France, Germany, the United Kingdom, the United States, and India) data sets for the period 1970–2005, which cover the fields of shareholder protection, creditor protection, and labour regulation; the other two datasets cover shareholder protection and creditor protection for a wider range of countries over a shorter period of time – 25 countries over the period 1995–2005. For more details on these data sets, see www.cbr.cam.ac.uk/research/projects/project2-20output.htm (homepage of the "Law. Finance and Development" project on the Cambridge Centre for Business Research website).

[98]   Nor do they find any relationship between common law legal origin and the first three indicators (stock market capitalisation, the value of stock traded, and the stock market turnover ratio). However, they obtain different results for the fourth variable, the number of listed companies. This variable is positively correlated with legal origin, but there is a negative relationship with the shareholder protection index.

causality between a shareholder-friendly corporate law and a prosperous stock market can find robust support neither from the legal practices across countries nor from empirical studies that use new data sets that have been shown to measure shareholder power (protection) more accurately.

3.4. LAW AND STOCK MARKETS: DOES SECURITIES LAW MATTER?

3.4.1. SECURITIES LAW IN BOOK

In addition to corporate law, securities law has also been endorsed by LLSV as an important factor contributing to the success of stock markets. For example, La Porta et al. (2006) examine the effect of securities law on stock market development in 49 countries, with a focus on mandatory disclosure, liability standards, and public enforcement (see chapter 2 for more details). Their regression results show that both disclosure requirements and liability standards are positively correlated with larger stock markets; conversely, public enforcement plays a modest role at best in the development of stock markets. Therefore, these authors conclude that "the answer to the question of whether securities law matter is a definite yes" (La Porta et al., 2006: 27).

This conclusion is consistent with a long-standing theoretical argument that securities law is indispensable for the prosperity of securities markets (Coffee, 1984; Mahoney, 1995; Fox, 1999; Black, 2001).[99] This conclusion also corresponds to the findings of numerous empirical studies that attempt to reveal the consequences of securities regulation, with special attention to (but not limited to) the US market experience. After reviewing this empirical literature, Cross and Prentice (2007: 63) conclude that "these studies … clearly support the economic value of securities regulation … U.S. legal governance appears to provide considerable value to firms as evidenced from the economic value of cross-listing and bonding with federal securities laws".

---

[99]   In fact, for some scholars, securities law in America has replaced corporate law as the most important tool to protect investors, and securities markets therefore flourish in the United States despite its manager-friendly corporate law. For example, Bebchuk and Hamdani (2006) argue that federal (securities) law "has systematically replaced state law arrangements with ones imposing tighter constrains on insiders". More specifically, federal securities law has deployed a significantly broader range of devices than state law: first, whereas state law primarily relies on judge-made standards to address corporate issues, federal law uses both judge-made law and detailed agency-made regulations; second, whereas state law imposes duties and restrictions only on company insiders – notably, directors and officers – federal law regulates both insiders and outsiders, such as gatekeepers and bidders for corporate control; third, whereas state law relies on enforcement by private parties, federal law employs both public and private enforcement; finally, whereas state law is limited to civil sanctions, federal law uses both civil and criminal sanctions. See also Thompson (2003), Thompson and Sale (2003), and Roe (2003) on this issue.

-Chapter 3. Law, Stock Markets,and Economic Growth

More specifically, the law of securities regulation may be divided into three broad categories: disclosure requirements, antifraud provisions, and insider-trading rules (Goshen and Parchomovsky, 2006; Prentice, 2006; Cross and Prentice, 2007). Accurate information is necessary to ensure that capital moves to those who can use it more efficiently. Fraud, conversely, reduces allocative efficiency because low quality corporations (projects, securities, etc.) disguise themselves as high quality firms by making bogus statements about their prospects, which in turn erodes the informational content of the market price. In addition, securities fraud reduces managerial accountability by impairing the ability of outside shareholders to monitor the performance of the firm (and firm managers) and increases the execution costs of securities trades by decreasing trading volume and thus the liquidity of the market (Pritchard, 1999). If fraud cannot be addressed effectively, investors will be reluctant to invest and trade and may finally withdraw from the market, which might then become dormant.[100]

High quality firms may take some measures to convince investors of their quality, such as allowing outsiders (accounts, for example) to review the books and records and having these outsiders certify the accuracy of the firms' representation. However, these private methods are not free. Investors may also expend resources on verifying the financial information of corporations to avoid being victims of fraud, which is costly and even socially wasteful if investors conduct duplicative investigations. Fortunately, these costs can be reduced by legal rules against fraud. As Easterbrook and Fischel (1984) posit, "the penalty for fraud makes it more costly for low-quality firms to mimic high-quality ones by making false disclosure. An antifraud rule imposes low or no costs on honest, high quality firms. Thus it makes it possible for high quality firms to offer warranties at low cost. The information warranty if enforced, makes it unnecessary for buyers to verify information or for sellers to undertake expensive certification. The expenses of offering high quality securities go down while the expenses of passing off low quality securities rise". With decreasing costs of verifying information credibility, investors' estimate of the value of a firm will be more accurate, the price of a stock will be more informative, and the stock market where these investors interact and these stocks are traded will be more efficient in allocating capital (Goshen and Parchomovsky, 2006).

The principal statutory weapon against fraud in the United States is Section 10(b) of the 1934 Act and Rule 10b-5 promulgated by the SEC under that section.[101] Such antifraud provisions seem to have reduced securities fraud to a

---

[100] Bernstein (2004) argues that the Dutch lost the preeminent position as financers of capital markets that they enjoyed during the 1600s and much of the 1700s because they failed to create regulatory bodies or otherwise protect investors from securities fraud and unfair dealing.

[101] For example, Rose (2010: 2174) describes Rule 10b-5 as the "primary antifraud provision in federal securities law"; Cross and Prentice (2007: 140) conclude that section 10(b) is "the most

large extent. For example, a 1963 SEC study reported that 99 of 107 SEC fraud actions in an eighteen-month period involved issuers that were not subject to the reporting requirements of the 1934 Act, which suggests the potency of the deterrent value of the Act (Seligman, 2003: 562). Recent empirical studies also show that there are significant monetary and non-monetary penalties for firms and their managers who commit fraud and therefore become targets of the SEC. For example, Karpoff et al. (2008a) track the fortunes of 2,206 individuals identified as responsible parties for 788 SEC and Department of Justice (DOJ) enforcement actions for financial misrepresentation from January 1, 1978 through September 30, 2006. These authors report that the majority of the culpable managers (93.4%) lose their jobs by the end of the regulatory enforcement period; many also face diminished employment prospects, monetary and non-monetary sanctions, and criminal penalties.[102] Karpoff et al. (2008b) examine the penalties imposed on the 585 firms targeted by SEC enforcement actions for financial misrepresentation during the period 1978–2002 and find that, on average, these firms lose 41% of their market value when the market becomes aware of their misconduct. In addition, these authors report that the penalties imposed on firms by the market are much higher than those penalties imposed by the legal system.[103]

The importance of antifraud provisions in protecting public investors, however, should not be overestimated. Antifraud rules prohibit materially false and misleading representation, but do not impose affirmative disclosure obligations on public corporations. Therefore, according to Easterbrook and

---

potent securities fraud provision ever enacted", and that "evolution of the law of section 10(b) cause of action created a securities fraud remedy many times more potent than any that existed before anywhere in the world". Section 10(b) of the 1934 Act prohibits the use of "any manipulative or deceptive device" "in connection with the purchase or sale of any security" (15 U.S.C. §78j (b)), and is regarded as a "catch-all" or "residual" antifraud provision because it outlaws types of manipulation not specifically proscribed by Section 9 of the Act (Seligman, 2003: 345). Under the authorisation of the Act, the SEC adopted Rule 10b-5 in 1942, which stipulates that it shall be unlawful for any person in connection with the purchase or sale of any security "(1) to employ any device, scheme, or artifice to defraud, (2) to make any untrue statement of a material fact or to omit to state a material fact necessary in order to make the statements made, in the light of the circumstances under which they were made, not misleading, or (3) to engage in any act, practice, or course of business which operates or would operate as a fraud or deceit upon any person" (17 C.F.R. §240. 10b-5).

102 The SEC has barred or is in the process of barring 693 individuals (31%) from future employment as officers or directors in a public firm. The average culpable manager owns 6.5% of the firm's equity and experiences a loss in stock value of $15.3 million when the misconduct is revealed. SEC fines average an additional $5.7 million. In addition, 617 (28%) of these individuals have been charged with criminal violations. Up to the publication of their paper, 469 of these individuals pled guilty or were convicted and sentenced to an average of 4.3 years in jail and 3 years of probation.

103 The penalties imposed on firms through the legal system average only $23.5 million per firm. By contrast, the reputational penalty – defined as the expected loss in the present value of future cash flows due to lower sales and higher contracting and financing costs – is over 7.5 times the sum of all penalties imposed through the legal and regulatory system.

Fischel (1984: 680), "in a world with an anti-fraud rule but no mandatory disclosure system, firms could remain silent with impunity".[104] Without additional methods of regulation, issuers would withhold significant amounts of material firm-specific information and investors would be unable to make reliable inferences regarding an issuer's integrity based solely on what an issuer chooses to disclose. In that case, it is difficult or even impossible for investors to differentiate between candid and opportunistic issuers. In general, a regulatory regime that relies exclusively on an antifraud prohibition "would likely result in socially deficient levels of firm-specific disclosure" (Franco, 2002: 277). It is thus necessary to complement antifraud rules with other regulatory arrangements – such as mandatory disclosure requirements – to increase the volume of firm-specific information.

Mandatory disclosure is a constant theme of the US federal securities regulation[105] and is embodied in the Securities Act of 1933 (the 1933 Act) and in the 1934 Act. The 1933 Act regulates issuance of securities and the 1934 Act imposes continuing and periodic reporting requirements in connection with subsequent securities trading. Pursuant to the 1933 Act, when corporations issue securities to the public, they are required to file a registration statement with the SEC. Then, a portion of the registration statement known as the prospectus must be circulated to potential investors. The 1934 Act requires periodic disclosure in the form of annual, quarterly, and interim reports, in addition to disclosure when corporate directors are elected and for votes regarding significant organic changes to the corporate form.

The United States undoubtedly has the most extensive disclosure requirements for public companies (Hertig et al., 2009). The scope of mandatory disclosure requirements in the United States is much broader than in many other countries. US firms are subject to a continuous reporting requirement if they are listed on a national securities exchange, have more than 750 shareholders and assets exceeding $10 million (whether or not they are exchange-listed), or have previously issued securities that were registered under the 1933 Act. By contrast, the EU's disclosure requirements are narrow because they extend only to firms traded on "regulated markets". In addition, the content of mandatory disclosure in the United States is also more comprehensive. While all jurisdictions require substantial disclosure regarding a basic description of the company (which can

---

[104] This logic can also be found in the US Supreme Court's admonition: "Silence, absent a duty to disclose, is not misleading under Rule 10b-5". Basic, Inc. v. Levinson, 485 U.S. 224, 239 n.17 (1988).

[105] See, for example, Easterbrook and Fischel (1984), who argue that federal securities laws "had and still have two basic components: a prohibition against fraud, and requirements of disclosure when securities are issued and periodically thereafter", and Prentice (2006), who concludes that mandatory disclosure and punishment for fraudulent disclosure are two "primary tools" employed by Congress to restore investor confidence in the nation's market after the Great Crash of 1929.

be described as "hard" information, ranging from an inventory of its assets to an accurate statement of its current financial position and past cash flows), the US is the leader in forcing the disclosure of "soft", "projective", or "forward-looking" information,[106] in addition to information related directly to governance issues and agency problems.[107] The United States has therefore earned the highest score when financial economists attempt to quantitatively compare the extent of mandatory disclosure in different countries (La Porta et al., 2006).

Mandatory disclosure has been justified by scholars from different theoretical perspectives.[108] For example, Coffee (1984) argues that corporate voluntary disclosures create serious externality problems that can lead to private over- or under-production of information. Disclosure regulation can be relied on to mitigate this problem by mandating a socially optimal level of disclosure, at least in theory. Mahoney (1995) contends that the principal purpose of mandatory disclosure is to help shareholders address certain agency problems – specifically, management compensation and self-dealing – by reducing shareholders' monitoring costs.

Hertig et al. (2004) summarise the arguments for mandatory disclosure as follows. First, without mandatory requirements, insiders are not likely to disclose bad news voluntarily because bad news will hurt managers by reducing their compensation and diminishing their job security and hurt controlling shareholders by decreasing the value of their shareholdings and raising the firm's cost of capital. Second, insiders might attempt to bond themselves ex ante to reveal all information, good or bad. However, ex post, the bonding costs may exceed the returns from bonding truthful disclosure, which makes these commitments incredible.[109] Third, there is a divergence between the private benefits of disclosure to the company and its social benefits. Disclosure can impose private costs on firms by aiding their competitors, although it enhances the welfare of diversified investors (and social welfare). Fourth, information is of less value to investors, to the extent that it is idiosyncratic, without standardised format, content, and quality. A mandatory disclosure regime can improve the

---

[106]   Such information includes management's predictions about likely price changes in each of the multiple markets in which the firm operates (i.e., product, supply, capital, and labour markets), in addition to management's best estimates of likely changes in demand for the firm's products, including any new products or cost-saving technologies that the firm plans to introduce.

[107]   This category includes information about top management compensation (salaries, bonuses, equity compensation, and severance payments), in addition to information about cash flows that find their way to controlling shareholders.

[108]   The value of mandatory disclosure is doubted by other scholars, according to whom the market gives corporations sufficient incentives to disclose all material information and mandatory disclosure is therefore useless. See, for example, Choi (2000), Romano (1998, 2001), etc. For helpful surveys on this topic, see Ferrell (2007a) and Leuz and Wysocki (2008).

[109]   The mandatory disclosure system in the US has therefore been described as a mechanism through which issuers can make a credible commitment to high quality, comprehensive disclosure for an indefinite period into the future (Rock, 2002).

comprehensibility and comparability of information through standardisation, which thus increases the value of information to investors.

Mandatory disclosure has therefore been regarded as "the most important device for protecting public investors" (Hertig et al., 2009: 280). However, the early studies of the US mandatory disclosure regime suggest a different story. In the first empirical study of the effects of mandatory disclosure, Stigler (1964) questions the value of mandatory disclosure after finding that the passage of the 1933 Act had no apparent effect on the average return earned by investors in new stock issuances. In another very influential study, Benston (1973) compares the effects that the imposition of mandatory disclosure had on a set of firms that were not voluntarily disclosing sales information prior to the 1934 Act relative to a set of firms that were already voluntarily disclosing sales information. Benston finds that there was no difference in stock return performance between the two groups around the period of the enactment of the 1934 Act and thus concludes that the 1934 Act was not socially beneficial.[110]

More recent studies, by contrast, provide increasing evidence of the benefits of mandatory disclosure.[111] One investigation finds that large over-the-counter (OTC) US firms realised highly significant positive abnormal returns when they were first subject to continuous mandatory disclosure requirements in 1964 (Greenstone et al., 2006).[112] Another study examines the impact of the 1964 imposition of mandatory disclosure requirements on the OTC market in terms of volatility and stock returns (Ferrell, 2007b) and finds that mandatory disclosure is associated with both a dramatic reduction in the volatility of OTC stock returns and with OTC stocks enjoying positive abnormal returns. Bushee and Leuz (2005) examine the economic consequences of the imposition of mandatory disclosure requirements on OTC Bulletin Board (OTCBB) companies and find that firms that were already complying with mandatory disclosure requirements experienced significant positive abnormal stock returns.[113] Other

---

[110] But see Ferrell (2007a), who criticises the validity of the Stigler and Benston studies. Ferrell shows that the Stigler study involves an inappropriate time period and uses no control group to attend to changed market conditions. He also questions the use of voluntarily disclosing companies as an effective control group in Benston's paper. See also Leuz and Wysocki (2008) on the limitations of these early studies.

[111] There continues to be disagreement in recent literature. For empirical studies that doubt the value of mandatory disclosure, see Battalio et al. (2011), and Mahoney and Mei (2008).

[112] The 1964 Securities Act Amendments extended the mandatory disclosure requirements that had applied to listed companies since 1934 to large firms traded on the OTC market. Greenstone et al. (2006) document that OTC firms most affected by the imposition of SEC disclosure regulation experienced abnormal returns of 11–22% from the time the regulation was proposed to when it went into force, and abnormal returns of about 3.5% in the weeks surrounding firms' announcements that they had first come into compliance.

[113] However, they show that the majority of OTCBB firms (over 2,600) did not wish to comply with the new mandatory disclosure requirements and thus were removed from the OTCBB. In addition, these noncompliant firms are smaller, more leveraged, and more profitable than newly compliant firms. These findings suggest that for a significant number of small, illiquid

SEC disclosure requirements, such as Regulation Fair Disclosure (FD)[114] promulgated in 2000, have also been found to enhance the operation of the stock markets (Prentice, 2006). In summary, recent empirical evidence "is consistent with mandatory disclosure often having socially beneficial effects" (Ferrell, 2007a).

Insider trading is defined as "trading in securities while in possession of material nonpublic information" (Bainbridge, 1999). Metrick (2008) offers two definitions of insider trading. The first definition refers to any purchase or sale of the stock of a publicly listed corporation by an insider of that corporation, such as an officer, director, or major shareholder. The second definition does not require the trader to be a corporate insider, but requires only that the trader possess material non-public information. Insider trading, as Bainbridge (1999) admits, "is one of the most controversial aspects of securities regulation". Theoretical debates over the benefits and costs of insider trading have continued for several decades (Beny, 2007). Some scholars argue that insider trading is economically efficient. For example, Manne (1966) contends that insider trading can act as an efficient compensation mechanism, through which insiders will be motivated to undertake more entrepreneurial innovations.[115] Similarly, Carlton and Fischel (1983) argue that insider trading is a solution to the contracting cost problem: insider trading enables managers to continually update their compensation in light of new information without incurring costs related to bargaining over the details of compensation contracts ex ante, monitoring the efforts and output of managers in the interim, and renegotiating ex post. In addition, insider trading is believed to increase stock price accuracy (Manne, 1966; Carlton and Fischel, 1983).

By contrast, other scholars suggest that insider trading might simply be an inefficient private benefit of control that accrues to managers and other insiders at the expense of public shareholders. For example, Kraakman (1991) argues that

---

firms, the benefits of mandatory disclosure can frequently be outweighed by the costs that it imposes.

[114] On August 15, 2000, the SEC adopted Regulation FD to address the selective disclosure of information by publicly traded companies and other issuers. Regulation FD provides that when an issuer discloses material nonpublic information to certain individuals or entities – generally, securities market professionals, such as stock analysts, and holders of the issuer's securities who may well trade on the basis of the information – the issuer must make public disclosure of that information. In this way, the new rule aims to promote full and fair disclosure. For more information, see www.sec.gov/hot/regfd.htm.

[115] According to Manne, entrepreneurs within the firm and their productive output are difficult to identify ex ante. Thus, if corporate insiders' compensation is set in advance, the compensation will be inefficient. Insider trading is sometimes understood as a mechanism to avoid such inefficiencies. With insider trading, entrepreneurs can be rewarded in direct proportion to, and contemporaneously with, their innovation. The entrepreneur who produces an innovation is the first person to know about the valuable new information related to the innovation. He or she can profit by buying the company's shares before the public learns about the innovation and before their value rises to reflect the positive news.

insider trading enables managers, on an ex post basis, to undo an efficient ex ante compensation contract and thereby sabotage performance-based compensation schemes intended to tie pay to productivity. Moreover, Kraakman (1991) claims that insider trading might give managers incentives to take on too much risk or undertake value-reducing projects.[116] Cox (1986) further cautions that in practice it is difficult to ensure that those who create valuable information (the entrepreneurs) are the only ones within the firm who can profit from it, and the inability of entrepreneurs to exclude other insiders from profiting on the valuable information might reduce rather than increase their incentives to innovate. Finally, when insider trading is pervasive, information traders (sophisticated professional investors and analysts) will be unable to recoup their investment in information and eventually will exit the market; as a result, the informational efficiency of the market will be damaged (Goshen and Parchomovsky, 2006).

Recent empirical evidence seems to favour the opponents. Bhattacharya and Daouk (2002)[117] measure the effect of insider trading laws vs. insider trading enforcement (as proxied by prosecution) on the cost of equity using four different approaches. Whichever approach they use, these authors find that insider trading enforcement is associated with a significant decrease in the cost of equity. The efficiency-enhancing role of enforcing insider trading laws is further confirmed by Daouk et al. (2006) and Fernandes and Ferreira (2009). Using data from a cross-section of 33 countries, Beny (2005, 2007)[118] finds that countries with more prohibitive insider trading laws have more diffuse equity ownership, more accurate stock prices, and more liquid stock markets. These findings suggest that, in addition to enforcement, formal insider trading laws also matter to stock market development. Beny (2008) further shows that stringent insider trading laws (and enforcement) are associated with greater corporate valuation, particularly in common law countries.

---

[116] Because insider trading is more profitable when stock prices are more volatile, insider trading may encourage managers to undertake excessively risk projects in order to increase volatility that would create private opportunities for profitable insider trading but that would reduce corporate value. For a formal model on the effect of insider trading on managers' choices among risky investments, see Bebchuk and Fershtman (1994).

[117] They provide a comprehensive survey that finds that 103 countries had stock markets at the end of 1998. Although 87 countries had promulgated insider trading laws, only 38 of these had enforced such laws (as evidenced by prosecutions). Before 1990, these respective numbers were 34 and 9.

[118] Beny first codes four elements of a country's insider trading laws: *tipping*, which measures whether a corporate insider is liable for giving price-sensitive private information to an outsider (tippee) and encouraging her to trade; *tippee*, which measures whether tippees, like corporate insiders, are forbidden to trade on price-sensitive private information; *damages*, which measures whether the potential monetary penalty for violating a country's insider trading law is greater than the illicit insider trading profits; and *criminal*, which measures whether insider trading is a criminal offence in the country. She then creates an aggregate insider trading law index, IT Law, which is the sum of these four elements.

Under current United States law, there are three basic theories under which trading on insider information is unlawful (Bainbridge, 1999; Newkirk and Robertson, 1998). The "disclosure or abstain rule" was adopted by the SEC in *In re Cady, Roberts & Co.*[119] and was upheld by a federal circuit court in *SEC v. Texas Gulf Sulphur Co.*[120] Pursuant to this rule, anyone in possession of insider information is required either to disclose the information publicly or refrain from trading in the shares of the corporation. In 1981, a federal circuit court adopted the "misappropriation theory" in *United States v. Newman*[121] to expand the scope of insider trading to include professionals such as lawyers, consultants, and even investment bankers who legitimately receive confidential information from a corporation within the course and scope of providing services to the corporation.[122] Finally, in 1980, the SEC promulgated Rule 14e-3 under section 14(e) of the 1934 Act, which made it illegal for anyone to trade on the basis of material nonpublic information regarding tender offers when they know the information emanated from an issuer.[123]

Thus, the United States pioneered the introduction of insider trading laws, and until 1967, when France established its insider trading laws, the United States was the only country that had such laws. The first enforcement of insider trading laws also occurred in the United States (1961). Until 1990, only nine countries had brought any charges under these laws. In addition, the enforcement record of the SEC is without equal. For example, from 1980 to 1997, the United Kingdom brought only 17 prosecutions for insider trading, 12 of which were successful; by contrast, the SEC brought 57 cases alleging insider trading in 1997 alone (Newkirk and Robertson, 1998). As generalised by Cross and Prentice (2007: 143), "for quite a long time only the United States showed any particular interest in punishing insider trading".

3.4.2. SECURITIES LAW IN PRACTICE

The text of the securities law is not the entire story. As Stigler (1970) states, "[a]ll prescriptions of behavior for individuals require enforcement". Without effective enforcement, a law, no matter how elaborate, cannot be expected to affect people's behaviour.[124] Legal enforcement can be divided into two categories:

[119] 40 SEC 907 (1961).
[120] 401 F.2d 833 (2d Cir. 1968), cert. denied, 394 U.S. 976 (1969).
[121] 664 F.2d 12 (2d Cir. 1981).
[122] The main distinction between these professionals and individuals formerly charged with insider trading is that these professionals owe no fiduciary duty to the issuer but are nonetheless liable for trading the securities of the issuer while in possession of the non-public information (Elisofon, 2008).
[123] 17 C.F.R. §240.14e-3.
[124] With respect to securities markets regulation, enforcement is so important that it is claimed to be "at the heart of a good national investor protection system" (Black, 2001: 822).

private enforcement, which is initiated by private litigation, and public enforcement, which relies on public authorities, such as the SEC or tax collection agents (Shavell, 2004: Chapter 25). More specifically, in the context of securities regulation, public enforcement includes "criminal and civil suits brought by public officials and agencies, as well as various ex ante rights of approval – such as for securities offering statements – exercised by public actors", while private enforcement encompasses "civil lawsuits brought by private parties, such as shareholder derivative suits and class actions" (Armour, Hansmann, and Kraakman, 2009).

Both private enforcement and public enforcement of securities law are shown to be connected with the prosperity of the stock market. For example, La Porta et al. (2006) show that private enforcement (both in terms of disclosure requirements and liability standards)[125] is positively correlated with larger stock markets, whereas public enforcement plays a modest role at best in the development of stock markets. By contrast, Jackson and Roe (2009) find that the depth of capital markets (as measured by market capitalisation, trading volume, the number of domestic firms, and the number of initial public offerings) is positively associated with stronger public enforcement (as measured by the size of the regulatory staff that oversees capital markets and the budget for securities regulation).

Private and public enforcement both play important roles in the operation of US capital markets. In the US, the shareholder class action is one of the most important mechanisms for enforcing antifraud rules and mandatory disclosure requirements (Hertig et al., 2004, 2009). During the 1990s, approximately 200 securities fraud cases seeking class-action status were filed every year in the federal courts, with a significant increase to 498 in 2001 and a return to the level of 200 in 2002–2008.[126] For jurisdictions without the procedures and monetary incentives that are necessary to support US-style securities class action, private enforcement plays much less of a role.[127] For example, the incidence of private law suits relating to disclosure violations is modest in France, Germany, and Italy, and almost non-existent in the UK (Hertig et al., 2009).

---

[125]   The problem with the study of La Porta et al. (2006) is that these variables only measure the extent to which investors can access valuable corporate information (disclosure requirements) and the procedural complexity in recovering losses from wrongdoers instead of directly measuring the intensity and scope of shareholder litigation across countries. It may therefore be concluded that they still focus on "law in book", rather than "law in practice".

[126]   See Stanford Law School, Securities Class Action Clearing House, at http://securities.stanford.edu/.

[127]   See Coffee (2007), who argues that "[c]lass actions remain rare to unknown in Europe (including the United Kingdom) … As a result, the entrepreneurial system of private law enforcement that characterizes the United States is simply not present in Europe". As the data presented in Jackson (2007) shows, private enforcement in the United States imposes greater financial penalties than public enforcement.

The United States also stands out because of its powerful public enforcement.[128] As reported by Jackson (2007), US securities enforcement is notable in several respects. First, the number of governmental agencies and quasi-governmental agencies is striking: in addition to the SEC, the Department of Justice,[129] state securities commissions, and the National Association of Securities Dealers (NASD) and NYSE play major roles and impose substantial sanctions on the securities markets and securities firms. Second, the overall number of public actions each year is high. For example, there were 3,624 actions on average per year during the period 2002–2004. And the level of public sanctions is substantial, averaging over $5.3 billion per year for the period 2002–2004. Not included in these administrative sanctions are substantial criminal convictions for securities-related crimes, averaging nearly 4,200 months of prison sentences at the federal level alone plus more than 1,500 months of probation per year during the period 2002–2004.

Public enforcement is much weaker in other jurisdictions. Jackson (2007) compares enforcement activity in the United States with that in the United Kingdom and Germany, and concludes that "even when adjusted for market size, the United States had substantially more enforcement actions than the United Kingdom and Germany". This conclusion is further confirmed by Coffee (2007), who uses updated information to show that the SEC imposed financial penalties that exceeded those of the Financial Service Authority (FSA, a quasi-judicial body responsible for the regulation of the financial services industry in the United Kingdom between 2001 and 2013) at a nearly ten-to-one margin (at least in 2004 and 2005). Coffee (2007) thus concludes that "[i]n terms of actual enforcement actions brought and sanctions levied, the United States is an outlier, which, even on a market-adjusted basis, imposes financial penalties that dwarf those of any other jurisdiction".

In summary, it may be argued that securities law (together with its enforcement) is a precondition for the development of stock markets, and the achievement of the United States in building up a large and successful stock market may be explained by its leadership in establishing investor-oriented securities law (as opposed to its shareholder-unfriendly corporate law) and a strong regulatory agency. For countries that want to develop a strong stock

---

[128] The following discussion focuses on the "output" of enforcement. In terms of regulatory "input", such as regulatory budgets and staffing levels of securities market regulators, Jackson (2007) and Jackson and Roe (2009) show that the intensity of enforcement in the United States is not very striking. For example, the staffing level (staff per million population) for the United States (23.75) falls below that found in Australia (34.44), Canada (38.93), Hong Kong (59.59), Luxemburg (315.12), Singapore (77.74), and Uruguay (46.64), but is higher than that found in France (5.91), Germany (4.43), Italy (7.25), United Kingdom (19.04), and 42 other countries.

[129] Coffee (2007) provides more details on the role of Department of Justice and concludes that "the prospect of criminal enforcement radically distinguishes securities enforcement in the United States from that of the rest of the world".

market, the optimal strategy seems to be to learn or even copy US-style securities regulation, with an emphasis on antifraud provisions, mandatory disclosure, insider trading restrictions, and effective enforcement. As we will discuss in the following sections, however, these conclusions still face serious challenges.

3.5. ROLE OF PRIVATE MECHANISMS AND POLITICS

3.5.1. PRIVATE MECHANISMS MATTER

The United States is not the only country with prosperous stock markets. For example, at least in terms of the ratio of stock market capitalisation to GDP, the United Kingdom has a higher value than the United States in recent years[130] (124% vs. 119% in 2012, and 118.7% vs. 104.3% in 2011, respectively). However, the regulatory environment in the United Kingdom is fundamentally different from that in the United States. For example, the disclosure requirements in the United Kingdom are less stringent than those in the United States. The SEC conducted a detailed comparison of US and UK disclosure requirements for companies that issue equity securities and concluded that "U.S. disclosure rules that govern the public offering of equity securities are in many respects significantly more specific and comprehensive than those of the United Kingdom. As a result, much information about equity securities issuers that is available to U.S. investors is not available to their U.K. counterparts under current law" (Landau, 1987: 468).

In addition, insider trading restrictions in the United Kingdom are weak. Coffee (2007) compares insider trading penalties in the US with those in the UK and identifies significant differences between them. The SEC pursues insider trading cases zealously. Between 2001 and the fall of 2006, the SEC brought over 300 insider trading enforcement actions against over 600 individuals and entities, i.e., approximately 50 insider trading actions per year. In addition to the SEC's civil enforcement efforts, the US Department of Justice also exerts consistent efforts in its steady prosecution of insider trading under the criminal law.[131] In sharp contrast, criminal prosecutions of insider trading are conspicuous by their absence in the United Kingdom, and civil actions are rare.[132] Even when insider trading prosecutions are brought in the United Kingdom, the penalties imposed for liability are modest by US standards. In

---

[130] http://data.worldbank.org/indicator/CM.MKT.LCAP.GD.ZS/countries/US?display=default.
[131] In just one year (2006), the Federal Bureau of Investigation participated in 95 insider trading prosecutions, which consisted of 56 pending cases, 24 indictments, and 15 convictions.
[132] From 2001 to 2007, the FSA was reported to have successfully brought just eight cases alleging insider trading.

addition, although the UK has an elaborate liability regime that broadly sanctions financial misstatements and fraud, its level of enforcement is far from that found in the US (Hertig et al., 2004).

In general, the United Kingdom relies more heavily on self-regulation to sustain its securities markets. For example, takeovers are regulated by the City Code on Takeovers and Mergers (the "Takeover Code"), a body of rules that is written and administered by the Panel on Takeovers and Mergers (the "Takeover Panel"). The Takeover Panel includes representatives from the LSE, the Bank of England, the major merchant banks, and institutional investors. Both the Panel and the Code were, "until recently, entirely self-regulatory"[133] (Armour and Skeel, 2007). After adopting the Financial Services Act in 1986, the self-regulatory character of the UK securities markets was weakened to some extent because regulatory powers were granted to a government entity, the Department of Trade and Industry. However, most regulatory powers were then delegated to the Securities and Investment Board (SIB), a private company limited by guarantee[134] and financed by a levy on market participants. The SIB sets the overall framework of regulation but does not itself act as the direct regulator of most investment firms. Second-tier regulators (such as the self-regulatory organisations (SROs), who were the most prominent group of these entities) performed those functions. The style of regulation in the United Kingdom is thus described as "self-regulation within a statutory framework" (Ferran, 2003). In 2000, the Financial Services and Markets Act brought a further reduction in self-regulation. Even after this legal reform, securities regulation in the United Kingdom is said to follow a "light touch" approach[135] (Langevoort, 2009) or a "flexibility model"[136] (Gadinis and Jackson, 2007), both of which emphasise the

---

[133] More specifically, City professionals (particularly institutional investors) avoided the need for ex post litigation by developing a body of norms that eventually gave rise to the Takeover Code. These norms were, and still are, enforced by reputational sanctions, such as the threat of exclusion from the LSE, which ensured that contentious issues were resolved ex ante without the need for court involvement.

[134] In British and Irish company law, a private company limited by guarantee is an alternative type of corporation that is used primarily for non-profit organisations that require legal personality. A company limited by guarantee does not typically have share capital or shareholders, but instead has members who act as guarantors. The guarantors give an undertaking to contribute a nominal amount (typically very small) in the event of the winding up of the company. See http://en.wikipedia.org/wiki/Private_company_limited_by_guarantee.

[135] According to Langevoort (2009), light touch is a term of art used to describe an approach that relies more on prudential dialog with the regulated community than ex post enforcement and more on principles than rules. Academically, it can be linked to the literature on so-called "new governance" strategies for regulation that seek to enlist the cooperation of the regulated community so as to overcome the inevitable informational disadvantage that authorities have in regulating rapidly changing markets. The basic idea is to let regulated entities experiment with compliance practices without a one-size-fits-all command, as long as outcomes satisfy the articulated principles.

[136] The flexibility model grants significant leeway to market participants in performing their regulatory obligations but relies on government agencies to set general policies and maintain

importance of self-regulation and rely on cooperation between the regulator and the regulated entities.

Recent historical and empirical studies have shown that private ordering, market-based solutions, and self-regulation – as opposed to legal rules and regulatory instruments – played essential and critical roles in sustaining the stock market in the United Kingdom. For example, Cheffins (2001: 469) finds that "from a legal perspective, the United Kingdom was not a protective jurisdiction for minority shareholders during the first half of the twentieth century". During this period, the listing requirements imposed by the LSE and the "quality control" function undertaken by financial intermediaries (such as stock-brokers, finance house, and merchant banks) combined to bolster the UK securities markets.

In the second half of the twentieth century, institutional investors, such as pension funds, insurance companies, and unit and investment trusts (collective investment vehicles that resemble the American mutual fund) emerged as major players in UK securities markets.[137] Compared with individual investors, institutional investors are wealthier, more sophisticated, and have more interests at stake. Acting together, they have both the motivation and power to push for

---

some enforcement capacity. Under this approach, a jurisdiction achieves flexibility by channelling agency rulemaking in the form of guidance, rather than, or in addition to, prescribing rules. Language in guidance is not prescriptive and is frequently phrased in "best practice" terms instead of as firm regulatory obligations. In many cases of noncompliance with guidance, agencies do not threaten sanctions against regulated entities but ask them instead to disclose noncompliance to the public and explain the reasons that led to it, leaving it to the market to appreciate their validity. The regulatory agency's enforcement philosophy is largely preventative: the agency conducts selected investigations of securities laws violations and the primary purpose is to deter potential violators rather than to unveil each separate instance of potential misbehaviour in the industry.

[137] By the beginning of the 1990s, UK institutions held about two-thirds of all public traded British stocks; the 25 largest institutional shareholders held an absolute majority of the stock of many UK companies; and for smaller UK firms, the five largest institutional holders controlled 30% or more of the shares (Black and Coffee, 1994). The rise of institutional investors can be attributed to the Labour government's egalitarian agenda, particularly with respect to tax policies (Coffee, 2012). Pension and insurance payments received relatively favourable tax treatment, thus creating a stronger market for these products. As a result, the total financial assets of pension funds grew 32 times between 1952 and 1979; by the 1970s, pension funds accounted for approximately one-third of all personal savings in the United Kingdom. As money flooded into pension funds, there was little practical alternative for UK money managers but to invest in equity shares. Insurance companies also increased the allocation of their assets to equities from 10% in 1946 to 16% by 1956 and 21% by the early 1960s. Tax law also contributed to the development of securities markets in the United Kingdom through another channel. As a response to high tax rates, especially a punitive estate tax regime, family businesses typically sold their control blocks and placed the case proceeds of these sales into long-term trusts. In summary, tax law forced blockholders to exit and the tax-induced flood of money into pension funds and insurance products crested a new class of investors. In that sense, law really matters for the development of UK securities markets, but here we refer to tax law rather than corporate or securities law. For a more detailed discussion, see Cheffins (2008).

good corporate governance and motivate managers to pursue wealth-maximisation strategies (Black, 1992). Institutional investors thus have been the driving force behind many corporate governance rules, such as preemptive rights in the LSE's listing rules, the Takeover Code, the Combined Code on corporate governance, etc., which give considerable power to shareholders in addressing managerial failure. With the help of these rules (and English company law),[138] institutional shareholders are able to question management decisions through informal communication in normal times and provoke CEO turnover in the event of severe underperformance.[139] The exercise of (institutional) shareholder power therefore has become a powerful means by which managerial opportunism problem is effectively addressed; more importantly, there is no more necessity to resort to a strong regulatory agency, such as the SEC – or to private enforcement mechanisms managed by the courts – to protect the interests of shareholders. Thus, according to Armour (2008), "institutional investors, who hold the majority of the shares in UK listed companies, have engaged systematically in the production of rules and norms that facilitate low-cost informal interventions in response to managerial failure", and "strong informal private enforcement has historically therefore been the flipside, in the UK, of weak formal private enforcement".[140]

Even the history of securities markets in the United States does not seem to fit very well with the "securities law matters" hypothesis that was discussed above. For example, although they acknowledge that the federal securities legislation introduced in the mid-1930s bolstered investor protection, Cheffins et al. (2013) argue that this reform effort did not energise the stock market to the extent that LLSV's study implies it should have.[141] In reality, stock markets in the US languished for at least two decades following the enactment of the federal securities laws. In addition, the OTC market, which was subject to less stringent regulation than national stock exchanges, grew much faster than the latter, a

---

[138] Compared with corporate law in the US, UK corporate law grants more power to shareholders. For a comparison, see Becht et al. (2009).

[139] For a more detailed report of how institutional investors in the United Kingdom intervene in corporate affairs, see Black and Coffee (1994), who emphasise that an important advantage of British institutional shareholders is that their world is close-knit; communication among these entities is easy and unregulated, which reduces the coordination costs and free-rider problems that can plague collective action.

[140] Armour's study shows that the level of formal private enforcement, in the form of shareholder litigation, is close to nonexistent. Private litigation therefore appears to play almost no role in controlling managerial agency costs in UK-listed firms. In addition, public enforcement agencies tend to engage with firms in ways that are characterised by informality – i.e., by relying on private conversation and ex ante intervention to secure compliance instead of an aggressive pursuit of ex post sanctions. His estimate suggests that up to 20% of listed companies may be subject to some type of informal engagement, and 3% to formal enforcement, from those public agencies every year.

[141] While US stock markets experienced great expansion during the Eisenhower administration, the SEC "reached its nadir" when "its enforcement and policy-making capabilities were less effective than at any other period in its history" (Seligman, 2003: 265).

phenomenon that contradicts the theory that regulatory structure is essential for the stock markets to become vibrant.

Before the enactment of the securities laws in the middle of the 1930s, Americans had previously witnessed the prosperity of stock markets. O'Sullivan (2007) reports that there was a more than fourfold increase in the numbers of stocks traded on the US stock market between 1900 and 1930 (from 1,028 in 1900 to 4,359 in 1930). The number of individuals owning stock in listed companies rose from 500,000 in 1900 to 2 million in 1920 to 10 million by 1930 (Baskin and Miranti, 1997: 190).[142] In addition, while it still ranked behind Denmark and Switzerland in terms of the stock market capitalisation to GDP ratio in 1900 (Musacchio, 2010), the United States ranked first by 1929 (La Porta et al., 2008).

It seems unlikely that the growth of the US stock markets during this period can be explained by the legal protection that was available to minority shareholders. At that time, an enterprise's state of incorporation largely determined the legal protections available to minority shareholders, and the most important development during this period was the interstate competition for corporate charters that occurred from the mid-1880s onward. This competition finally led to a process of "race to the bottom"[143] in which states watered down shareholders' rights to attract incorporating firms (or, more precisely, the insiders of firms who generally make the decision about the state of incorporation) (Seligman, 2003: 43–44). The statutory rights accorded shareholders by state corporate law therefore substantially diminished. During this period, some states sought to protect investors with so-called "blue-sky" securities laws.[144] By 1914, 24 states had blue-sky laws and, by 1931, that number had grown to 47 of the 48 states in the US (Nevada was the exception). However, these laws had limited impact (O'Sullivan, 2007; Seligman, 2003) because they did not apply across state lines and were replete with exemptions for certain types of securities; in addition, most states exempted securities listed on specified stock exchanges, which was the most important limitation in such regulatory schemes.

The gap left by law and regulation was filled by self-regulatory institutions, such as investment banks and stock exchanges, that found that it was in their self-interest to foster the development of securities markets (Coffee, 2001, 2012). Investment banks frequently placed one or more representatives on the issuer's

---

[142]   See also Cheffins and Bank (2009) on the significant development of US stock markets during this period.

[143]   There has long been a debate about the desirability of state competition for corporate charters. See, for example, Cary (1974), and Winter (1977).

[144]   State securities laws were known as "blue sky" laws because they were intended to check stock swindlers who were so barefaced they "would sell building lots in the blue sky". Such laws regulated the sale of securities within state boundaries by requiring issuers of securities to submit certain types of information prior to gaining approval for their public sale. See Seligman (2003: 44–46).

board to protect public investors from opportunistic managers and (maybe more importantly) predatory corporate raiders. In frequently rejecting listings and insisting on an adequate earnings track records before listing an issuer, the NYSE was distinguishing itself from its competitors and marketing itself as "the guardian of public shareholders"[145] (Coffee, 2001: 34). In general, in the early development of the US stock markets, "private ordering and self-regulation played decisive roles"[146] (Coffee, 2012: 36). The situation changed fundamentally in the 1930s with a series of New Deal securities and banking law reforms. The banking reforms hindered banks from becoming significant players in the governance of America's large corporations, and the creation of the strong SEC with the authority to oversee stock exchanges minimised the influence of self-regulatory organisations. As generalised by Armour and Skeel (2007: 1727, 1779), "U.S. federal regulation in the 1930s both pre-empted self-regulation and restricted the ability of institutional investors to coordinate", and "the interests of shareholders were represented not by shareholders themselves, but by the SEC".

Because a prosperous stock market predates a sophisticated and investor-oriented legal framework in the United States (and in the United Kingdom), it is more reasonable to argue that law follows rather than leads the development of stock markets, notwithstanding the arguments suggested by LLSV to the contrary. Thus, only after stock markets develop to such an extent that minority shareholders have become a powerful constituency whose concerns must be taken seriously by politicians and it has been shown that private mechanisms are unable to sustain the markets anymore will the legislature "supply" the legal protections that investors "demand".[147] Of course, these legal rules will then

---

[145] This guardian role manifested itself in two concrete ways: (1) the NYSE, beginning in 1900, insisted that its listed companies publish annual audited financial statements, and (2) it protected shareholder voting rights by resisting attempts by issuers to deviate from the norm of "one share, one vote". According to Seligman (2003: 46), the NYSE's listing requirements were "far more precise than any found in the blue sky laws", and they "more closely resembled the standards subsequently adopted in Schedule A of the 1933 Securities Act than those found in the English Companies Act, which proponents of the federal Securities Act usually identified as their model". However, Seligman doubts the effectiveness of the NYSE's listing requirements because they were purely voluntary standards and therefore could be easily avoided.

[146] See also Cheffins (2003: 12), who examines the development of US securities markets during the early decades of the 20th century and concludes that, "it is therefore fair to say that the various market-oriented factors offering protection to investors in fact proved highly effective in mobilizing capital and assuaging perceptions of risk".

[147] Coffee (2001) first makes this argument, which has been supported by subsequent studies, such as Callaghan (2009), who finds that sudden increases in the number of people owning shares (due to privatisation, tax changes, etc., as opposed to legal reform) in Britain, Germany, and France since the 1950s were followed by political efforts to champion the interests of small shareholders. She then concludes that "a causal arrow runs ... from ownership structures to politics and corporate law. Outside shareholders must first emerge as a sizable constituency before a political party will advance their cause ... political and legal efforts to protect shareholders have historically tended to follow, rather than precede, the appearance of securities markets". See also Milhaupt and Pistor (2008).

influence the direction, speed, and size of future development of stock markets. Unfortunately, this dynamic dimension in the relationship between law and stock markets has been ignored by LLSV and their followers because these scholars are focused exclusively and excessively on the contemporary connections between law and finance.

Although stock markets can develop to a certain extent with the help of private ordering, they cannot grow to their full potential under a purely voluntary regulatory regime. Thus, according to Coffee (2001: 66), "[w]hile markets can arise in the absence of a strong, mandatory legal framework, they neither function optimally nor develop to their potential in the absence of mandatory law that seeks to mitigate the risks of crashes". As markets grow in size, the net benefit of opportunism (even with repeated transactions and reputational concern) increases with the distance (geographically, culturally, linguistically, etc.) between the parties, and private monitoring becomes less and less effective in controlling agency problems.[148] Formal law is required to fill the vacuum; otherwise, there may be a serious market failure. Indeed, legal change in the area of shareholder protection seems driven by crisis.[149]

Whether legislation can be expected to fill the gap left by private mechanisms, in turn, depends on political factors such as (1) the political power and influence of investors versus other stakeholders, such as managers and workers, and (2) the responsiveness of the legislature to shareholders' legal needs. As Milhaupt and Pistor (2008: 40) have argued, "law is a political product not only at its inception but in the way it affects and is shaped by the interests of political, social and economic actors. It is impossible to understand where law comes from and where it is going without venturing into the realm of the political economy". An examination of the role of politics is therefore required.

3.5.2. THE ROLE OF POLITICS

Recent studies have shown that it is difficult or even impossible for stock markets to thrive in a country in which investors are politically weak and their interests are subordinate to or sacrificed in the interests of other social purposes. Rajan

---

[148] For a detailed discussion of this issue, see Cross and Prentice (2007: chapter 2).

[149] This trend has been systematically discussed by Milhaupt and Pistor (2008). In general, these authors argue that "law is not an endowment like a fixed capital investment that, once in place, provides a firm foundation for capitalist activity. The vibrancy of a capitalist system hinges on creative destruction in the sphere of governance as well as the economic sphere. Governance structures of all types, including law, must adapt and respond to changes in the economy. Rather than thinking of a legal system as a fixed endowment for the economy, it is more productive to view the relationship between law and markets as a highly iterative process of action and strategic reaction" (Milhaupt and Pistor, 2008: 5). Similarly, Coffee (2001: 66) concludes that "a 'crash-then-law' cycle has characterized the history of securities markets".

and Zingales (2003a) have revealed that many countries, particularly those countries with a civil law system, have experienced "great reversals" of financial development[150] in the twentieth century, a phenomenon that is hard to explain using LLSV's legal origin hypothesis. Political explanations seem more convincing. For example, Perotti and von Thadden (2006) argue that the damage and consequences of the First World War seem to have had different redistributive effects on the middle class in different countries, which shaped public policies and social attitudes toward stock markets. Those countries that experienced no inflation (and where the median voter thus still held a sufficient equity stake), such as the United Kingdom, the Netherlands, Switzerland, Australia, Canada, and the United States, had a more securities-market-friendly response to the Great Depression (such as 1930s US securities laws). By contrast, in countries in which the financial interests of middle class were ravaged by inflation, such as in Austria, Belgium, Germany, France, and Italy, more restrictions were placed on stock markets.

In addition to inflation, the World Wars, invasions, and military occupation have also been shown to be related to the (non)development of stock markets. Roe (2006) constructs a "total destruction" variable that combines both economic measures (the ratio of GDP in 1945 to that in 1913) and military measures of destruction (whether a country was occupied during the World Wars), and shows that this variable strongly predicts the strength of late-twentieth-century securities markets: those countries that were destroyed in the early part of the twentieth century (mainly civil law countries) had weaker securities markets than those that fared less poorly (mainly common law countries). Roe (2006) concludes that "if the financial savings of a nation's middle class were devastated first by interwar hyperinflation and depression and then by wartime destruction of the underlying physical assets, it is possible that, for decades after 1945, typical voters in such a nation would have cared little about protecting financial capital because they had little of it and because their well-being was tied more to their human capital".[151]

---

[150] By most measures, the civil law countries were more financially developed in 1913 than in 1980, and only recently have most surpassed their 1913 levels.

[151] Several channels have been identified by Roe (2006) to connect wartime destruction and the subsequent development of securities markets. First, military occupation weakened institutions overall, and when the time came to rebuild, the polity rebuilt human institutions in early decades and waited until later to rebuild stock markets. The second channel ties destruction to postwar domestic politics. Stunned voters were averse to risk, labour was powerful, and savings were meagre. Those background political conditions were not market-friendly. The third channel is postwar international politics. The program in many nations was to fight communism, inducing most Western European and East Asian governments to befriend international communism's most likely domestic allies – voting workers. Political leaders therefore frequently turned not to markets but to governments to mobilise capital. A fourth channel is that destroyed nations do not immediately need large pools of capital from financial markets. Banks are adept at allocating capital to known technologies, whereas securities markets are more adept at allocating capital to new and untried technologies. After

After the Second World War, many European countries adopted the so-called "social democratic"[152] pattern, which has been argued to constrain the development of stock markets. As Roe (2003) shows, in social democratic regimes, employees are systematically protected from actions that shareholders (and managers) might otherwise prefer to take. Lay-offs are difficult to implement, the range of managerial discretion is limited, and unemployment benefits are high and easy to obtain. To maintain social peace, the means by which shareholders can tie managers to ownership interests, such as high incentive compensation via stock options, shareholder wealth maximisation norms, and hostile takeovers are disfavoured in social democracies. The pressures from social democracies therefore increase managerial agency costs for shareholders and thus decrease the firm's value to diffuse shareholders who can hardly monitor, influence, and control managers. Shareholders must seek alternatives to reduce those agency costs, such as concentrated ownership, under which shareholders can counterbalance the political power of workers and monitor managers more effectively. However, concentrated ownership also means a weak stock market. Roe (2003) further shows that there is a tight correlation between politics and ownership concentration: countries on the political left (mainly continental civil law courtiers) have less diffuse ownership and right-leaning countries (mainly common law countries) have more diffuse ownership. The theory from Roe (2003) is supported[153] by subsequent studies, including Belloc and Pagano (2009), who find that there is a negative cross-country correlation between an economy's degree of employment protection and its degree of corporate ownership dispersion.[154]

---

the Second World War, reconstruction was largely a known task for which banks were well suited – perhaps better suited than volatile equity markets – and which fit with a polity that preferred steady and low-risk reconstruction.

152 Social democracy is defined as a policy regime involving a universal welfare state and collective bargaining schemes within the framework of a capitalist economy, which is often used to refer to the social models and economic policies prominent in Western and Northern Europe during the later half of the 20th century. See http://en.wikipedia.org/wiki/Social_democracy.

153 Roe's theory still faces serious challenges. For example, Cioffi and Hopner (2006) show that since the mid-1990s, in Germany, France, Italy, and the US, centre-left political parties have pushed for pro-shareholder corporate governance reforms, while the right has generally resisted these reforms to protect established forms of organised interests, concentrated corporate stock ownership, and managerialism. Schnyder (2010) further argues that centre-left parties are neither invariably a pro-reform force nor an anti-reform force. Their preferences depend on whether labour is excluded from the formation of the corporate governance structure. If there is cooperation between labour and employers rather than exclusion of the left, the left will not favour dismantling current corporate governance structure. For a systematic review of Roe's theory, see Gourevitch (2003).

154 Belloc and Pagano (2009) argue that causation may run in both directions: from strong employee legal protection to strong concentrated ownership and vice versa. Thus, not only is concentrated ownership a necessary response to powerful employment protection but also powerful employment protection is a necessary response to controlling shareholders who have both the incentives and the means to expropriate the interest of stakeholders, including

Rather than classifying countries as either left-wing (social democratic) or right-wing, Hall and Soskice (2001) draw a distinction between two types of political economies, namely liberal market economies (LMEs) and coordinated market economies (CMEs).[155] In LMEs, firms coordinate their activities primarily through competitive market arrangements. Market relationships are characterised by the arm's-length exchange of goods or services in the context of competition and formal contracting. In response to the price signals generated by such markets, the actors adjust their willingness to supply and demand goods or services, often on the basis of marginal calculations, such as those stressed by neoclassical economics. Conversely, in CMEs, firms depend more heavily on non-market relationships to coordinate their endeavours with other actors and to construct their core competencies. These non-market modes of coordination generally entail more extensive relational or incomplete contracting, network monitoring that is based on the exchange of private information inside networks, and more reliance on collaborative – as opposed to competitive – relationships to build firm competencies. In contrast to LMEs in which the equilibrium outcomes of firm behaviour are typically dictated by demand and supply conditions in competitive markets, the equilibria on which firms coordinate in CMEs frequently result from strategic interaction among firms and other actors.

In general, LMEs are more compatible with a diffuse shareholder governance model, while CMEs are more in harmony with a blockholder model. Gourevitch and Shinn (2005) empirically examine the relationship between an economy's degree of coordination and its level of financial development. These authors construct a coordination index (CI)[156] and find a positive correlation between CI and ownership concentration and a negative correlation between CI and minority shareholder protections, which is further confirmed by Hall and Gingerich (2009).

---

employees. The consequence is an institutional complement between legal protection for employment and ownership concentration. For more detailed discussions on this issue, see Gelter (2009) and Brunner (2009).

[155] According to Hall and Soskice (2001), among the large OECD nations, six can be classified as liberal market economies (the US, Britain, Australia, Canada, New Zealand, and Ireland) and another ten as coordinated market economies (Germany, Japan, Switzerland, the Netherlands, Belgium, Sweden, Norway, Denmark, Finland, and Austria). In addition, they argue that six other countries (France, Italy, Spain, Portugal, Greece, and Turkey) may be characterised by another type of capitalism, which can be described as "Mediterranean". This type of capitalism is marked by a large agrarian sector and recent histories of extensive state intervention that have left these economies with specific kinds of capacities for non-market coordination in the sphere of corporate finance but more liberal arrangements in the sphere of labour relations.

[156] The index is constructed from country scores based on six values: shareholder power, dispersion of control, stock market capitalisation, level of wage coordination (at what level wages are set: local, intermediate, or national), degree of wage coordination, and labour turnover (a proxy for job security). The index was calculated for 20 countries for the period 1990–1995.

A major channel through which the degree of economic coordination can influence corporate governance and stock market development in a country is its electoral system. Iversen and Soskice (2009) show that election systems of proportional representation are strongly correlated with CMEs, whereas majoritarian electoral systems are correlated with LMEs.[157] Gourevitch and Shinn (2005) then show that countries with proportional representation systems tend to have higher ownership concentration and lower investor protections, and majoritarian countries have the reverse, being correlated with lower concentration and higher investor protections.[158] Similarly, Pagano and Volpin (2005) provide empirical evidence for a negative correlation between investor protection and the proportional system in a panel of 45 of 49 countries studied by LLSV (1997, 1998) and a positive correlation between labour protection and the proportional system in a panel of 21 OECD countries.

Most CMEs can also be classified as corporatist countries. Morck and Yeung (2010) draw a distinction between "fundamentalist corporatism" and "reformed corporatism", in which corporatism in its original sense is identified using four key characteristics. First, corporatism endorses hierarchy that is based on innate human inequality. Second, to safeguard this social order, the state, businesses, and labour must cooperate, which constrains the role of the state because policies that would disrupt society's innate order are unacceptable, even if democratically endorsed by the (erring) electorate. Corporatism thus endorses authoritarianism. Third, Corporatism separates itself from socialism by endorsing private property and from liberal capitalism by rejecting market-based wages, prices, employment, and production levels. Fourth, corporatism applies a type of principle of subsidiarity: authority subsides to the lowest feasible level of the hierarchy. Such a fundamentalist corporatism can be found in Fascist Italy,

---

[157]   See also Cusack et al. (2007, 2010) on the evolution of electoral systems in different countries and the compatibility between electoral systems and styles of capitalism.

[158]   According to Gourevitch and Shinn (2005), the logic behind these correlations is as follows. An organised production regime (CMEs) rests on a high degree of interdependence among the various players in the firm: it rests on arrangements among stakeholders, managers, blockholders, and workers to preserve the firm's institutions against outsiders. In so doing, they seek a high degree of stability in the policy regime that favours this outcome – to protect their stake in the high level of specific assets that they have invested in that regime. Proportional representational systems are more likely to do that than majoritarian systems because they give a "veto" to all players on the shape and rate of change. According to Gourevitch (2003), "[m]ajoritarian systems magnify the impact of small shifts of votes, thus allowing large swings of policy; consensus systems [proportional representation systems] reduce the impact of vote shifts by giving leverage to a wide range of players through coalitions, thus resulting in minimal policy swings". Conversely, majoritarian institutions undermine the incentives of producers to commit to specific assets because such institutional systems have greater policy variances than do proportional representation systems. As a result, because firms want flexibility, the ability to hire and fire, to cut production, shift assets, sell, close, and move as market conditions require in the moment, they prefer policies that support the liberal governance model, i.e., policies that stress the primacy of the external shareholder, not the various stakeholders.

Falangist Spain, Vichy France, etc. Elements of corporatist thought found new vigour after the Second World War in many high-income European countries. These elements typically include centralised wage-setting, labour union leaders' involvement in government policy, labour market regulation, or some mixture of the above; such policies are named as "neocorporatist".

Scholars have argued that the legacy of corporatism (at least in its fundamentalist version) is that it is detrimental to financial development and economic growth. Morck and Yeung (2010: 38) conclude that "[c]orporatism sanctifies established hierarchies, endorsing the perpetual power of entrenched elites ... Corporatism ... necessitates extensive state intervention ... Corporatism sanctifies the status quo – existing jobs must pay traditional wages and existing firms must continue providing these jobs – so a low tolerance for risk emerges naturally, as do rigid labour laws and lofty entry barriers ... corporatism deters both trust in strangers and trustworthy behaviour towards strangers ... corporatism legitimizes barriers against foreign trade and investment". Indeed, Gourevitch and Shinn (2005) introduce corporatism values for 18 OECD countries and show that there is a positive correlation between the corporatism value and ownership concentration and a negative correlation between such value and minority shareholder protections.[159]

In addition to social ideology, political conflict and compromise, and election systems, rent-seeking efforts by interest groups also matter for stock market development, whether these efforts are undertaken directly or through their influence on the legal protections offered to outsider investors. When wealthy individuals or families have controlled a large part of the corporate sector (through control pyramids or other arrangements), they may wield their economic and political influence to attain policies that preserve and expand their corporate governance powers and thus sustain their concentrated corporate control (Morck et al., 2005), which, in turn, preserves and increases the resources at their disposal for further political lobbying. The objects of this lobbying presumably are policies that limit public investors' rights, impede entry by upstarts, and raise the barriers for international trade and capital.

---

[159]   In their study of corporatism, Gourevitch and Shinn (2005) focus on the grand bargains (sometimes termed the Historical Compromise) among shareholders, workers, and managers during the interwar years in many European countries. In order to repress class conflict, forge a framework for social peace, and build a welfare state, managers and workers joined together in a broad bargain to provide job security, stability, and regularity – workers ceded authority to managers in exchange for stable jobs and pay increases while managers presided over a large organisation secure from hostile takeover. Blockholders were also drawn into this bargain: they kept certain benefits of control, but must share authority and rewards with workers and managers. Corporate governance outcomes were therefore rooted in labour-management cooperation but at the expense of outsider shareholders. In addition, for the grand bargains to be successful, interests should be effectively organised and even institutionally centralised so that negotiation costs can be economised. Therefore, where corporatism is strong, there will be blockholding rather than diffusion of ownership.

Stock market development, or more generally, financial development, will hurt not only the aforementioned controlling shareholders but also other groups with vested interests, such as incumbent financiers who benefit from inadequate financial development. Financial development breeds competition, and competition erodes incumbents' profits; in addition, financial development requires more transparency that will directly damage incumbents' traditional methods of doing business through contracts and relationships (Rajan and Zingales, 2003b). Incumbents therefore have strong incentives to retard financial development, and (because of their accumulated wealth, influence, and power) sufficient resources to manipulate the political process through which the orientation of legislation and style of financial regulation will be determined. If incumbents cannot be curbed by effective institutional arrangements, their rent-seeking efforts will lead, in the end, to the "great reversal" of financial development (Rajan and Zingales, 2003a).

It is therefore not surprising to find that stock markets prosper in common law countries such as the US and UK instead of in continental European countries, which have suffered more from the World Wars, have strong social-democratic, corporatist, and/or coordinated features, and that adopt proportional representation systems. In addition, compared with the US and UK, continental European countries are known to have other problems that may retard the development of stock markets. For example, Rajan and Zingales (2003a) argue that in civil law countries, it is easier for a small group representing private interests to influence policy implementation because a centralised governance system is easier to capture. In a highly centralised economy, it is easier for the government to intervene in the securities markets and ultimately stunt such markets' potential growth (Coffee, 2001).

In summary, the relationship between law and stock market development cannot be fully understood without considering political factors, such as social preferences, partisan systems, and the influence wielded by interest groups. Thus, according to Gourevitch and Shinn (2005: 5), "corporate governance structures are fundamentally the result of political decisions". Politics may influence stock market development directly when politically connected companies enjoy easier access to external finance, lower taxation, and thus higher market valuation, particularly in highly corrupt countries (Faccio, 2006). Politics can also shape the direction of stock market development indirectly not only by determining the level of legal protection offered to minority shareholders but also by (among other options) defining the extent of labour market regulation, which thus affects the bargaining power of workers versus shareholders inside the company. Certainly, politics is not only a cause but also a consequence. Shareholders, managers, and workers will use their economic resources, legal weapons, and social influence to defend their interests in the political arena. In that sense, the stock market is embedded in a dynamic and interconnected political economy, and its development can hardly be explained by a single factor, such as an investor-friendly securities law or a powerful SEC-like regulatory agency.

3.6. CONCLUSION

The importance of stock markets in promoting economic growth has been demonstrated by theoretical studies and confirmed empirically. Stock markets can be expected to perform functions that are crucial to an economy's operation, such as producing information, monitoring investments, allocating risk, mobilising savings, and facilitating the exchange of goods and services. Mishkin (2006: 25) therefore concludes that "developing a well-functioning financial system that directs funds where they can do the most good is thus a ... crucial step on a nation's path toward producing wealth". Similarly, Bernstein (2004: introduction) argues that capital markets are one of the four factors[160] that "are the essential ingredients for igniting and sustaining economic growth and human progress".

The development of stock markets, in turn, requires certain mechanisms to address corporate governance problems, such as information asymmetry and misaligned incentives between shareholders and managers (or between controlling shareholders and minority shareholders). Without these mechanisms, managers (or controlling shareholders) will pursue their own self-interest at the expense of shareholders (or minority shareholders), who can only protect themselves by leaving the markets. If there is a massive withdrawal of shareholders, stock markets will inevitably decline and shrink, and the capability of an economy to accumulate capital, to encourage innovation, and to stimulate economic growth will be damaged to a large extent.

LLSV and their followers have argued that law – particularly corporate law and securities law – is the most important mechanism through which agency problems inside the corporation can be effectively controlled. However, this chapter shows that LLSV and their colleagues may have overestimated the significance of law in stock market development. Stock markets can emerge and prosper in an environment in which self-regulation, reputation mechanisms, and other informal institutions can be relied on to assure outside investors without resorting to investor-friendly types of legislation and public enforcement mechanisms; when private ordering finally reaches the limit of its capacity, whether and to what extent the legislature can fill the gap left by informal mechanisms is determined by political factors, such as the distribution of political power, the social ideology, electoral systems, etc. An omitted variable

---

[160] The other three factors are property rights, scientific rationalism, and improvements in transport and communication.

error will occur if politics is not considered when we try to understand the connection between law and the stock markets.

Politics is important, but again, its role should also not be overestimated. Other factors matter as well. For example, in the introduction to a book that examines the history of corporate governance in eleven countries (Canada, China, France, Germany, India, Italy, Japan, Sweden, the Netherlands, the United Kingdom, and the United States), Morck and Steier (2005) conclude that "the clearest lesson, evident in every chapter, is that 'things happen', and constrain what can happen next. The history of corporate governance, like other historical processes, is *path dependent*" (italics in original). In other words, history matters. In addition, religion, economic openness, technology, etc. are also shown to matter to stock market development (Stulz and Williamson, 2003; Rajan and Zingales 2003a; Zagorchev et al., 2011; Graff, 2005).

The relationship between law and stock markets is therefore more complicated than suggested by LLSV. It is dynamic rather than static, bidirectional rather than unidirectional, and context-dependent rather than universal and unconditional. Both law and the stock markets are embedded in highly sophisticated institutional environments in which political, economic, and social factors influence, complement, and strengthen one another.[161] This is a world in which institutional complementarity, multiple equilibrium, and path dependence prevail; however, this world can hardly be addressed by the new classical economics that underlies the works of LLSV. A deeper understanding of the role of law in stock market development can hardly be reached before we take this complexity into consideration and pay more attention to social context, historical background, and underpinning political institutions in future studies.

---

[161]   As Aoki (2001: 207) puts it clearly, "an economy as a whole may be viewed as robust and coherent overall cluster of mutually interdependent institutions".

CHAPTER 4

THE ROLE OF PROPERTY LAW
IN ECONOMIC GROWTH*

4.1. INTRODUCTION

The institution of property rights is as old and ubiquitous as mankind. Even in aboriginal societies in which there were no formal legal authorities, some type of claim to land and other objects emerged as a consequence of an adaptive response to the natural environment, which might be explained in efficiency terms (Bailey, 1992, 1998). Ancient precepts, such as the Eighth Commandment prohibiting theft, clearly illustrate the value of property rights to our ancestors as a means of establishing and maintaining basic social order. The importance of property rights has increased as human societies have grown more complex as a result of the dynamic relationships among population growth, economic development, and resource exploitation. Rising population pressure means scarcer resources and more intensive utilisation of those resources, which in turn necessitates a well-designed property rights system to guide human behaviour in a more productive, cooperative, and innovative direction.

Property rights also revealed their power in one of the greatest events of the twentieth century, the fall of the centrally planned economies. In addition to the informational limitations of planning (and the superiority of market prices in conveying decentralised information) that was emphasised by Hayek (1945), the preponderance of state ownership in planned economies (in lieu of private property) contributed significantly to the economic failure of communist regimes all over the world. As Demsetz (1996) posits, the larger a society, the more likely it is that underlying conditions favour private ownership. Societies as large as those of China and Russia simply cannot function well on a centralised, state-controlled basis because the bureaucracy lacks incentives to manage assets efficiently without bearing the consequences of their actions; ultimately, the cumulative bureaucratic costs result in the downfall of planned economies.

While never underestimating the significance of property rights, economists paid little attention to the origins, operations, and consequences of property

---

*   A paper based on this chapter has been published in *Law and Development Review* under the title "Property Rights, Law and Economic Development" (2013, Vol. 6, No. 1, pp. 117–142).

rights for a long time; instead, they simply assumed that the property rights system was exogenously determined and focused on understanding the price mechanism from different angles (Demsetz, 1998). A fatal flaw then followed: because of the way it treated property rights, new classical economic theory was unable to discriminate among certain economic situations that are in reality quite different. For example, an economy based on private property could not be distinguished from a communist economy, and the theory of price would seem equally applicable to a communist and to a capitalist society (Lerner, 1944; Lange, 1936, 1937). Consequently, traditional economic theory could not understand the various institutional settings in the real world, failed to predict the collapse of planned economies, and opened the door for ineffective policy suggestions for transitional and developing countries (Roland, 2000; Easterly, 2002, 2006).

Although the topic was not completely ignored by economists, the path-breaking economic analysis of property rights did not occur until 1960, when Ronald Coase published "The Problem of Social Cost". Coase's seminal work was gradually extended and refined by Alchian (1965), Demsetz (1967), Furubotn and Pejovich (1972), De Alessi (1980), and Barzel (1997), among others; eventually, it gave birth to a general approach that focuses on the relationship between property rights and the allocation and use of resources. According to the Coasean analysis of property rights, property rights are crucial to economic performance: "in all societies, primitive and modern, property rights are an important part of social technology that helps to determine economic efficiency" (Bailey, 1998).

Thanks to the growing literature on the economic analysis of property rights that has been compiled over the past several decades, our understanding of the nature, evolution, and effects of property rights has been greatly enriched. In addition, policy options based on property rights have been proposed to solve the problem of market failure in a broad array of fields, including fisheries management, pollution control, etc. Nevertheless, when we look at the specific area of property law rather than the broad domain of property rights, the situation is noticeably different. As Lueck and Miceli (2007) admit, the economic analysis of property law is substantially less well developed than the economic analysis of property rights, and there is a longstanding disconnection between these two fields.

The current economic analysis of property law manifests its insufficiency most obviously when we attempt to explore the role of property law in economic growth. First, there is no general theoretical framework available for understanding property law as a whole, not to mention the complicated interrelationships among law, political systems, and economic forces. Second, great attention is paid to property laws in developed countries, particularly in common law countries such as the US, whereas transitional and developing countries in which property law is supposed to be more important are virtually ignored. Finally, property law is frequently treated as static rather than dynamic; thus, the time dimension is missing from these analyses and history is ignored in descriptions of the transformation of property law. In view of these shortcomings, we must look beyond the economics of property law literature and bring contributions from the economics of property rights, development economics, economic history, comparative law and economics, etc., into our study of the role of property law in economic growth to reach a more comprehensive and profound understanding of the value of property law.

The rest of this chapter is organised as follows. Section 2 discusses the definition and taxonomy of property rights. Section 3 reviews theoretical arguments and empirical studies regarding the relationship between property rights and economic performance. Section 4 offers explanations about the failure of formal property rights in most developing countries. Finally, we conclude in section 5.

4.2. SOME BASICS OF PROPERTY RIGHTS AND PROPERTY LAW

4.2.1. DEFINITION

It is important – but apparently difficult – to offer an incontrovertible definition of property rights, given that property rights are specified variously and inconsistently in the law and economics literature and no consensus appears to exist. As Eggertsson (1990: 34) and Cole and Grossman (2002) note, the principal disagreement about the concept of property rights is rooted in the incompatibility of economic and conventional legal conceptions of the nature and scope of property rights. For economists, property rights are nothing but a mechanism that can be used to allocate authority for the access to and use of resources. This mechanism may or may not be related to and supported by formal law: for example, Allen (1999) regards property rights as "the ability to freely exercise a choice over a good or service", with no reference to any social institutions;[162] alternatively, Demsetz (1998) describes property rights as "socially acceptable uses to which the holder of such rights can put the scarce resources to which these rights refer", and therefore suggests the importance of social underpinnings,[163] formal or informal.

---

[162] Umbeck (1981) expresses a similar view by arguing that "a person may acquire rights in coconuts simply because he is the only one who can climb a tree. Similarly, an individual may have rights to fish because he alone knows where to catch them. Or, a pretty woman may have the rights to a seat on a crowded bus because she is pretty".

[163] This understanding of property rights echoes the arguments in Alchian (1965) and Furubotn and Pejovich (1972).

For legal scholars, however, property rights have a different meaning: they are relations among people respecting things. As Cole and Grossman (2002) put it clearly, if A holds a "right" to something, at least one other person must have a corresponding duty not to interfere with A's possession and use. If A claims a "right" but cannot point to a corresponding duty that is enforceable against at least one other person, then what A possesses may not be a "right" at all but some lesser entitlement such as a privilege, liberty, or mere use. Consequently, to assert a property right is to assert a claim that is enforceable against others by formal law, or by some other social alternative that inevitably involves public authority of some type. Thus, doing something, or having the ability to do something, has nothing to do with the (legal) *right* to do something.

Barzel (1997) attempts to clear up the confusion by introducing a taxonomy of economic (property) rights and legal (property) rights and defines the economic (property) rights an individual has over a commodity or an asset "to be the individual's ability, in expected terms, to consume the good (or the services of the asset) directly or to consume it indirectly through exchange". Moreover, legal rights, which are recognised and enforced by the government, as a rule, enhance economic rights, but the former are neither necessary nor sufficient for the existence of the latter. An example that can be used to clarify the distinction between economic and legal rights is theft: thieves lack legal rights over the goods they steal, but they are able to consume the goods, to exclude others from using them, to derive income from them, and to alienate them; each of these capabilities is an attribute of ownership and hence thieves have economic rights over stolen property. Posner (2002: 46–47) makes a similar distinction between formal legal rights and de facto rights and argues that formal legal rights are merely a subset of property rights in a broader economic sense.

Admittedly, "when transaction costs are positive, rights to assets will not be perfectly delineated" (Barzel, 1997: 4); with this stipulation in mind, a legitimate claimant will never fully own a commodity or an asset from an economic perspective. It is also true that some entitlements created by legislation, regulation, or even community-based norms that are not recognised as legal rights nonetheless demonstrate identical features as legal property rights, such as transferability, exclusivity, and perpetuity. Thus, we must extend the definition of property rights to incorporate the complexity of the real world, which had been disregarded by traditional legal understanding for a long time. Nonetheless, to posit that thieves have economic rights over stolen property, or that a person may acquire rights in coconuts simply because only he can climb a tree, is so aberrant from common sense and contrary to legal practice that any resulting research will risk being rejected by the public as irrelevant to social policies. In addition, equating property rights with ability or use also leads to inefficient economic outcomes because ability- and use-based property rights are not entitled to compensation and other remedies in the face of encroachment, expropriation, etc., and such weak and insecure property rights will in turn discourage investment, production, and exchange.

In summary, we cannot talk about property rights without referring to enforcement mechanisms, remedial methods, and legitimacy or social recognition. We therefore prefer definitions that relate property rights to social underpinnings or public authority, such as the aforementioned definition provided by Demsetz, Libecap's (1989: 1) definition that describes property rights as "the social institutions that define or delimit the range of privileges granted to individuals to specific assets", Pipes's (1999: Introduction and Definitions) definition that emphasises the importance of formal acknowledgement by public authority, etc. Property law is thus a set of rules that are enforced by courts and govern the acquisition, use, and transfer of property rights to specific assets.

4.2.2. TAXONOMY

Basically, four types of property rights are identified in law and economics, namely open access, private property rights, common property rights, and state property rights (Lueck, Miceli, 2007). Open access to a piece of property can be defined as a state under which "there is no delimitation or delineation of its use rights to any private party, and hence no one has the right to exclude others from using it and all are free to compete for its use" (Cheung, 1987).[164] The adverse consequences of open access can be summarised under two headings: supply effects and demand effects (Eggertsson, 2003). On the supply side, aggregate wealth is not maximised because of an insufficient supply of resource units as a result of inadequate provision, maintenance, and investment in improvement, whereas on the demand side excessive withdrawal of resource units leads to the loss of wealth. Open-access resource values also fall because exchange is limited due to the absence of property rights; in addition, under open access, competing claimants will divert labour and capital inputs from socially valuable production to predatory and defensive activities (Libecap, 1998). In sum, the problem of open access can be formalised as a prisoner's dilemma in which the lack of cooperation among users of an open-access resource leads to the least-optimal result for all, or, in Harding's (1968) classic term, the tragedy of the commons.

---

[164] In his analysis, Cheung imprudently uses the term "common property rights" to define a state of open access, a move which inevitably leads to some confusion that clouds his argument. For extensive discussions on the difference between open access and common property rights, see Ostrom (1999) and Eggertsson (2003). The confusion may be traced back to Hardin (1968)'s famous "The Tragedy of the Commons", which uses the term "commons" to describe a situation of actual open access, in which rational individuals, acting independently without any restrictions or regulations, will ultimately deplete a shared limited resource on which their collective long-term interests depends heavily.

The most salient open access resources are those that exist in a vacuum of effective rules defining property rights, such as marine resources in international waters, the air, the atmosphere, etc. Other open access resources are the consequence of conscious public policies that ensure the access of all stakeholders (real or potential) to the domain of a resource. In addition, even those resources with *de jure* clear property rights may be transformed into *de facto* open access resources when claims are ill defined and/or ineffectively enforced. For example, in poorly protected national parks and forest reserves, villagers from the surrounding areas may perceive it as legitimate and of little risk to encroach upon park resources (Heltberg, 2001, 2002).

In the state of open access, nobody owns the resource; thus, the external cost in terms of reduced resource availability is not internalised by individual users. An obvious and straightforward solution to open access is to create and distribute private ownership through which an externality can be internalised to a great extent: under perfect private ownership, owners capture the full benefits of their decisions and bear the corresponding costs by excluding others from using the resource. Thus such owners have a strong incentive for optimal asset use, maintenance, and investment (Demsetz, 1967; Pejovich, 1990: 28; Lueck, Miceli, 2007). In addition, private property rights are extolled because resources governed by this regime are transferable from owners to others by sale or gift upon mutually agreed upon terms. Transferability, then, acts as an effective mechanism through which resources can move from less productive to more productive owners (Posner, 2002: 33; Pejovich, 1990: 29). Compared with other forms of property rights, such as common property regimes, private ownership saves on the costs of delineating rights and monitoring for compliance because "monitoring boundary crossings is easier than monitoring the behavior of persons situated inside boundaries" (Ellickson, 1993).

Generally speaking, private property rights pave the way for the operation of market mechanisms that make full use of available knowledge (Cheung, 1970), particularly that dispersed and tacit information that by its nature cannot be measured, processed, and integrated by any central authority (Hayek, 1945). In addition, such rights help realise the fruits of specialisation and division of labour by coordinating decisions and activities among different parties in a cost-effective manner (Demsetz, 2002) and encourage organisational and technical innovations by rewarding productive entrepreneurship instead of unproductive rent-seeking activities (Baumol, 1990; Murphy, Shleifer, and Vishny, 1991, 1993).

Unfortunately, private property rights are not a panacea for all economic problems that result from open access or other market failures. First, creating, distributing, and enforcing private property rights is not free. In other words, cost benefit calculations[165] will leave some resources, or some attributes of a

---

[165]   There is a long tradition in law and economics and new institutional economics, dating back to at least Demsetz (1967), that inquires about the emergence (or non-emergence) of property

resource, unregulated and relinquish them to what Barzel (1997) called the "public domain", where unproductive wealth capture prevails. Second, well-organised interest groups can maximise their wealth by seeking favourable changes in legal rules and policies that have a negative influence on the structure of property rights in a given society.[166] Finally, when the government is the definer and enforcer of rights, information costs, rent-seeking costs, and agency costs as results of bureaucratic incompetence and opportunism will frequently render the definition and enforcement of rights ineffective or invalid, and in some extreme cases lead to the partial or complete destruction of private property (McChesney, 2003).

When private property rights are not available or do not allocate resources efficiently because of the aforementioned problems, other forms of property rights, such as common property rights and state property rights can be relied upon to address the open access problem. Common property rights may be viewed as an intermediate step between open access and private ownership; such common property rights emerge as an institutional solution when a resource is sufficiently valuable to justify the cost of organising a user group but not the cost of defining and enforcing private property rights. More specifically, five attributes are most conductive to the development of common property rights: (1) low value of production per unit of area; (2) high variance in the availability of resource units on any one parcel; (3) low returns from intensification of investment; (4) substantial economies of scale derived from utilising a large area; and (5) substantial economies of scale in building infrastructure to utilise the large area (Ostrom, 1999).

A typical common property regime does not give members full rights to alienate their property rights. In other words, they cannot transfer their rights to those outside the group. This attribute of a common property regime is related to a fundamental problem faced by community members, i.e., the task of designing an effective internal governance structure that prevents excessive use and that ensures continued maintenance and improvement. The most common method of allocating the use of common property is to grant equal access to all members of the group, which avoids the explicit cost of measuring and enforcing individual use (when the access to the resource is shared) or effort (when final output is shared); however, in a group with heterogeneous[167] members, an

---

rights in terms of the costs and benefits of exclusion. Eggertsson (1990: chapter 8) provides an excellent survey on this tradition. For some recent studies on the emergence and evolution of property rights, see articles published in *Journal of Legal Studies*, Volume 32, Issue 2.

[166] For extensive discussions on the relationship between property rights and interest groups, see Eggertsson (1990: 271–280) and Libecap (1989).

[167] Heterogeneity indicates both economic inequalities in wealth, income, access to credit, etc. and social-cultural differences including differences in ethnicity, caste, class, religion, and/or cultural views of the resource (Ruttan, 2008). Heterogeneity has long been argued to be associated with inefficient common property management. However, recent studies doubt the negative impact of heterogeneity on the efficiency of common property management and

incentive is created for overuse in the former case and shirking in the latter (Lueck, 1994). Fortunately, inefficiencies arising from the equal sharing rule can be moderated by homogenous membership requirements, which provides an economic rationale for preserving homogeneity by screening potential members, by indoctrination, or by restricting the transfer of memberships (Lueck, Miceli, 2007).

Despite obvious weaknesses such as the absence of the right to transfer ownership shares and the internal governance costs incurred to reach a collective agreement and organise a community of users, a common property regime is recognised as an efficient institutional solution to the tragedy of the commons in many cases (Fitzpatrick, 2006). Taking irrigation as example, a series of studies of the performance of communal proprietorship systems contrasted with government-owned and -managed systems clearly demonstrates the higher productivity of the communal systems when controlling for appropriate variables (Ostrom, 1999).

In traditional law and economics, state ownership is justified in view of its function in correcting market failures that arise from the provision of public goods. The value of state ownership may be better understood in the theoretical framework of the so-called new comparative economics (Djankov et al., 2003). To Djankov et al. (2003), there are two central dangers that any society faces, i.e., disorder and dictatorship.[168] Four social strategies – private orderings, private litigation, regulation, and state ownership – can be used to control the twin dangers of dictatorship and disorder. These four strategies are ranked in terms of the growing powers of the state vis-à-vis private individuals: whereas there is no public involvement required with private orderings, the government takes complete control over an activity with state ownership. Given the fundamental tradeoff between dictatorship and disorder that is inherent in such control strategies, the efficient strategy for a given society is that which might minimise the total social costs of dictatorship and disorder. In some situations, if disorder is too high for private orderings or courts or regulations to counter successfully, government ownership is the last resort. For example, Hart et al. (1997) argue that prisons should be publicly owned because the risk of private jailers mistreating inmates is too high. Compared with a government employee, the private prison owner has a stronger incentive to engage in cost reductions, which

___

present empirical evidence on the positive effects of heterogeneity. The issue is not yet resolved, and we now have a mixed picture at best. For more extensive discussions, see Faysse (2005) and Ruttan (2008).

168 Disorder refers to the risk to individuals and their property of private expropriation from banditry, murder, theft, violation of agreements, torts, or monopoly pricing. Disorder is also reflected in the private subversion of public institutions (such as courts) through bribes and threats, which allows private violators to escape penalties. Dictatorship refers to the risk to individuals and their property of expropriation by the state and its agents in such forms as murder, taxation, or violations of property. Dictatorship is also reflected in expropriation through other means, such as occurs when state regulators help firms restrict competitive entry.

can – at least in principle – substantially reduce the quality in some important dimensions, such as prison violence and the quality of personnel.

Even in most situations in which state ownership is apparently desirable because cost reduction has adverse consequences, private ownership remains superior for several reasons (Shleifer, 1998). First, in industries in which innovation is crucial, the greater incentives for private entrepreneurs to innovate may shift the efficiency balance in their favour. Second, the adverse effects of cost reductions present fewer problems when there is enough competition among private suppliers who face lower demand if their quality drops. Third, some private firms may work hard to establish a reputation for quality to ensure that they have customers in the future. These considerations thus point to a rather narrow set of circumstances in which state ownership is likely to be efficient: (1) when opportunities for cost reductions that lead to non-contractible deterioration of quality are significant; (2) when innovation is relatively unimportant; (3) when competition is weak and consumer choice is ineffective; and (4) when reputational mechanisms are weak. In addition, once politics is taken into account, the case for government ownership is further weakened. In an economy with weak institutions, the government may use its control of state firms and other assets as a means of channelling benefits to its political supporters.

4.3. PROPERTY RIGHTS AND ECONOMIC PERFORMANCE: THEORY AND EVIDENCE

4.3.1. THEORY

It has become conventional wisdom among economists and lawyers that effective property rights, particularly private property rights, play a fundamental role in economic development[169] by shaping the incentives of individuals to undertake productive activities such as investment, trade, and wealth creation. As we discussed above, private property rights can be relied on to reduce externalities and encourage resource transfers, which can pave the way for the market mechanism to operate.

In addition, private ownership is typically enforced by public authorities, such as courts, and thus can be characterised as a claim that is enforceable against others by formal law. Formal property rights defined and enforced by the state – an organisation "which has a comparative advantage in violence" (North, 1981: 21) – are believed to be clearer and more secure than informal

---

[169]   In the words of Eggertsson (1990: 40), "subtle changes in the content of property rights can change the macroperformance of an economic system and lead to economic growth or stagnation".

property rights enforced by private power or community-based norms; thus, the former are more helpful for economic growth. First, as a (credible) third party, the state can lower the transaction costs related to property rights by developing an impartial judiciary, which will help capture important economies of scale[170] by providing more standardised enforcement of property rights to more people in a broader territory and make the punishment of wrongdoing more credible by isolating the enforcers from the enforced parties. Second, informal substitutes for the legal enforcement of property rights can function only to a limited extent and result in inefficient outcomes in some cases; for example, reliance on extralegal norms for enforcement may limit one's possible business partners to a small number of individuals with whom one is familiar, which might prevent potentially mutually beneficial exchanges involving strangers (Cross, 2002).

Formal property rights can also be justified from other perspectives. For example, as Merrill and Smith (2000) argue, if property owners are allowed to create idiosyncratic rights to property at will, they will not take into account the full magnitude of the measurement costs they impose on strangers to the title. In that case, property law can be relied on to address this measurement-cost externality problem through compulsory standardisation of property rights. Moreover, property law can be expected to limit the right to subdivide private property into wasteful fragmentations and to keep resources well-scaled for productive use (Heller, 1998, 1999). Finally, the security and stability of property rights that is provided by property law enables the temporary separation of ownership and possession, which in turn increases the joint wealth of the parties and allows for increased net value resulting from learning how best to use assets, particularly those complex assets whose full economic potential cannot be realised right away and helps to extract more utility from other interoperable assets (Bell, Parchomovsky, 2005).

More specifically, there are five channels through which formal private property rights (FPPR) can affect economic activities. The first claim is that private property encourages individuals to use their resources in the most socially efficient way because, under a private property regime, all costs and benefits of individual action are internalised by decision makers (Demsetz, 1967; Alchian, Demsetz, 1973).[171] Studies on open access have shown that resources are highly prone to over-exploitation and degradation without private property

---

[170] For a more extensive discussion on economies of scale in the public enforcement of property rights, see Bell and Parchomovsky (2005).

[171] In the words of Demsetz (1967), "A primary function of property rights is that of guiding incentives to achieve a greater internalization of externalities". Alchian and Demsetz (1973) argue that "the difficulty with a communal right is that it is not conducive to the accurate measurement of the cost that will be associated with any person's use of the resource". Conversely, "*private* rights can be socially useful precisely because they encourage persons to take account of *social* costs" (italics in original).

rights, particularly with increased population densities or with commercially valuable resources (Hardin, 1968).

The second mechanism through which private property influences economic efficiency is that when property is relatively secure, resources will be maintained in productive uses rather than being diverted to unproductive uses, such as invasion and self-defence[172] (Skaperdas, 1992; Grossman, Kim, 1995). Even in developed countries with well-functioning governments, private protection of property rights, such as private security guards hired by firms and neighbourhood watch groups organised by homeowners, is not uncommon. In some extreme cases in which the government does not enforce property rights, individuals will seek out alternative enforcers of property rights, such as organised crime in Japan and Sicily. These organisations frequently employ threats and sometimes violence (Milhaupt, West, 2000; Gambetta, 1993).

The third channel, which has attracted the most attention in theoretical and empirical research, concerns the effects of property rights on investment. Property rights, or more precisely, security of property, influence investment decisions in two ways (Johnson, 1972; Besley, 1995, 1998). First, the values of all investments attached to an asset will decline when the asset faces the risk of expropriation; thus, the volume of such investments will be reduced. Second, the risk of expropriation changes the relative returns on different investments, diverting investments toward assets that are more certain but less productive. For example, investments move from fixed assets, such as trees and irrigation, to more portable assets, such as livestock, and from long-term to short-term projects.

Assets with formal titles, such as registered or titled lands, are widely believed to improve access to credit for their owners (Atwood, 1990; Besley, 1998; Deininger, 2003). When a lender is assured that an asset pledged as collateral is secure and free of competing claims, he will be more willing to make loans based on the collateral because it reduces the lender's cost of information regarding the borrower's creditworthiness and risk of default. Consequently, the interest rate for the borrower is lowered and the volume of credit offered is expanded, which encourages investment in assets. According to de Soto, the most influential advocate of formal property rights in spurring economic development, the lack of formal titles to land and other assets has prevented the poor in the developing

---

[172] The basic logic behind the theories is that in a state of anarchy in which there are no property rights, the Nash equilibrium of the social game is inefficient in the sense that everyone has a temptation to engage in some aggression, and everyone requires defensive expenditures to counter the aggression of others. In a simple economy with two agents, the ideal would be that neither agent spends anything on aggression against the other's resources, and both can thus devote their entire resource to production. However, when one is defenceless, the other can steals his entire output by spending a little of his resource on predation. Anticipating this, each responds with some defensive expenditure, and the process escalates. In the resulting equilibrium, the resources spent on defence by one player equal those spent on offence by the other.

world from using such assets as collateral and thereby capturing their full value. These assets therefore become "dead capital", rather than the capital-generating assets that prevail in developed countries (de Soto, 2000).

Finally, when property rights are clear and secure, the transaction costs involved in identifying the real owner of the property and making and enforcing a lease or sale contract are reduced to the extent that property markets can function effectively in transferring the property from less efficient uses to more efficient uses (Johnson, 1972; Barrows, Roth, 1990; Deininger, 2003). In addition, improving property's transferability can improve investment incentives when the gains from trade increase the owner's marginal return from the property (Besley, 1998).

4.3.2. HISTORICAL AND CROSS-COUNTRY EVIDENCE

The significance of property rights for economic development has been an appealing subject in economic history studies, among which the works of North stand out as the most innovative and influential contributions. In *The Rise of the Western World*, North and Thomas (1973) attribute the rise of the Western world – more precisely, the success of the Netherlands and England as opposed to the failures of France and Spain – to the creation and evolution of an efficient property rights regime, which provided the incentives necessary for sustained economic growth. In *Structure and Change in Economic History*, North (1981) developed a neoclassical theory of the state and argued that the existence of a state is essential for economic growth because "it is the state that is responsible for the efficiency of the property rights structure, which causes growth or stagnation or economic decline" (North, 1981: 17). The theory of the state is then used to explore human history from the Neolithic Age to the beginning of the twentieth century, in which two major discontinuities in the population/resource rates, namely the First (Neolithic or Agricultural) and Second (Industrial) Economic Revolutions are paid the most attention and explained by the complicated interaction among property rights and organisations. In *Constitutions and Commitment*, North and Weingast (1989) argue that the Glorious Revolution of 1688 gave rise to certain fundamental constitutional changes that allowed the government to commit credibly to upholding private property rights. The resultant decrease in risk premiums enabled the government to borrow at an unprecedented level, advanced the development of a market for private debt, and finally led to a financial revolution that triggered the industrial revolution.

A long line of economic research supports North's conclusions, from the general understanding of the importance of property rights to the more specific issue of the economic effects of the Glorious Revolution.[173] For example,

---

[173] However, North's theory, particularly his interpretation of the Glorious Revolution has been criticised from different perspectives. For example, Quinn (2001) offers evidence to show

Rosenberg and Birdzell (1986) argue that the immediate sources of economic growth in Western countries are innovations in trade, technology, and organisation, which in turn rely on effective property rights to grant decision-making power to entrepreneurs rather than to political or religious authorities and protect the fruits of innovation from expropriation. Pipes (1999) reviews the development of property in mankind's history, with special attention to the institutional differences between England and Russia, and concludes that the different status of private property with respect to the threat of expropriation by the state was the crucial distinction in the different historical paths of the social, political, and economic development in the two countries. The significance of property rights in explaining economic history is also endorsed by Jones (1981), Mokyr (1990), and Landes (1998).

Moreover, North's propositions are backed by some empirical studies indirectly. For example, Klerman and Mahoney (2005) find that abnormal equity returns near the time of the 1701 Act of Settlement, which mandated that judges enjoyed tenure for good behaviour rather than at the pleasure of the Crown, are large and statistically significant, a result that is consistent with the view that judicial independence as a shield for private property should have a beneficial economic impact that in turn can be reflected in equity returns. Another empirical study conducted by Delong and Shleifer (1993) shows that over the period from 1050 to 1800, absolutist governments are associated with low economic growth, as measured by city growth. These authors therefore conclude that the rise of absolutism in regions such as Italy and Spain, and absolutism's failure to enrich itself in Holland and early modern England, diverted the economic centre of Europe from the Mediterranean to the English Channel and the Atlantic.

The relationship between property rights and economic development has been examined in certain empirical studies[174] using cross-country data. The

that, although the risk premium on sovereign debt declined after the Glorious Revolution, interest rates on private debts increased. Sussman and Yafeh (2006) find that the level of interest rates in Britain continued to be fairly high for several decades following the Glorious Revolution, and increased substantially in response to the outbreak of military conflicts. Stasavage (2003, 2007) argues that the British state's credibility as a borrower was only consolidated after 1715, once the Whig party, which was intimately associated with government creditors, established lasting political supremacy. Regarding the effect of institutional reform on property rights, Clark (1996) finds that the Glorious Revolution had no significant impact on either rates of return on capital or land values and concludes that "stable property right may have been a necessary condition for the Industrial Revolution, but, since they had existed in England and Wales for more than 200 years prior to the Industrial Revolution, they were certainly not a sufficient condition". The importance of the patent system in encouraging innovation in the British Industrial Revolution is also doubted (Mokyr, 2009). All the evidence leads Mokyr (2008) to caution that "the traditional emphasis on formal institutions has been over-emphasized, and the enforcement of property rights by the state was less crucial than the Northian interpretation has suggested".

[174] For a comprehensive review of the literature that uses cross-country regression to study the relationship between institutions and economic growth, see Pande and Udry (2006).

most influential may be Knack and Keefer (1995), who use institutional indicators compiled by two private international investment risk services (ICRG and BERI) to measure the security of property rights in individual countries, and find significant correlation between property rights and economic growth. The same indicators are used by Clague et al. (1999), Hall and Jones (1999), and Acemoglu et al. (2001), among others, who confirm that property rights have a positive and important effect on growth. The cross-country studies on the institutional foundations of growth, however, have been challenged in the recent literature. For example, Glaeser et al. (2004) argue that most indicators of institutional quality used to establish the proposition that institutions (property rights) cause growth are constructed to be conceptually unsuitable for that purpose. These measures of institutions reflect what actually occurred in a country, or ex post outcomes of institutions, rather than institutions per se. As such, these measures change with per capita income and are highly volatile; in addition, they cannot be used to differentiate a dictator's choice of respecting property rights from a democratic government's obligation to protect private property.

4.3.3. MICRO EVIDENCE

Numerous academic efforts have examined the effects of property rights, particularly FPPR, on economic performance empirically along the five dimensions we have discussed. Some studies of the relationship between property rights and resource management confirm the superiority of private property rights over open access (and common ownership) in guiding efficient resource use. In one of the pioneering works on this topic, Bottomley (1963) finds that Arab tribesmen in the Libyan province of Tripolitania employed communal land for low-valued uses, such as growing occasional crops of barley and grazing privately owned sheep and goats, rather than for more profitable activities, such as almond-tree planting. Using both cross-sectional and time series data from the US East Coast and Gulf Coast oyster industry, Agnello and Donnelley (1975) show that labour productivity was higher in privately leased oyster grounds than in government-regulated open-access grounds. Anderson and Lueck (1992) exploit a sample of 39 Indian reservations to estimate the effect of land tenure on agricultural productivity. They find that the per-acre value of agricultural output is 85–90% lower on tribal-trust land than on fee-simple land and 30–40% lower on individual-trust land than on fee-simple land.[175] Grafton,

---

[175] Tribunal trust land is managed by the tribe subject to trust constraints administered by the Bureau of Indian Affairs (BIA). Under fee simple, the land is privately owned by individuals who are free to use, lease, and sell it. Under individual trust, the land is held by individual Indians, but their rights are subject to trust constraints that are administered by the BIA.

Squires, and Fox (2000) test for changes in efficiency in the same resource (the British Columbia halibut fishery) following privatisation of property rights, and they find that privatisation leads not only to efficient input usage but also to a substantial producer surplus. In addition to the negative effects on productivity, common ownership is demonstrated to be ineffective in controlling resource over-exploitation problems and thus is conducive to land degradation and resource depletion (López, 1997; Ahuja, 1998).

There are plenty of cases, however, that challenge the reported inefficiency of common property in resource allocation and exploitation (Ostrom, 1990, 1999; Baland, Platteau, 1996). For example, in Töbel, Switzerland, a village of only 600 people, communal space for cattle grazing is regulated by an alp association, which is governed by the villagers themselves. Although yields are relatively low, the land in Töbel has maintained its productivity for many centuries, and overgrazing has been prevented by tight controls. Successful management of common property resources can also be found in Nepal (Arnold and Campbell, 1986), Japan (McKean, 1982), Turkey (Berkes, 1992), India (Wade, 1994), and medieval Northern Europe (Smith, 2000), among others. Furthermore, some studies find that privatisation of resources has not served as a panacea for their conservation; in fact, in many cases, it has contributed to accelerated resource destruction. For example, privatisation of land in India accelerated the destruction of native vegetation (Jodha, 1992).

There is clear evidence that individuals will divert resources to unproductive uses, such as inefficient investment, expensive self-protection, and even violent conflict, when property rights are insecure. For example, De Vany and Sanchez (1979) find that *ejidatarios*[176] in Mexico exhibit higher fertility than comparable groups because children help parents secure their rights to land. The relationship between land security and fertility can also be observed in Thailand, the Philippines, Iran, Egypt, and India (Stokes, et al., 1986). Similarly, Field (2007) shows that a titling program issued by the Peruvian government with the aim of converting informal property in urban squatter settlements into formal property has greatly reduced the human resources that untitled households devote to maintaining tenure security through informal means. This change resulted in both an increase in total labour force hours and a reallocation of work hours from inside the home to the outside labour market. In Buenos Aires, Argentina, when squatters obtained formal land rights as a result of an expropriation law enacted by Congress in 1984, this change was found to increase squatters' housing investments, reduce household sizes, and improve the education of

---

[176]   An *ejidatario* is a member of an *ejido*, an agrarian community that has received and continues to hold land in accordance with an agrarian law established after the Mexican Revolution. In a typical *ejido*, all rights to crop lands are granted to individual families on a usufruct basis. The land cannot be sold, leased, mortgaged, or disposed of in any similar fashion. Rights to these lands may be passed on to heirs, but they may also be lost if the land is not under cultivation for two consecutive years.

their children[177] (Galiani, Schargrodsky, 2006). In Brazil, unfortunately, the inconsistency between the civil law that supports title held by landowners and the constitutional law that supports the rights of squatters leads to pervasive violence between landowners and squatters (Alston, Libecap, and Mueller, 1999, 2000). Violence resulting from squatting was also universal in California and other western states of the US in 1860; in addition, squatters are found to have lower production than non-squatters because squatters must allocate part of their labour to protect their property rights (Clay, 2006).

The empirical linkage between property rights and investment has been of the utmost concern to economists and is the subject of numerous studies covering the majority of developing countries; unfortunately, the evidence does not systematically confirm the linkage that the theory suggests. The evidence from Asian and Latin American countries is stronger. For example, in two provinces in Thailand, Feder and Onchan (1987) find that farmland security (possession of land title) implies greater capital formation, higher capital/land ratios, and higher levels of land improvement. In China, Li et al. (1998) and Jacoby et al. (2002) use household data from northeast China to show that land tenure security[178] significantly affects land-specific investment and investment in soil quality (organic fertiliser), in particular. In India, Pender and Kerr (1998) find that soil and water conservation investment is significantly lower on leased land in two of the study villages and lower on plots that are subject to sales restrictions in one village. In Vietnam, the land law of 1993, which gave households the power to exchange, transfer, lease, inherit and mortgage their land-use rights, is found to lead to a significant increase in the share of total area devoted to multi-year crops and to some increases in irrigation investment (Do, Iyer, 2003). In Brazil, the results of a household survey confirm that ownership security (i.e., whether the farmer holds the title to his land) plays an important role in promoting investment in land improvements (Alston et al., 1996). Land titling and registration are also found to be associated with increased investments in Guatemala and Nicaragua (Schweigert, 2006; Deininger, Chamorro, 2004). In addition to rural areas, tenure security is demonstrated to influence residential investment in urban squatter neighbourhoods in Peru and Argentina (Field, 2005; Galiani, Schargrodsky, 2006).

---

[177] As Becker and Lewis (1973) state, there is a tradeoff between the quantity and quality of children faced by parents. Therefore, if land titling causes a reduction in fertility, it might also induce households to increase educational investment in their children.

[178] Most cultivated land in rural China remains collectively owned and the state has purposely provided localities flexibility in land management; the government has explicitly allowed leaders the right to make periodic adjustments to household land holdings if conditions so require. Tenure insecurity induced by frequent reallocation by local leaders of collective land is thus believed to weaken farmer investment incentives in the land, particularly in longer-term, land saving investments (Wen, 1995). By contrast, some scholars suggest that the inefficiencies are not so great and that even farmers are not in favour of tenure reform (Kung, 1995).

For Africa, the picture is mixed. An early study reviews empirical evidence from Kenya, Uganda, and Zimbabwe and concludes that "there is little empirical evidence to support the hypothesis that registration, through increased tenure security, has increased investment in agriculture" (Barrows, Roth, 1990: 290). Migot-Adholla et al. (1991) use cross-sectional evidence from Ghana, Kenya, and Rwanda in 1987–1988 to show that the relationship between land rights (the level of individualisation of land rights and particularly the extent of transfer or alienation rights) and land improvements is far from clear. In a book based on eight case studies in seven African countries (Burkina Faso, Rwanda, Ghana, Kenya, Uganda, Somalia, and Senegal), several cases (Matlon (1994) on Burkina Faso, Blarel (1994) on Rwanda, and Roth et al. (1994) on Uganda) confirm the positive impact of land rights on investment, whereas others failed to do so. The relative insignificance of the effects of land ownership on investment is further supported by findings from Uganda (Place, Otsuka, 2002; Pender et al., 2004) and Madagascar (Jacoby, Minten, 2007). By contrast, in an influential paper, Besley (1995) uses data from two regions of Ghana (Wassa and Anloga) and finds that land improvements in Wassa (in the form of tree planting) are significantly related to land rights, whereas land improvements in Angola (including drainage and continuous fertilising) have no such relationship. Similarly, Gavian and Fafchamps (1996) find evidence that tenure insecurity incites farmers to divert scarce manure resources to more secure fields (fields that are owned rather than borrowed) whenever they can. Furthermore, Place and Otsuka (2001) confirm the effects of tenure security on incentives for making long-term investments to boost agricultural production in their study of Malawi.

Even if investment is empirically confirmed to be positively correlated with tenure security in general, and land titling in particular, it remains too early to conclude a causal relationship from that. As Sjaastad and Bromley (1997) argue, the causal direction may be from investment to tenure security rather than vice versa. In other words, investment, particularly the "conspicuous" investment, such as planting leguminous trees (as opposed to "inconspicuous" investment, such as fallow land), can be viewed as a commitment to the long-term productive use of the land, and thus undertaken to increase tenure security.[179] Some

---

[179] See also Deininger and Jin (2006), who argue that when tenure security is exogenously given, higher security will lead to higher investment when the investment is for the purposes of increasing productivity; however, the relationship becomes ambiguous when tenure security is endogenous, i.e., when security can be enhanced through investment. For example, a higher level of tenure insecurity could result in more investment for fencing that has no impact on productivity but enhances tenure security. In fact, planting eucalyptus trees is an important strategy used by farmers in Ethiopia to enhance their tenure security although eucalyptus trees do not improve soil fertility and have adverse productivity impacts.
   Deininger and Jin (2006) therefore suggest that security and transferability should be considered separately in empirical studies and claim that greater transferability of land rights will enhance investment at any level of tenure security because it allows farmers to capitalise on their investment if they are not able to self-cultivate in the future. They also distinguish

empirical evidence, for example, Gray and Kevane (2001) and Brasselle et al. (2002) on Burkina Faso, Quisumbing et al. (2001) on Ghana, and Place and Otsuka (2002) on Uganda, seems to be consistent with this hypothesis.

The evidence about the credit effects of formal property rights is also ambiguous. An early study conducted by Feder and Onchan (1987) demonstrates that land security for farms in Thailand (possession of land title) increased access to institutional credit, yielding greater capital formation. In Peru, land titling is found to be associated with a 9–10 percentage point increase in approval rates from the public sector bank for loans to be used for housing construction materials (Field, Torero, 2004). In Argentina, the evidence indicates a positive (but modest) effect of land titling on access to mortgage credit and no effect on access to other forms of credit, such as credit cards and bank accounts (Galiani, Schargrodsky, 2006). Again, empirical studies in rural Africa fail to find a significant relationship between the possession of title and the use of formal credit (Migot-Adholla et al., 1991; Place, Hazell, 1993; Pinckney, Kimuyu, 1994). A more subtle conclusion is reached by Carter and Olinto (2003), who find that land titling has differential effects across wealth classes and disproportionately benefits larger scale farmers (farms in excess of 15 hectares).

Some studies claim that land titling stimulates land transactions and increases the value of titled property relative to untitled property. For example, Jimenez (1984) compares unit housing prices between the non-squatter (formal) sector and the squatter (informal) sector in the city of Davao, the Philippines, and finds that unit dwelling prices are 58% higher in the formal sector than in the informal sector. Based on interviews with real estate brokers in Jakarta, Dowall and Leaf (1991) show that land prices were affected strongly by the level of tenure security. Feder and Nishio (1999) report that three to four years after the issuance of title deeds under the Land Titling Project, the land market in Thailand was more active in the project area compared with the non-project area. In Brazil, Alston et al. (1996) find that the effect of a title on land value is positive and significant. In Nicaragua, registration increases land values by 30% (Deininger, Chamorro, 2004). In Ecuador, Lanjouw and Levy (2002) find that holding a title is associated with a sizable increase in the market value of properties (on average, 23.5% more than untitled property values).

Conversely, the evidence also shows that formal property rights are not a prerequisite for the development of an active land market, particularly in African countries. In Kenya, a well-functioning land market has not been created as a

---

between two types of investment: planting trees that is highly visible and can therefore be used to manifest property rights, and establishment or maintenance of terraces that enhance productivity more but are less visible. The evidence shows that: (1) insecure tenure (proxied by past land redistribution) encourages planting of trees but discourages terracing; (2) both tenure insecurity and low levels of transferability reduce the propensity to invest, particularly with respect to productivity-enhancing but less visible assets; and (3) transferability has a larger impact on investment.

result of land registration (Barrows, Roth, 1990). A survey of sixteen different areas of six African countries with titling programs (Kenya, Rwanda, Burundi, Uganda, Malawi, and Zambia) showed that, on average, only 16% of the land parcels were acquired through market purchases, whereas 63% were obtained through inheritances and various types of gift transfers and the rest through other means, primarily state allocation (Platteau, 2000: 151–152). Similarly, in Ho Chi Minh City (HCMC), Vietnam, Kim (2004) shows evidence of a flourishing real estate market in spite of the fact that approximately half of the houses did not have legal titles.

4.4. WHY FORMAL PRIVATE PROPERTY RIGHTS MAY FAIL

4.4.1. MALFUNCTIONING OR NONEXISTENCE OF RELATED FACTOR MARKETS

Whether FPPR can bring about desirable economic outcomes, as many economists and lawyers expect, depends significantly on the existence and operation of related factor markets, such as credit markets, labour markets, and insurance markets, which cannot be created or maintained by a property rights regime per se. For example, Feder and Feeny (1991: 145) find that most of the impact of land ownership on investment in Thailand "stemmed from the fact titles increased farmer's access to credit, rather than from the elimination of actual risk to the land rights of the farmers". Deininger (2003: Chapter 3) also argues that land rental markets and land sales markets[180] will not function well

---

[180] In rural labour markets, wage workers' true efforts are not easily observable, which is a typical agency problem that is exacerbated by spatial dispersion of the agricultural production process and the need to constantly adjust to micro-variations of the natural environment. By contrast, fixed-rent tenancy will provide optimum incentives for the tenants' efforts and thus is widespread in all developed countries, such as the US and Canada, in which approximately one-third of the agricultural land is cultivated by tenants. However, fixed-rent tenancy might be too risky for the tenant to participate, if markets for credit and insurance are so incomplete that the tenant is prevented from either borrowing to obtain working capital or to smooth consumption in case of an unfavourable shock. In addition, landlords will tend to enter into fixed-rent contracts only with tenants who are wealthy enough to pay the rent under any possible output realisation. Some empirical evidence indicates that a large number of potential tenants are actually rationed out of the tenancy market due to wealth constraints. Therefore, the ability of the land rental market to bring about efficiency-enhancing transfers is constrained by the functioning of markets for credit and insurance, in addition to potential tenants' asset endowment. In areas with poorly developed insurance and capital markets, land sales will likely be few and limited mainly to distress sales; because returns from agricultural production are highly covariate, demand, and therefore land prices, will be high in good crop years when savings are high, sellers are few, and potential buyers of land are many. Simultaneously, the need to satisfy basic subsistence constraints might also give rise to a large supply of people who are forced to

if there are imperfections in the aforementioned factor markets. Therefore, when factor markets cannot be introduced or sustained or when there are significant distortions and imperfections in these markets (as we can observe in many developing countries), the effects of property rights tend to be invalidated.

Taking credit markets as an example, the World Bank (2001: 134) reports that most African countries opted to create at least one large state bank after gaining their independence to support indigenous industries and state ventures and to make banking services available for the broad population, including those in rural areas. In many countries, these large state banks continue to dominate the banking sector. After decades of politicised management and soft budget constraints, they have found it difficult to restructure or privatise. Higher government ownership of banks is shown, however, to be associated with slower financial development (La Porta et al., 2002) and with lower efficiency and stability in the banking sector (Barth et al., 2004).

Financial market distortions impose significant barriers on access to financing for households and small and medium enterprises (SMEs). Beck et al. (2009) report that although more than 90% of households in several European countries have a bank account, less than half of the households in many developing countries have one, and in many African countries fewer than one in five households has an account. In addition, small firms report lack of financing to be one of the most important business constraints they face: for example, less than 20% of small firms use external financing. In this type of economic environment, the impact of land title or registration on credit-related increases in capital investment will be reduced substantially, as Atwood (1990) argues.

In addition, where informal credit markets function well and can substitute for formal markets to a great extent, land titling will also be of limited value. For example, in one Thai province in which informal lending was predominant, Feder and Onchan (1987) find that the impact of land titling on credit access was negligible. Atwood (1990) also argues that, although informal lenders in other parts of the world may accept informal, unregistered land claims as collateral if the lenders are close enough to the community to have low-cost information about the legitimacy of informal land claims and if they can foreclose on land when a borrower defaults, informal lending in Africa is seldom, if ever, secured by land but by other property or by a combination of social custom and goodwill.

Finally, when the judicial system is ineffective or partial, or when people do not recognise formal land ownership as legitimate and do not like to accept its distributive consequences, or when administrative agencies fail to maintain a valid titling and registration system, titled land will not be considered reliable

engage in distress sales of their land in bad years. In addition, during periods of macroeconomic instability, nonagricultural investors may use land as an asset to hedge against inflation, and such excess demand for land will therefore increase the price of land as a speculative asset. In that case, it will be difficult for poor but efficient producers to gain access to land through the purchase market.

collateral by lenders because it is more difficult to foreclose upon (Platteau, 2000: 144–146). Moreover, there are supply constraints that result from lenders' strategies: commercial banks and financial institutions typically prefer lending against more reliable streams of income than those found in agriculture, and considerations of administrative costs may lead banks and other credit agencies to set a minimum size of loans which frequently exceeds the capital needs of small landholders (Platteau, 2000: 148).

4.4.2. COSTS OF FORMAL PROPERTY RIGHTS

There are a variety of costs in terms of creating and maintaining a formal property regime, including the costs of establishing a property registration system. Taking land registration as an example, there are two different systems of land registration, namely a land records system, which prevails in the United States and France (and some other countries, most with a French legal background), and a land title registration system, which was created within the German legal tradition and is now used in most of the world[181] (Arruñada, 2003; Arruñada, Garoupa, 2005; Hanstad, 1998; Miceli, 1998). According to Miceli (1998), the land records system, which originated with the recording acts, requires the maintenance of a public record of land transfer that can be inspected by prospective buyers to establish evidence of good title, thereby easing land transfer. However, examination of the record does not guarantee title; depending on the thoroughness of the search and differences in lawyer's opinions about the title history, there remains a risk in the claim to title.[182] As a result, the history is searched anew with each land transfer, and owners typically purchase private title insurance to provide monetary compensation in the event of future claim. By contrast, under the land title registration system, a landowner registers his land with the government, at which time a legal proceeding is undertaken to determine the status of title. In the absence of a legitimate claim, the government issues a certificate that gives the owner good title against any future claims. Subsequent purchasers need only inspect the certificate to verify ownership; if a

---

[181]   Land titling systems also include the Australian "Torrens" variety, which has also been introduced in some other common law jurisdictions. The term "Torrens" derived from the name of Sir Robert Torrens, who created a system of registration of title to land in Australia while he was serving as Register General of the Province of South Australia in 1858.

[182]   Under a land records system, title disputes are solved by using a property rule. If the seller's right is shown to be defective, the buyer loses the property right to the benefit of the true owner. The buyer is left with contractual rights against the seller, the title examiner, and/or title insurer (Arruñada, 2003). By contrast, the use of a liability rule for solving title disputes dominates in the title registration system. That is to say, a good faith buyer acquires a property right if the purchase is based on the information provided by the register. If the seller's right is later shown to be defective, the buyer keeps the property right and the true owner gets a contractual right against the seller and the register.

claimant should later appear, he is only entitled to monetary compensation from a public fund financed by registration fees.

There have long been debates over the comparative merits of these two systems. On the one hand, a land records system is believed to be less costly and more flexible (Arruñada, 2003). Under a records system, some minor defects not worth clarifying can be insured either by the parties or a third-party insurer, which helps to avoid holdout problems (and associated bargaining costs) in title purging. Moreover, costs will tend to be minimised and flexibility (in terms of rapid innovation and adaptation to changes in technology and demand) can be achieved because title examination and clarification are conducted by business firms or professionals who are paid with a residual profit, at least when the competition is sufficiently strong. On the other hand, a land title registration system can provide more security for property rights and can realise economies of scale in information production that must be forgone under a land records system. A land title registration system is also given credit for the fact that it awards the land to the party who values it most (the current owner rather than the claimant) (Miceli, Sirmans, 1995), induces optimal investment in land improvement (Miceli, Sirmans, Turnbull, 1998), and reduces dynamic inefficiency in land development (Miceli, Sirmans, Turnbull, 2000). In summary, a land title registration system is favoured by the majority of scholars because it "not only makes land titles more reliable, but is also simpler, more logical, and less costly"[183] (Hanstad, 1998), and is therefore recommended by most land registration projects that are funded by multilateral agencies in developing countries as a more efficient policy option (Deininger, Feder, 2009).

An effective land title registration system is, however, expensive. Establishment of the system will likely take several years to complete and will consume valuable physical and human resources that might otherwise be used for unrelated socially desirable projects. Moreover, operation and maintenance of the system, once established, require significant additional resources. In the World Bank's 2008 "Doing Business" report, the mean cost associated with property registration in 173 countries amounted to 6.6% of the property's value, and the mean waiting time was 81 days.[184] The cost of registering property is highly bimodal; whereas it is 2% or less of property values in 32 cases, it amounts to 5 or

---

[183] One empirical study conducted by Janczyk (1977) shows that, in Cook County, Illinois, in which the two title systems coexist, the cost of transferring a title in the records system was approximately twice that of a transfer in the Torrens system. In addition, Cook County could have saved $76 million once all of the property in the records system was registered into the Torrens system.

[184] However, as Deininger and Feder (2009) warn, these figures are based on expert opinion for unencumbered property in the capital city, and they should thus be treated with proper care and are likely to constitute a lower bound for the cost of registration than that faced by the average landholder. For example, a field-based study in St Lucia found transaction costs for what was considered a "typical" transaction by the local population to be almost three times the 7% given in the Doing Business survey.

10% and over 10% of property values in 92 and 41 cases, respectively (Deininger, Feder, 2009). In some extreme cases, such as Syria, the costs of registering property is approximately 28.05% of property value, while in Kiribati it takes 523 days to register property. Consequently, as Barnes and Griffith-Charles (2007) show, when the costs exceed the benefits (in terms of increased security) that users obtain from registering, they will return to the informal system to convey and divide their land, and the sustainability of the land registry system will be seriously compromised by such processes of "deformalisation".

In addition to the direct costs of a land registration system, the discrepancies between title documents and reality that results from ineffective operation of this system constitute another major disappointment of land titling programs in developing countries (Platteau, 2000: 146–147; Trebilcock, Veel, 2008). Without sufficient administrative capabilities, succession and other transfers of title are largely unregistered, such that the land registration system poorly reflects the present-day reality, which destroys the utility of the system and engenders new uncertainties. In other cases, such as in Nicaragua and Bolivia, title to the same piece of land may be delivered to separate parties when more than one government agency has the authority to title land but there is neither a clear distinction between their geographic jurisdictions nor any cooperation between the two agencies (Barnes, Stanfield, and Barthel, 2000). Finally, in some Latin American countries, such as Guatemala, over-centralisation of registry institutions renders the registration service highly inaccessible for residents of remote areas.

4.4.3. PROPERTY LAW AND CUSTOMARY LAND SYSTEM

In many developing countries, customary land ownership continues to be more important in governing land issues than formal property law is (Barrows, Roth, 1990; Pinckney, Kimuyu, 1994). Generally, in most African countries, the formal land system covers at most 2–10% of the total land area (Deininger, 2003: 62). In addition, the customary law tenure has been flexible enough to adapt to a new environment[185] and secure enough to warrant land-related investments. Studies from all parts of Africa indicate that, under normal circumstances, customary land ownership guarantees basic tenure security (measured in terms of use rights and transfer rights) to all villagers (even migrants), and it is sufficient to induce

---

[185]　When the advantages of individualised tenure have grown because of increased population density and/or market integration, many communal tenure systems either recognise a user's property rights if the land has been improved or compensate the user for improvements when the land is redistributed, which attenuates tenure-related investment disincentives (Sjaastad, Bromley 1997; Deininger, Binswanger, 1999). Moreover, although communal systems prohibit land transactions with outsiders, rentals – and often even sales – within the community (and possibly beyond) are normally allowed, providing the scope for efficiency-enhancing transfers (Place, 2009).

investment; there is thus no increased security with formal title and therefore no direct impact on investment (Atwood, 1990; Pinckney, Kimuyu, 1994; Place, 2009). It is also not surprising to find an ambiguous relationship between land markets and land titling because market-style land transfers have developed in customary regimes, particularly in which land is relatively scarce and the efficiency gains from market transfers are high (André, Platteau, 1998; Platteau, 2000: 158–159).

When the state in the developing world tries to replace customary land tenure with formal property law but fails to fill the gap in providing important social services left by the withdrawal of a communal regime, such as the social safety net function of communal land,[186] a significant efficiency loss will be incurred. As Bromley and Chavas (1989) posit, the absence of a right to exclude someone desperately in need of the means for living means that risks are more effectively pooled, and a common property regime can therefore be understood as an integral part of risk sharing strategies. Therefore, when there are incomplete insurance markets because of either information asymmetries or the limits of contract, if individuals are sufficiently risk averse and the efficiency gains from privatisation are sufficiently limited, privatisation of communal land can be welfare-decreasing (Platteau, Francois, 2005).

Many empirical studies have confirmed the insurance-providing role of common property resources (CPRs). For example, Ellickson (1993) shows that in each of the three pioneer settlements in US history (the Jamestown settlement of 1607, the Plymouth settlement of 1620, and the Mormon settlement at Salt Lake in 1847), settlers began with group ownership of land as a response to an environment characterised as highly dangerous. In the context of the modern developing world, this insurance function performed by CPRs is shown to favour the poor: Jodha (1992) reveals significant contribution of CPRs with respect to the employment and income generation for the rural poor in India. In the Tapajos region of Brazil, in which there are 18 traditional communities along the border of the Tapajos National Forest, Pattanayak and Sills (2001) find that non-timber forest products have played a substantial role in providing local people with a form of "natural insurance" against agricultural risk; in Zimbabwe, Cavendish (2000) shows that communally owned environmental resources, such

---

[186] Commonly held land can provide insurance against external shocks in two different ways (Platteau, Francois, 2005). First, communal land typically acts as the "asset of last resort": those who work on communal land receive not only a return on their labour but also an imputed form of resource rent, and the amount of rent they obtain is directly proportional to their labour contribution; those in most need, i.e., those with relatively poor outside earnings chances who allocate relatively more effort to gathering resources from the common property, obtain a relatively higher share of the resource rent. Second, communal land can fulfil a role as the "employer of last resort": across individuals, the productivity of labour allocated to the common land is relatively homogeneous in comparison with productivity outside; this feature allows the commons to provide a fallback form of employment in cases in which labour cannot find profitable employment elsewhere.

as forests, fisheries, land, and water, make a significant contribution to average rural incomes and to the well-being of poorer households, in particular. Therefore, when common property resources are privatised and the vulnerable segments of the community (the poor) cannot be adequately compensated, they will try to resist the alleged efficiency-increasing institutional change.

As Meinzen-Dick and Mwangi (2008) show, in many rural communities that remain largely dependent on agriculture and natural resources for their livelihoods, property rights to land are better understood as a "web of interests", with many different parties that have rights to use, regulate, and/or manage the resource.[187] Therefore, most land is subject to multiple and overlapping claims by several different types of groups. In addition, customary land tenure is considered to be adaptive, flexible, and dynamic, given that "land rights are subject to intermittent or on-going negotiation, and tenure security depends more on a person's standing with his/her relatives and neighbours than on the way in which a claim was originally acquired" (Berry, 1997: 1233). It is hard, or even impossible, to codify and register the complex bundles of rights associated with given parcels, particularly in view of the substantial information and transaction costs faced by most developing countries. When customary group rights are extinguished by formalisation, the state's failure to record all existing land rights will therefore lead to a shearing of this web, and legitimate claimants, such as women, children, and seasonal users, among others, may be denied legal recognition of their traditional rights to land. The formalisation of property rights thus becomes an important source of social conflict.[188]

In other cases, land tenure formalisation may even be regarded as illegitimate when the elites manipulate titling programs to the extent that the poor or otherwise vulnerable land users are dispossessed of their rights to land.[189] In the

---

[187] For example, the same plot of land can be used to provide many products: a food crop; fodder for animals; fruits, sticks, and timber from its trees; wild medicinal plants nectar for bees; and a spring for drinking water for people and animals. If it is in a flood plain, there may be fishing in the wet season and cultivation in the dry. In many agrarian societies, rights to each of these uses can be separated and accessed by different individuals and groups.

[188] Disputes were found to vary from fewer than 10% of agricultural parcels in Rwanda and Ghana to between 25% to 30% in Uganda and Kenya, and from 21% in Zambia to 43% in Burundi (Place, 2009).

[189] For example, in Thailand, land records have been manipulated by government officials so as to allow elites with a high level of political connections to obtain ownership of land that, under the traditional system, would have been controlled by homesteading cultivators, whereas the original occupants (particularly when they belong to non-Thai minorities) have found it difficult to protect their customary rights because of land dispute claimants' differential access to the Thai bureaucracy. In Kenya, those few well-connected Kenyans who succeeded in having pasture lands registered in their own names on the grounds that they would bring them into cultivation were finally found to use the land as collateral in order to obtain loans from banks in Nairobi and to use the proceeds of these loans to finance their children's university studies abroad, with the intention of shunning repayment and letting the land be foreclosed upon. In Mauritania, good irrigated lands traditionally claimed by local Negro-African communities have been adjudicated to private owners with a view to

words of Barrows and Roth (1990: 274) words, "registration effectively provided a mechanism for transfer of wealth to those with better social or economic positions, thereby creating tenure insecurity for less influential right-holders". Therefore, the transition from customary land tenure to formalised, individual ownership becomes a "race for the prize", and "it is mostly the wealthy, the powerful, and the informed who succeed in a race contested under such murky conditions" (Benjaminsen, Sjaastad, 2002: 129). Insofar as it encourages unequal land capture by powerful elites, formalisation of land rights will inevitably be rejected by those whose traditional claims are weakened or even denied in the process of formalisation (by accident or design), and debates and conflicts will then continue to plague society. As a consequence, valuable resources are wasted on unproductive uses, such as pervasive recourse to courts, exclusion of other users through various types of enclosures, and even illicit and semi-criminal acts of theft (Peters, 2004). In extreme cases, apparently trivial land conflicts can be kept alive for generations and may suddenly erupt into large-scale civil strife and violence (André, Platteau, 1998; Fred-Mensah, 1999).

Generally speaking, when most developing countries try to replace the customary land system with formal (individualised) land rights, their supply-side constraints, such as insufficient budgets, incompetent agencies, and inadequate legitimacy, will frequently cause so-called "legal pluralism" (Fitzpatrick, 2006). For example, in Kenya, Barrows and Roth (1990: 273) show that "the land law failed to gain popular understanding or acceptance, individuals continued to convey rights to land according to customary law, and a gap developed between the control of rights as reflected in the land register and as recognized by most local communities." Under legal pluralism, the question of which institution defines and enforces property rights is ambiguous because "traditional authorities have lost much of their power of control over land, but the state has not developed the capacity to take full control" (Fred-Mensah, 1999: 952). Thus, instead of complementing one another, formal and informal land institutions compete with one another, and these parallel systems give rise to so-called "institutional shopping", where different parties pursue disputes through different channels (e.g., formal vs. informal, legal vs. administrative) (Deininger, 2003: 35; Deininger, Feder, 2009).

Legal pluralism, institutional ambiguity, and institutional shopping will further undermine the social conditions that enable customary land tenure to function effectively, such as norms of reciprocity and cooperation, low-cost internal governance mechanisms, and informal sanction systems (Fitzpatrick,

---

encouraging their efficient exploitation; however, in the end, these lands were allocated to people of Moorish origin by an essentially Moorish administration and in many instances were not actually brought into cultivation (Platteau, 2000: 165–167). This phenomenon is termed "land grabbing" by Feder and Nishio (1999), who define the grabbers as "those who are better informed, are more familiar with formal processes, and have better access to officials and financial means to undertake procedures for registration".

2006). Norm-based common property arrangements may therefore become dysfunctional,[190] or even break down entirely, particularly under pressure from rising resource values. Alternatively, legal pluralism may also damage the legitimacy and credibility of formal property systems, which can lead to efficiency costs,[191] in view of the local population's determined resistance to drastic reshuffling of land rights. In the worst-case scenario, the norm-based resource governance system will disintegrate without the provision of effective substitutes by the state, and open access (and resource depletion) will follow.

4.4.4. PROPERTY LAW AND THE STATE

This discussion has finally led us to an evergreen issue that is attracting much attention from scholars of new institutional economics, i.e., the relationship between property rights and the state. As Eggertsson (1990: 40, 317) puts it clearly, "the property rights approach is not complete without a theory of the state" because "without the state, its institutions, and supportive framework of property rights, high transaction costs will paralyse complex production systems, and specific investments involving long-term exchange relationships will not be forthcoming". In the words of North[192] (1981: 17), "[a] theory of the state is essential because it is the state that specifies the property rights structure. Ultimately it is the state that is responsible for the efficiency of the property rights structure, which causes growth or stagnation or economic decline". Finally, the state is a two-edged sword: "[t]he existence of a state is essential for economic growth; the state, however, is the source of man-made economic decline" (North, 1981: 20).

The importance and desirability of the state has been endorsed by social scientists since Thomas Hobbes, given its allegedly irreplaceable role in maintaining social order, providing public goods and services, and redressing market failure. Although they are far from perfect, states in the developed world

---

[190] For example, it was reported that customary land tenure in Somalia was secure and that titling programs actually decreased security by calling into question the applicability of customary law and creating the possibility of the dispossession of unregistered farmers who continued to abide by customary law (Trebilcock, Veel, 2008). See also Lanjouw and Levy (2004), who argue that "if one takes an area with a long-standing and well-understood customary property rights system and overlays a formal state titling program, it can make residents less secure because they are unsure which system will apply in any given situation".

[191] There may be three forms of such efficiency costs (Platteau, 2000: 156). First, new uncertainties arise that tend to multiply precisely the kind of transaction costs (search, enforcement, and litigation) that some studies predict will be reduced by the creation of formal land rights. Second, there are all the costs that the new "illegitimate" owners must bear to protect the land they have acquired in violation of local customary norms. Third, social turmoil in the countryside can give rise to serious labour market imperfections that may entail considerable efficiency costs at the level of the entire economy.

[192] North (1981) first develops a neoclassical theory of the state. For other economic theories of the state, see Olson (1993, 2000) and McGuire and Olson (1996), and Barzel (2002).

indeed conform to such stereotypes and effectively fulfil their responsibilities. Unfortunately, worldwide, properly functioning governments that protect property rights and supply public goods are the exception, not the rule (Leeson, 2007; Leeson, Williamson, 2009). For example, according to the 2010 Failed States Index,[193] which is compiled by Foreign Policy magazine and the Fund of Peace, nearly 21% of the world's countries (37 countries) are "failing states". In these countries, governments are typically ultra-predatory, dysfunctional, and near collapse. Another 51% of the world's countries (91 countries) are states that are in imminent danger of failing. If these measures are correct, in over half the world, states are either critically or dangerously dysfunctional.

Weak and failed states[194] cannot be expected to perform the functions that they are supposed to perform, such as defining and protecting property rights, because their governments lack either the capacities or the incentives required for effective governance (Acemoglu, 2005). Weak countries therefore fail to create and maintain a variety of institutions that are directly or indirectly responsible for the functioning of a formal property rights regime, such as a reliable and inexpensive land titling system, a competent and uncorrupt judiciary, and a functional police force (Trebilcock, Veel, 2008). In some extreme cases, the effects of weak states are so detrimental that they are said to "kill growth" (Easterly, 2002: Chapter 11) and are better replaced by a state of anarchy[195] (Leeson, 2007; Leeson, Williamson, 2009).

More generally, weak states are susceptible to capture by powerful elites and therefore easily become a vehicle for rent-seeking. As the models of Glaeser et al. (2003), Polishchuk and Savvateev (2004), and Sonin (2003) have shown, in an institutional environment in which the state is likely to be captured, influential

---

[193] The index's ranks are based on twelve indicators of state vulnerability: four social, two economic and six political. Social indicators include demographic pressures, massive movements of refugees and internally displaced persons, a legacy of vengeance-seeking group grievance, and chronic and sustained human flight. Economic indicators consist of uneven economic development along group lines and sharp and/or severe economic decline. The political indicators group consists of criminalisation and/or delegitimisation of the state, progressive deterioration of public services, widespread violation of human rights, security apparatus as "state within a state", rise of factionalised elites, and intervention of other states or external factors. For more details, see http://ffp.statesindex.org/rankings-2010-sortable.

[194] Eizenstat et al. (2005) make a distinction between weak and failed states. The weakness of states can be measured along three functions performed by the governments of strong states: security, the provision of basic services, and the protection of essential civil freedoms. Failed states do not provide any of these functions whereas weak states are deficient in one or two of these functions.

[195] Leeson (2007) compares the state of 18 key development indicators in Somalia before and after its government collapse and finds that by nearly all indicators Somalia is doing significantly better under anarchy than it was under government. See also Powell et al. (2008), who rank Somali welfare on 13 development indicators before and after anarchy relative to 41 other sub-Saharan Africa (SSA) countries and find that on five of the indicators, Somalia is in the top half of SSA countries. In addition, Moselle and Polak (2001) provide a theoretical model demonstrating that if a state is highly predatory and its behaviour goes unchecked, the government may not only fail to add to social welfare but may actually reduce welfare below its level under anarchy.

elites and/or rich agents can subvert the political, regulatory, and legal institutions of society for their own benefit. When this type of subversion occurs, such elites and/or rich agents have no interest in, and even object to, strong protection of property rights provided by the state in a non-discriminatory manner. On the one hand, they can protect their own property by appealing to their de facto political power or other available strategies that can be used to shelter them from expropriation.[196] On the other hand, they will benefit from weak protection of property rights, which allows them to engage in profitable but unproductive activities such as rent-seeking and other redistributive actions.[197]

The evidence from transition economies demonstrates that public officials in high-capture economies appear to have created a private market for the provision of ordinarily public goods, such as the security of property rights, and for rent-seeking opportunities that a relatively small number of firms can obtain through capture. State capture generates individualised gains to captor firms while creating substantial costs for the rest of the economy in terms of deteriorating sales and investment growth (Hellman et al., 2003). In Russia, the public property rights enforcement mechanism has been replaced by private (mafia-type) enforcement to the extent that the state and the government are claimed to have effectively been "privatized" (Braguinsky, 1999). Consequently, markets are subject to extremely high transaction costs because the number of participants in each segment of the divided market (caused by private enforcement) is strictly limited and the flows of goods, capital, labour and information are severely disrupted; the intrinsic uncertainty inherent in these private enforcement systems orients the economy toward extremely short-term profit maximisation. Thus, many small businesses and much of the population are driven to the shadow economy when they believe that they are being unfairly taxed and exploited by small but well-organised pressure groups.[198]

In the developing world, particularly in the post-colonial states of Africa, rulers rely on alliances with local strongmen, whom they allow to exploit local economic opportunities and to create a so-called "neo-patrimonial" system of governance. In some extreme cases, as with Mobutu Sese Seko of Zaire, a neo-patrimonial regime

---

[196] For example, during the political instability resulting from the Mexican Revolution, the Mexican oil industry effectively defended its property rights by making use of two powerful weapons (Haber et al., 2003). First, the oil companies could make effective appeals to the US government to intervene on their behalf. Second, they were able to coordinate their actions, which meant that they could threaten the Mexican government with production boycotts.

[197] In the words of Gradstein (2007), "When the political machinery is controlled by small wealthy elite, it will not be interested in state protection against appropriate rent seeking despite its growth enhancing potential because rent seeking benefits the rich relative more".

[198] In three Russian cities, Frye and Zhuravskaya (2000) find that shopkeepers who faced particularly extensive (predatory) regulations were more likely to have had contact with private protection rackets than shopkeepers who faced a lighter regulatory burden. The Sicilian mafia is also understood as a substitute for public enforcement of property rights at a time when state provided security was scarce and banditry widespread (Bandiera, 2003).

results in the theft of a large part of the society's resources by a single individual, whereas in others, it merely amounts to rent seeking, i.e., the use of the public sector to reallocate property rights for the benefit of a particular interest (Fukuyama, 2004: 16). For example, in Northwest Cameroon, land conflicts have increased because local elites seek to acquire large tracts of land under individual title, a process facilitated by the 1974 land ordinance and by the links between local elites and national politics. In Kenya, a critical contributing factor to the growing social inequality in access to land is the capacity of the patron-client chains that link the national elite to the local level to gain control over resources that offer opportunities for accumulation. In Nigeria, political and civil elites benefit disproportionately from the 1978 Land Use Decree by manipulating the allocation authorities. Finally, in Somalia, the tragic civil strife is rooted in an earlier process of land occupation and expropriation by the state and its governing elites; in particular, the Land Law of 1975 enabled those with privileged access to the mechanisms of registration to obtain title to land that local farmers had used for generations (Peters, 2004).

In summary, good governance, such as a consistent legal and institutional framework, broad access to information, and competent and impartial agencies, is a necessary precondition for the functioning of formal property rights. However, many developing countries are characterised by serious deficiencies in governance, and the state's monopoly on the exercise of power may therefore be abused to appropriate property or to assist in the unfair acquisition of land by elites (Deininger, Feder, 2009). The property law enacted and enforced by the state will then become a so-called "empty institution" (Ho, 2005: 13) rather than a credible institution[199] that property owners can appeal to in case of invasion, regardless of whether the invader is a government official or an ordinary citizen.

4.5. CONCLUSION

For a substantial amount of time in economics and jurisprudence, property rights in general and property law in particular have been regarded as the

---

[199] Diermeier et al. (1997) argues that, "unless property rights are credible, reform is unlikely to be effective in promoting economic growth and political stability", and "the credibility of formal rules established by the government plays an important role in shaping economic activity and promoting economic growth". Central to the credibility of the institution is the time-inconsistent exchange between state and private agents. More precisely, laws and policies frequently promise benefits in the future for changes in behaviour today. For example, to encourage investment, a government may pass a law promising tax benefits for certain years to firms that make certain investments. After a firm invests, however, it is vulnerable to ex post violations of its property rights by state agents. If courts do not constrain such state agents, the latter may impose confiscatory taxes regardless of legal rules to the contrary. Anticipating this possibility, rights holders view their property as vulnerable and remain reluctant to invest in the first place. See also Root (1989), North and Weingast (1989), and North (1993) on the credibility of institutions.

fundamental preconditions for sustainable economic growth and have been used to explain the differences in economic performance across countries. Property rights, or more precisely, those formal and individualised property rights, are expected to encourage efficient resource management, to stimulate investments in production and innovation, and thus to push the economy to a faster growth trajectory. The alleged desirability of formal private ownership has been embraced by a large number of economists and lawyers, who present much supportive evidence from historical and comparative perspectives (typically on the macro-level), which eventually becomes theoretical foundation for policy recommendations for developing countries (World Bank, 2002).

When we examine those studies conducted on the micro-level, particularly those from African countries, however, the picture is more mixed. Whereas some of the studies report positive and significant effects of formal private ownership on investment and other measures of economic performance, others fail to find a strong link between individualised property rights and economic outcomes. In general, three factors can be identified to account for the failure or insignificance of formal property rights in most developing countries. First, the malfunctioning or even nonexistence of other factor markets, particularly financial markets, tends to invalidate the effects of formal private ownership. Second, the merits of formal property rights may frequently be outweighed by their costs, which includes both the direct costs of defining, measuring, and enforcing property rights through the use of state power, and opportunity costs in terms of the forgone benefits supplied by customary (common) property regimes, such as scale economies, risk reduction, etc. Finally, when the state is captured by elites and degenerates into a rent-seeking machine, or when the state itself acts as a tyrannical leviathan whose interests consist of exploitation, plunder, and confiscation primarily, property law will only be regarded as a scrap of paper by property owners who will then be driven to the underworld economy to rely completely on private enforcement.

The main point here is not a simple conclusion, such as that property rights do or do not matter, but an exhortation to focus more on the complexity inherent in the functioning of property rights, such as their dependence on the extent and depth of the market, their dynamic rather than static characteristics, and their complicated interactions with economies, polities, and societies. It is therefore too optimistic, or even naïve, to embrace property privatisation and formalisation as a panacea for economic backwardness, given the context-contingent and environment-dependent nature of property rights that is hard to generalise into an optimal model of a property regime.

As Rodrik (2007) indicates, as a first-order economic principle, property rights should be protected to induce individuals to act productively and cooperatively. However, such a principle does not map onto any unique institutional framework; on the contrary, there may be multiple ways of overlaying such principle onto institutional arrangements. Therefore, "There is no unique correspondence between the *functions* that good institutions perform and the *form* that such institutions take" (Rodrik, 2007: 15; italics in original). In other words, one size cannot fit all. At least for some countries, economic growth can be achieved despite apparently weak *de jure* property rights, provided that some substitute strategies can be found to assure investors and entrepreneurs that their fruits will not be appropriated in the future, such as the Mexican oil industry's reliance on the US government's intervention (Haber et al., 2003), or some unorthodox institutional practices that have been adopted in China's transition.[200] Conversely, as our study has shown, well-designed property law may be shown to be *de facto* dysfunctional or impractical when it is not supported by effective enforcement mechanisms or not compatible with local norms and traditions.

It is thus not surprising to find that property law seems inessential in some scenarios, at least in the short term. In the long run, however, it is more plausible to argue that an impartial and effective property law is irreplaceable and indispensable, in light of the reality that "igniting economic growth and sustaining it are somewhat different enterprises" (Rodrik, 2005). More specifically, the former generally requires a limited range of (often unconventional) reforms that need not overly tax the institutional capacity of the economy. The latter challenge is in many ways more difficult because it requires constructing a sound institutional foundation to maintain productive dynamism and endow the economy with resilience to shocks over the longer term. Therefore, less developed countries do not need an extensive set of institutional reforms to begin growing because "when a country is so far below its potential steady-state level of income, even moderate movements in the right direction can produce a big growth payoff" (Rodrik, 2007: 39). By contrast, sustaining growth is more difficult, and an economy may finally find itself having outgrown its institutional underpinnings without extensive institutional reform. As a part of these growth-sustaining institutions, property law will justify itself if the observation period is long enough, as we have seen from the historical evidence.

---

[200] For example, the township and village enterprises (TVEs) were the growth engine of China until the mid-1990s, with their share in industrial value added rising to more than 50% by the early 1990s. However, TVEs had a special ownership structure: property rights were vested not in private hands or in the central government, but in local communities (townships or villages). According to Qian (2003), in the environment characteristic of China, property rights were effectively more secure under direct local government ownership than they would have been under a private property regime. The efficiency loss caused by the absence of private control rights was probably outweighed by the implicit security guaranteed by local government control (Rodrik, 2007: 24). In addition, fiscal decentralisation combined with mobile capital has created intense regional competition for private capital (such as foreign direct investment) in China and has led local governments to provide strong de facto protection for business investment, which can be used as a substitute for the weak formal property rights and legal systems that otherwise prevail in China (Zhang, 2007).

CHAPTER 5

DOES LAW MATTER FOR CHINA'S ECONOMIC GROWTH?[*]

5.1. INTRODUCTION

On the basis of studies of the relationship between law and economic prosperity, it is natural to argue that an efficient legal system precedes and underlies sustainable economic growth and that less developed countries cannot achieve the same level of economic success as industrialised economies without certain fundamental legal changes. This "law matters" hypothesis has been embraced by many economists and lawyers and has become the theoretical foundation for policy recommendations proposed to developing countries (World Bank, 2002).

However, certain apparent anomalies exist to the "law matters" hypothesis, of which China is the most notable. Despite its weak legal framework, China has undergone remarkable economic growth over the past three decades and has surpassed Japan as the world's second-largest economy. According to Allen et al. (2005: 57), "China is an important counterexample to the findings in the law, institutions, finance, and growth literature: Neither its legal nor financial system is well developed, yet it has one of the fastest growing economies". Ohnesorge (2003)[201] similarly argues that China's economic miracle has been accomplished "with a minimal legal system, and one placing few if any checks on political authority".

On the basis of the foregoing, scholars argue that China's economic growth has been primarily supported by nonlegal substitutes, such as governance mechanisms based on reputation and relationships (Allen et al., 2005). However, certain studies question whether formal law in China is entirely irrelevant. For example, Milhaupt and Pistor (2008) show that formal laws such as corporate and bankruptcy laws are an important tool that the Chinese central government uses to manage the state-owned sector. Peerenboom (2002) also indicates that

---

[*]   A paper based on this chapter will be published in the first volume of *Asian Journal of Law and Society* under the title "Is China an Anomaly for the 'Law Matters' Hypothesis?".

[201] According to Ohnesorge (2003), the key precondition to China's economic success is the substance of political commitment to capitalist development. See also Gehlbach and Keefer (2011), who argue that an institutionalised ruling party, such as the Chinese Communist Party (CCP), allows an autocratic ruler to make credible commitments to investors (members of such party) and, hence, to promote "investment without democracy".

China's legal system contributed to increased foreign direct investment during the second decade of reforms.

This chapter adopts a unique perspective in contributing to the argument on the role of law in China's economic development. We focus on the law's contribution to China's unbalanced macroeconomic structure, which facilitated China's extraordinary economic growth in the short run at the cost of environmental quality, ordinary citizen welfare, and long-term economic health. The primary conclusion of this chapter is that law does matter for China's economic development, though in a more complicated way. China's legal system is dysfunctional, property rights are weak, and the operation of the market economy is distorted. However, in contradiction to the prediction derived from the "law matters" hypothesis, China has achieved remarkable economic success. The secret lies in the fact that in such a legal environment, factor prices are lowered, investment and production are subsidised, and growth is therefore be accelerated.

The remainder of this chapter is organised as follows. In section two, we challenge the "law matters" hypothesis by referring to the growth experience of East Asian economies. In section three, we describe the apparent paradox of the coexistence of a weak legal system and a fast-growing economy in China. In section four, we attempt to solve this paradox by exploring the relationship between China's legal system and its imbalanced growth model. In section five, we present some general conclusions and discuss the policy implications of our findings.

5.2. THE "LAW MATTERS" HYPOTHESIS FACING EAST ASIAN EXPERIENCE

The most influential version of the "law matters" hypothesis is certainly the "legal origin" theory that we have discussed extensively in previous chapters. The major conclusion of LLSV is that legal origins are central to understanding the divergence in living standards across the regions and countries of the world. Furthermore, compared with civil law countries, particularly countries with a French civil law tradition, common law countries have enjoyed superior economic outcomes. One important channel through which legal origin influences economic performance is politics (Beck et al., 2003). More specifically, legal traditions differ in their emphasis on the rights of private property owners versus the power of the state. Civil law tends to emphasise the power of the state rather than the rights of private property owners to a greater degree than common law. A powerful state will tend to create policies and institutions that divert the flow of society's resources toward favoured ends, which is harmful to the operation of a free market economy.

One serious problem with LLSV's theory is that it oversimplifies the complicated relationship between the law and the market. According to LLSV, the legal world is clear and simple. There are either "good" legal rules, such as those that have been enacted in common law countries, that are believed to help to reduce transaction costs, encourage productive activities, and hence foster economic growth, or "bad" legal rules, such as those that can be found in (French) civil law countries, that are argued to be inefficient, unproductive, and hence detrimental to economic prosperity. The major difference between "good" and "bad" law lies in the intention of the law with respect to the market and the state: "good" law "seeks to support private market outcomes", whereas "bad" law "seeks to replace such outcomes with state-desired allocation" (La Porta et al., 2008: 286).

However, the actual effects of laws on real-world economies fall outside the scope covered by LLSV's dichotomy. As the growth experience of East Asian countries has shown, in certain developmental stages, a fast-growth economy and a weak or "bad" legal system can coexist. In countries in which such coexistence can be observed, laws and regulations were designed as manipulative tools through which economic activities and market transactions could be controlled and directed by the government; in addition, legal rules were enforced discriminatorily or selectively to favour particular interest groups, industries, or enterprises (Pistor and Wellons, 1999). The case of East Asian countries is therefore in conflict with LLSV's theory.

Despite their weak and flawed legal systems, many East Asian countries experienced extraordinary growth between 1965 and 1990 (World Bank, 1993). During this period, eight East Asian economies (Japan, Hong Kong, the Republic of Korea, Singapore, Taiwan, Indonesia, Malaysia, and Thailand) grew more than twice as fast as the remainder of the East Asian economies, roughly three times as fast as Latin American and South Asian economies, and five times as fast as sub-Saharan African economies. These East Asian economies also significantly outperformed industrial economies and the oil-rich economies in the Middle East/North Africa region.

In contrast to the prediction of "legal origin" theory, weak or "bad" legal systems in East Asian economies helped rather than hindered economic growth because such legal systems could be manipulated more easily by the government to intervene in the nation's economy. With the help of these legal systems, East Asian states were able to implement a unique development strategy: distorting relative prices so that (compared with a laissez-faire environment) more economic resources can be directed to capital accumulation, which, in turn, allows for faster economic growth. In Amsden's (1989: 14) words, in East Asian economies, "economic expansion depends on state intervention to create price distortions that direct economic activity toward greater investment", and in that sense, the state "has set relative prices deliberately 'wrong'". A similar conclusion is reached by Wade (1990: 29), who argues that "[g]overnment policies deliberately got some prices 'wrong', so as to change the signals to which decentralized agents responded, and also used nonprice means to alter the behaviour of market agents. The resulting high level of investment generated fast turnover of machinery and hence fast transfer of newer technology into actual production".

For example, in Taiwan, the government manipulated relative prices to enhance industrialists' profits and thereby to encourage more investment (Wade, 1990). In the 1950s and 1960s, it fixed low agricultural prices, allowing industrial wages to be lower and industrial profits and investment to be higher. The Taiwanese government also ensured that labour costs were not driven by union power, and it used fiscal investment incentives and concessional credit to lower costs of production and thus drove investment, first in heavy and chemical industries and more recently in electronics and machinery. Lastly, it lowered the costs of export production by establishing subsidies, duty drawbacks, and similar measures.

While successful in accelerating economic growth, these unorthodox institutional arrangements finally led East Asian countries to a trajectory of so-called state-guided capitalism, which, according to Baumol et al. (2007), suffers from problems due to failures on the part of the government, such as making excessive investment, selecting the wrong winners and losers, and becoming susceptibility to corruption. More important, the East Asian growth model has been proved to be unsustainable given its input-driven rather than productivity-driven economic growth. Kim and Lau (1994: 264) find that "[b]y far the most important source of economic growth of the East Asian newly industrialized countries (Hong Kong, Singapore, South Korea, and Taiwan) is capital accumulation, accounting for between 48 and 72% of their economic growth, in contrast to the case of the Group-of-Five industrialized countries (France, West Germany, Japan, the United Kingdom, and the United States), in which technical progress has played the most important role, accounting for between 46 and 71% of economic growth". A similar conclusion is reached by Kim and Lau (1995, 1996) and Young (1994, 1995).

The inescapable problem encountered with the input-driven growth model is that diminishing returns are associated with the addition of any one factor of production. With a given labour force, the addition of increasingly more machines will produce more output – but at a steadily declining rate. Therefore, more investment can raise the level of total output of an industry but not its long-term growth rate. As the famous Solow model has shown, regardless of the level of capital with which an economy begins, without technological progress, the economy will end up at a steady state in which no per capita growth occurs (Solow, 1956). To avoid diminishing returns, an economy must transform its growth style from investment-based growth to technology-based growth, from "growth by brute force" to "smart growth" (Baumol et al., 2007).

Historical evidence shows that in the process of pursing sustainable economic growth, winners (such as many economies in Western Europe and North America) and losers (such as the former Soviet Union) distinguish themselves by their ability to change their economies from investment-based economies to technology-based economies (Hayami and Godo, 2005). East Asian countries do not seem to provide a counterexample to the regularity of economic evolution. The East Asian financial crisis of 1997–98, which brought economic growth in many countries to an abrupt halt, can be cited as the strongest evidence for the unsustainable nature of the East Asian "miracle" (Crafts, 1999; Haggard, 1999).

The most important attribute that can be used to differentiate the "growth by brute force" and the "smart growth" models is the role of entrepreneurs versus bureaucrats in resource allocation. Compared with "growth by brute force", "smart growth" is driven by a process of incessant innovation, which, in turn, results from the risk-taking behaviour of entrepreneurs who attempt to increase profits by introducing new goods and new production methods in response to changes in both demand and production (Schumpeter, 1961; Baumol, 2002).

Obviously, entrepreneurship and innovation cannot be directly planned, ordered, or controlled by a government. By contrast, they can only be induced and motivated by appropriate institutional arrangements that set the basic reward structure of the economy so that wealth is created rather than redistributed. Such institutional arrangements can be classified into four categories: institutional arrangements that encourage the formation of innovative entrepreneurial enterprises, such as low-cost procedures for business registration, effective bankruptcy regimes, and easy access to finance; institutional arrangements that secure the rewards for productive entrepreneurial activity, such as reliable property rights protection, modest taxation levels, and proper regulation; institutional arrangements that discourage unproductive and rent-seeking activity; and institutional arrangements that use measures that keep successful entrepreneurs on their toes, such as antitrust laws (Baumol et al., 2007).

The key to converting a country's growth pattern to a sustainable one is therefore redesigning the institutional framework under which the economy operates to transfer the decision-making power from bureaucrats to entrepreneurs. This transition should be accompanied by a process of systematic and extensive market liberalisation so that entrepreneurs can be directed and motivated by a free market to meet actual social preferences with the most suitable production methods. Market-augmenting laws and regulations, such as those suggested by LLSV, will thus become a requisite for economic success during periods of innovation-directed growth.

On the basis of the growth experience of East Asian countries, a deeper understanding of the relationship between law and economic development can be reached. A less-developed economy may initially adopt a capital-driven economic growth model to ignite economic growth as quickly as possible. Under this approach, economic growth is easily initiated, controlled, and directed by the government, whose main task is to use a combination of policies and institutions (such as those used in East Asian countries) to maximise capital accumulation to push forward the economy. Law and regulations will be either weakened or ignored if they are in conflict with the development strategy of the government or enacted and enforced with the intention of augmenting the power of economic policies by, in Amsden (1989) and Wade (1990)'s words, "getting the prices wrong". The unusual combination of a fast-growth economy and a weak legal system then emerges.

Such a growth pattern will finally face a watershed, however. Without some fundamental institutional reforms from which a productivity-driven growth model can be expected to arise, the economy will be trapped in the status quo, or, in Solow's term, a steady state. Laws and regulations that sustain the functioning of a competitive market system from which entrepreneurship, innovation, and efficiency can stem will play a crucial role in shifting a country's growth trajectory to a sustainable one, such as that of Western European and North American economies. The connection between law and economic growth will therefore be more in line with the prediction of LLSV in the long run. In summary, law plays different roles in different growth trajectories (investment driven versus technology driven), and the relationship between law and economic growth is therefore context-(growth model or stage) dependent, dynamic, and more complicated than the relationship that can be inferred from LLSV's theory.

5.3. CHINA'S LEGAL SYSTEM AND ITS ROLE IN ECONOMIC DEVELOPMENT

Over the last 30 years, China has experienced a great transformation from a planned economy to a market economy, beginning with the restoration of household agriculture. The most remarkable consequence of this transformation is the massive expansion of China's economy, which is now the second largest in the world (the United States' economy is the first), with a nominal GDP of $8.227 trillion in 2012.[202] Another important outcome of this process is the general increase in the standard of living, which has lifted hundreds of millions of Chinese out of absolute poverty and helped China become a middle-income country. This transformation allowed China to become a global economic superpower and, with the current slowdown of other principal economies (particularly that of the United States), the chief driver of world growth.

---

[202] http://data.worldbank.org/indicator/NY.GDP.MKTP.CD.

Since 1978, China's legal system has also experienced a great transformation. Numerous legislations have been passed by the National People's Congress (NPC) to lay the foundation for China's economic reform and social change.[203] Today, virtually all the areas in which law is important, such as property, contracts, and business organisations, are covered by national legislation as well as low-level regulations. Law has therefore come to play an increasingly important role in regulating economic activities, resolving civil disputes, and shaping state behaviour. In addition, as part of China's efforts to merge into the international community, many legislative efforts, particularly those in business law and intellectual property law, have sought to bring China into line with international practice.

Courts have undertaken significant reforms that were designed to strengthen both the competence of judges and the professionalism of the court system (Liebman, 2007). One of the most important accomplishments of such court reforms is the dramatic increase in judges' education levels. Prior to the 1995 Judges Law, the only requirement to be a judge was to be a cadre. Since 2002, however, all new judges in China have been required to possess bachelor's degrees and to pass the national unified judicial exam, which had a pass rate of approximately 10% before 2007. In 2005, for the first time, more than 50% of Chinese judges had university degrees, which marks a sharp increase from 6.9% in 1995. Other measures, particularly those addressing technical or administrative problems rather than changing the court's power relative to other state actors (such as reforming the appointment system,[204] improving the quality of court decisions,[205] and fighting corruption), have also been adopted by the Supreme People's Court (SPC, which is responsible for the administration of the judiciary) in recent years.

As a result of China's legal reform, the number of commercial, civil, and administrative lawsuits has dramatically increased since the early 1980s, which may be considered evidence that courts are performing a more important role in resolving various conflicts in Chinese society. For example, Clarke et al. (2008) report that between 1983 and 2001, economic disputes accepted by courts of first

---

[203] For example, Pei (2001) reports that in the two decades since 1978, the NPC passed 165 major laws, amended 32 laws, and issued 88 resolutions. For a timeline of China's legislative developments, see Clarke (2007) and Clarke et al. (2008).

[204] Peerenboom (2002: 290–293) shows that Chinese authorities have passed a series of regulations and have taken a number of steps to reform the appointment system and to improve the quality of the judiciary, such as making the promotion system more merit based and imposing sanctions if judges fail to perform their duties adequately.

[205] Peerenboom (2002: 293) argues that the move away from an inquisitorial to an adversarial system placed pressure on judges to improve their performance. In addition, judges are now required to write more extensive judgments that set forth their reasoning and legal analysis rather than to just recite the facts of the case and state the conclusion. For example, in 2005, the SPC issued a notice stating that opinions should include accurate descriptions of the facts and evidence as well as logical arguments and legal reasoning.

instance increased at an average annual rate of 18.8%, that civil disputes increased at 8.3% per year on average over the same period, and that administrative cases increased at an average annual rate of 21.8% for the period 1987–2001.[206] In addition, from 1983 to 1998, the total value of disputes increased by 40.9% per year on average, whereas the average value of disputes increased by 11.9% per year on average.

Although far from ideal, courts in China do enforce court judgments and arbitral awards, as demonstrated by some empirical studies. Peerenboom (2002: 463–464) reports that applicants who turned to the courts for compulsory enforcement of arbitral awards were able to recover at least half of the award in 40% of the cases. Moreover, in many cases, nonenforcement is for legitimate reasons set forth in international treaties and Chinese law or due to the respondent's lack of assets. Put differently, the rate of nonenforcement for suspect or illegitimate reasons, such as local protectionism, judicial incompetence, and corruption, was between 17% and 29%. He (2009) finds that the enforcement outcomes in the Pearl River Delta of China are reasonable: in 50 cases, or 76% of the selected 66 cases, the plaintiffs recovered fully or partially; overall, 61% of the plaintiffs recovered more than 50% of the awarded sums. In addition, He (2009) shows that the enforcement process is relatively efficient, that the problem of local protectionism is not serious, and that the plaintiffs' impressions of the courts are quite positive.

Despite the considerable improvements that have been made during the last three decades, China's legal system is still under severe criticism for several reasons. First, there is widely dispersed legislative authority or, in Lubman's (2006: 33) words, "disorderly allocation of jurisdiction and power among law-making agencies". According to China's Constitution and the Law on Legislation, the NPC and its standing committee, which stand at the apex of China's legal system, have the power to pass statutes that are more authoritative than any kind of rule other than the Constitution. The State Council, which is at the head of the executive branch of the government, has the authority to enact "administrative regulations". In addition, People's Congresses, which exist at the provincial level and in certain large cities, may enact "local regulations" that govern local issues. All the preceding enactments have the formal status of law within the Chinese legal system and are, at least in theory, enforceable by the courts. Finally, ministries of the State Council and local governments may issue "rules", and although these rules are not generally enforceable by courts, they can

---

[206]   However, Liebman (2007) shows that caseloads have increased only modestly since 1999. In fact, the total number of first instance cases decreased by 2% between 1996 and 2006. He therefore concludes that courts are not necessarily playing a greater role relative to other institutions engaged in dispute resolution, such as the letters and visits system (also known as *xinfang* system, is the administrative system for hearing complaints and grievances from individuals in China).

substantially alter the rights of individuals and can be used by one party in private litigation against another (Clarke et al., 2008).

In addition to the dispersion of legislative authority, another factor that contributes to the problem with China's legal system is that there is no effective system to clearly define the lawmaking power of different organs of the state and to authoritatively resolve conflicts between different rules. The multiple sources of law therefore inevitably lead to disorder, inconsistency, and confusion in China's legal system. The most notable example of such disorder is that regulations promulgated by lower levels of government, in practice, often seem to trump theoretically superior regulations promulgated by higher levels of government. For example, long-term land leasing was first permitted under local rules in Shenzhen at a time when it was prohibited by national legislation and by the Constitution (Clarke et al., 2008). Similarly, Corne (1996) reports that in the mid-1980s in Hebei, Beijing, and Tianjin, approximately two thirds of local regulations were inconsistent with the Constitution, and Lubman (2006) shows that provincially approved tax incentives for foreign investors have sometimes varied widely from national legislation. The authority of the law is therefore diminished, and property rights cannot be considered to be secured by such a weak legal underpinning.

Another important weakness of China's legislation is that most legal rules remain poorly drafted and are characterised by excessive generality and vagueness. It has been argued that laws and regulations in China are intentionally drafted in broad terms to allow for sufficient flexibility in implementation to meet diversified local conditions in a quickly changing environment (Lubman, 2000). For this reason, certain drafting techniques, such as the use of general principles, undefined terms, broadly worded discretion, omissions, and general catch-all phrases, are often used to create wide scope for administrative discretion in interpreting the law.

The case of land ownership in rural China can be presented as an example that illustrates the vague nature of China's legislation. According to China's Land Administration Law, the land in rural areas is owned by farmers' collectives. However, the law does not provide a clear definition of the term "farmers' collectives". While various levels of rural organisation, including collective economic organisations of the townships (town), village collective economic organisations (or villagers' committees), and villagers' groups, are entitled by law to manage and administer rural land, whether they can legally represent and exercise land ownership or reap the profits from ownership is unclear.[207] Such "intentional institutional ambiguity", in Ho's (2005: 3) terms, is created to avoid potential large-scale social conflict resulting from the collapse of

---

[207]   The situation has been improved since the enactment of the Property Law, which came into effect on October 1, 2007. According to Article 60 of the Property Law, these rural organisations "shall, on behalf of the collective, exercise the ownership".

the commune system. The resulting legal indeterminacy, however, often leads to widespread confusion. For example, in a survey of 250 rural households in Anhui and Shandong provinces, the farmers who were interviewed reported certain misconceptions regarding land ownership: in Anhui and Shandong provinces, 68.85% and 44.44% of the respondents, respectively, considered rural land to be owned by the state, while 21.31% and 40.74%, respectively, considered rural land to be owned by individual farmers (World Bank, 2012a).

The excessive generality and vagueness of laws in China gives local authorities great discretion in interpreting and implementing laws, often leading to the application of greatly divergent patterns rather than of universal rules and thus undermining the predictability and certainty of the law. As described by Peerenboom (2002: 251), the outcome is that "[a]t minimum, it typically increases transaction costs by making it more difficult, time-consuming, and expensive to figure out just what the rules are at any time in a given place. At worst, it breeds corruption and a reliance on connections that erodes the normative force of law". Such a situation can hardly be argued to create a market-friendly legal environment.

While courts are a key institution for translating the law into social reality, they remain weak and lack independence from political interference. The most powerful influence comes from the Chinese Communist Party (CCP, hereinafter the Party), which possesses the ultimate power in China's society. In practice, the Party influences the courts in various ways and through various channels (Peerenboom, 2002). The Party primarily exerts influence in ideology, policy, and personnel matters, although it is sometimes directly involved in deciding the outcome of particular cases, such as cases that are politically sensitive, cases that could have a significant impact on the local economy, and cases that involve conflicts between the courts and the procuracy or government.

Interference from administrative bodies and officials is another serious threat to the independence of the courts.[208] Such interference takes various forms, such as harassing witnesses, approaching judges to "inquire" about a case and to "exchange" views about the case to ensure favourable treatment, and pressuring plaintiffs to have a case withdrawn from the courts (Hung, 2004). As a consequence, courts accept a relatively small number of administrative cases. From 1990 to 2002, courts across the country accepted approximately 60 million first instance criminal, administrative, civil, and commercial cases; administrative cases, however, accounted for only slightly more than 1% of this

---

[208]   Gechlik (2005) argues that like interference from the Party and administrative agencies, intracourt and intercourt influence within the Chinese court system is another major cause of judges' lack of independence. For instance, the practice of *qingshi* (instructions) – that is, junior judges or judges at lower courts frequently reporting to and seeking advice from senior judges or those in upper courts – is widespread. According to Hung (2004), the common practice of *qingshi* results from several problems: (1) an improved but still poorly qualified judiciary; (2) deficiencies in Chinese legislation; and (3) the existence of a system under which judges can be disciplined if their judgments are considered erroneous.

caseload, even though approximately 75% of Chinese laws are administrative laws and regulations (Hung, 2004). Pei (2006) further reports that winning cases against the government in courts has become increasing difficulty for plaintiffs, and this "pro-government bias" among courts generally discourages many citizens from taking their cases to the courts.

The independence of the courts is further undermined when the economic and political interests of the local governments are involved. Judges are selected and paid by local governments rather than by the central government, and this relationship pressures the courts to favour the localities in litigation that involve foreigners and parties from other parts of China (Clarke, 1996; Lubman, 1999). For example, courts may favour local litigants in commercial disputes with parties from other provinces, government agencies and local banks may shield the assets of local litigants from seizure by courts from other jurisdictions, and courts may refuse to enforce or assist in enforcing the civil judgments of courts in other jurisdictions, as required by law (Pei, 2001). The effectiveness of China's judiciary is seriously impaired by such local protectionism.

Political interference, a lack of independence, and local protectionism have been serious impediments to the effective enforcement of court judgments. In March 2004, Xiao Yang, the former president of the SPC, stated in his work report to the NPC that "[t]he difficulty of executing civil and commercial judgments has become a major 'chronic ailment', often leading to chaos in the enforcement process; there are few solutions to the problem" (China Law and Governance Review, 2004: 10). According to Ge Xingjun, the head of the SPC's Judgment Enforcement Division, only approximately 60% of civil and economic judgments can be enforced in basic-level courts, 50% can be enforced in intermediate-level courts, and 40% can be enforced in provincial high-level courts (China Law and Governance Review, 2004).

When faced with difficult or sensitive cases, courts may even close their doors. For example, the Guangxi High People's Court issued a notice in 2004 listing thirteen categories of cases that courts in Guangxi will not accept (Liebman, 2007). Such cases include real estate disputes arising from government decisions or institutional reforms, claims brought by workers who were laid off due to corporate restructuring, and lawsuits from a party's failure to implement a government decision on property ownership or usage rights. The weak judicial system exemplified by these events can hardly be relied on to protect property rights against private infringement or public intrusion. In Clarke et al.'s (2008: 400) words, "the courts in China do not play the role nor do they have the power that would be consonant with a legal regime that provided secure property rights".

At the heart of the problems that plague China's legal system is the tension that exists between the unchallenged power of the Party and the authority of law. Despite 30 years of economic, political, and social change, at its core, China is still a Leninist party-state in which the Party plays a leading role in politics and enjoys a monopoly of power through the exclusion of all other parties (McGregor, 2010). To the Party, law is merely an administrative tool that can be used to maintain and implement Party policies rather than a fundamental source of authority to which the Party should also be subject. Accordingly, judges are tailored as loyal servants of the party-state rather than as independent adjudicators to whom ordinary citizens can appeal. This instrumentalist approach to law finally leads to a situation in which "law in China is distinctly subordinate to the state bureaucracy" (Clarke, 2005: 64), and "if there is any conflict between party policies and law, judges are expected to handle a case in accordance with party policies" (Hung, 2004: 98). Thus, China's legal system can be compared with a bird constrained by the cage of the Party's dictation (Lubman, 1999, 2000).

Such a mixed picture of legal reform leads to different or even contradictory assessments of the relationship between legal reform and economic growth in China. On the one side, some scholars argue that formal legal rules matter for China's economic growth, at least when the attention is paid to the formal sector, when the observation is made in the long run, or when the analysis is undertaken with respect to necessary rather than sufficient conditions. For example, Yu and Zhang (2008) document and analyse the informal contracts developed in the city of Wenzhou, Zhejiang Province, and three formal contractual arrangements (Bills of Exchange, Documentary Credit, and Secured Lending) that have been increasingly used in China. They argue that as a general pattern, economic actors tend to rely on self-enforcing informal contractual arrangements first and to adopt more formal arrangements when such formal arrangements are feasible. The authors therefore conclude that "if viewed as a gradual process, formal law has indeed played an important role in Chinese economic development and will continue to do so". Peerenboom (2002: 463) also shows great sympathy for the hypothesis that "the high levels of foreign investment, coupled with the high growth rates, might be explained at least in part by improvements in the legal system". He argues that "property rights are more enforceable and rule-of-law issues less pressing than the oftentimes scathingly critical accounts of China's legal system would suggest" and that "there clearly has been considerable progress in providing investors with a framework with at least a somewhat higher degree of predictability".

On the other side, more scholars doubt the significance of formal law in explaining China's economic miracle,[209] and some of them claim that a reverse

---

[209] Some alternative mechanisms are argued to have sustained China's economic growth in an environment of weak rule of law. One such mechanism that has attracted much attention is informal contract enforcement institutions, such as negotiation, mediation, and self-enforcement through reputation and long-term relationships. Clarke et al. (2008) show that these measures are used extensively by Chinese businesses. Politics is another explanation. For example, Yao (2010a) claims that since the Party lacks legitimacy in the classic democratic sense, it has been forced to seek performance-based legitimacy instead by continuously

causal relationship is more likely to exist: economic development paves the way for legal reform rather than vice versa. For example, one scholar of Chinese law characterised the situation in 1999 as follows: "A striking feature of economic reform ... is the ambiguity of rights over the acquisition, management, and disposition of property. Chinese economic reforms have been successful to date despite the absence of any systematic attempt to clarify what economists call ... 'property rights'" (Lubman, 1999: 116–117). After reviewing the evidence concerning the role of law in China's economic development, Clarke et al. (2008: 420) reach a similar conclusion by stating, "[a]lthough the legal system has made great strides since the beginning of reforms and currently has a role of some significance in the economy, it is impossible to make the case that formal legal institutions have contributed in an important way to China's remarkable economic success. If anything, economic success has fostered the development of law, rather than the reverse".

China is not included in the sample of countries covered by LLSV's studies of law and stock market development. Allen et al. (2005) fill this research gap by giving China scores on shareholder and creditor rights on the basis of the methodology developed by LLSV. They find that the "overall evidence thus suggests that the majority of LLSV-sample countries have better creditor and shareholder protection than China" (Allen et al., 2005: 64). In addition, they show that "for two key categories of law enforcement, the rule of law and (government) corruption, China's measures are significantly below all average measures of LLSV-sample countries, regardless of their legal origins" (Allen et al., 2005: 67).[210]

World Bank's *Doing Business* reports also borrow their methodology from LLSV and attempt to measure the efficiency of the legal environments of different countries, to establish the rank of these countries according to certain variables, and to provide policy recommendations accordingly. According to *Doing Business* 2012, China's overall "Ease of Doing Business" rank was 91 out of 183 economies in 2012 (World Bank, 2012b). Some of China's indicators, such as "enforcing contracts" and "registering property", are strong. However, other indicators tell a different story. Regarding "protecting investors", a measure of

---

improving the living standards of Chinese citizens. Such performance-based legitimacy can be further transformed into a "credible commitment" to continuous economic development (Trebilcock, Leng, 2006). In addition, fiscal decentralisation combined with mobile capital has created intense regional competition for private capital (for example, foreign direct investment, FDI) in China, leading local governments to provide strong de facto protection for business investment, which can be used as a substitute for the weak formal property rights and legal systems that prevail in China (Zhang, 2007).

[210] They conclude that the secret of China's growth miracle lies in the fact that the nonstate sector, including both privately owned companies and hybrid structure firms (township and village enterprises, TVEs, for example), has flourished largely beyond the reach of formal laws promulgated by the central government and has become the dominant driver of China's economic growth. The quality of China's legal system is therefore irrelevant, at least when effective, alternative governance mechanisms can be relied on to support the growth of the nonstate sector.

the strength of minority shareholder protections against directors' misuse of corporate assets for personal gain, China ranks 97th out of the 183 economies. In terms of "starting a business", an indicator recording all procedures that are officially required for an entrepreneur to start and formally operate an industrial or commercial business, China ranks 151st. The worst score that China has received, 179th, is for "dealing with construction permits", an indicator that records all procedures that are required for a business in the construction industry to build a standardised warehouse.

The foregoing considerations support the idea that China represents an obvious anomaly to the "law matters" hypothesis suggested by LLSV. As we have shown, the power and effectiveness of China's legal system has been intentionally weakened by the design of its legislative and judicial processes; as a result, functions that are intended to be performed by a reliable legal system, such as securing property rights and enforcing contracts, can hardly be relied on by economic agents when they are needed. According to LLSV, the presence of a market-hostile legal system of this type will prevent an economy from achieving continuous economic growth; however, this prediction is obviously at odds with China's 30 years of double-digit economic growth and status as a dominant economic power in the world.

5.4. LAW AND CHINA'S UNBALANCED ECONOMY

In this section, we will show that, as in other East Asian economies, laws and regulations have been intentionally used by the Chinese government to distort prices, particularly the prices of factors of production related to land, capital, labour, environment, and energy, to subsidise production, to encourage capital accumulation, and to depress consumer spending. As a result, a structural imbalance has emerged that has helped China achieve excessive economic growth in the short run but that endangers its long-term economic sustainability. China's experience is therefore more in line with that of other East Asian economies but in contradiction to the prediction of "legal origin" theory.

In recent years, scholars and politicians have expressed concerns regarding the sustainability of China's growth.[211] Most of the concerns are based on the existence of a fundamental imbalance in China's economy, namely, the imbalance between investment and consumption. Theoretically, in all economies, output expansion is the sum of growth in consumption, investment, and the net

---

[211] For example, Yongding Yu, a respected Chinese economist, argues that "China has reached a crucial juncture: without painful structural adjustments, the momentum of its economic growth could suddenly be lost" (Yu, 2010). At his press conference after the annual meeting of China's legislature in March 2007, Primer Jiabao Wen also noted that China's economic growth is "unstable, unbalanced, uncoordinated, and unsustainable".

export of goods and services. A key feature of China's growth pattern is that increasing investment rather than increasing consumption, which is the most significant factor in GDP growth for other major economies, has been a major and increasingly important driver of growth (Prasad and Rajan, 2006; Lardy, 2007). Therefore, China can be described as an investment-driven economy.

Figure 5.1. Capital formation as percent of GDP

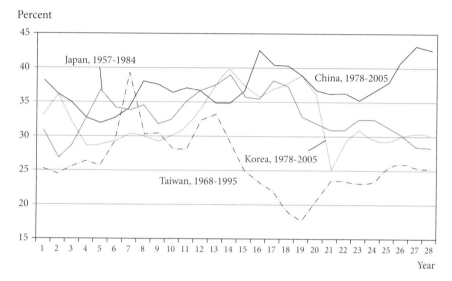

Source: Lardy (2007).

As Lardy (2007) shows (see figure 5.1), investment averaged approximately 36% of GDP over the first decade of economic reform in China. This average is relatively high by developing country standards but is not high compared with the percentage values achieved by China's East Asian neighbours when their investment shares were at their highest. However, since the beginning of the 1990s, the trend of China's investment rate has been increasing. In 1993, as well as in both 2004 and 2005, investment as a share of GDP was 43%, a level well above those of China's East Asian neighbours during their high-growth periods. In 2009, this ratio reached an unprecedented 47% owing to China's economic stimulus program, which was enacted in response to the global economic crisis that originated in the United States in 2008. In addition, while the longest period over which any other Asian country has maintained an investment-to-GDP ratio greater than 33% is nine years (Thailand from 1989 to 1997 and Singapore from 1991 to 1999), China is now in the fourteenth year of its investment boom (Pivot Capital Management, 2009).

While TFP (Total Factor Productivity) has significantly contributed to China's economic growth since the introduction of reforms at the end of the 1970s, its importance is thought to have declined over time. By contrast, the contribution of capital accumulation to GDP growth is increasingly high. For example, Kuijs and Wang (2006) show that growth in capital stock contributed to more than half of China's GDP growth from 1978 to 2004. However, TFP growth contributed one third of GDP growth, and employment growth contributed the modest remainder. In addition, by splitting the sample into two periods, Kuijs and Wang find that between 1993 and 2004, the contribution of capital accumulation to GDP growth was even higher, 62%.

Although the growth of consumption in China has been rapid in absolute terms throughout the reform period, it has lagged behind the underlying growth of the economy (Lardy, 2007). In the 1980s, household consumption in China averaged slightly more than half of GDP. This share fell to an average of 46% in the 1990s. However, after 2000, household consumption as a share of GDP fell sharply; by 2005, it was only 38% of GDP, the lowest share of any major economy in the world. In the United States in the same year, household consumption accounted for 70% of GDP, while in India, it was 61%. Even in Japan, which is famous for its high household savings, household consumption in 2005 was 57% of GDP.

The formation and continuation of the current economic growth pattern in China can be traced to the laws and regulations that are used by the government to distort factor prices. The laws regarding rural land provide a remarkable example that illustrates the distorting nature of Chinese law. As we have mentioned, the ownership of rural land in China has not been clearly defined by legal provisions, and in many cases, such ownership is unknown in practice. In addition, farmers are often deprived of their rights to benefit from urbanisation and industrialisation, which demands that a tremendous amount of land be converted from agricultural to nonagricultural uses. According to the Land Administration Law, unless collective land is to be converted to state-owned land through a land-taking process, such land cannot be sold, transferred, or leased for nonagricultural construction, such as industrial development. Thus, the only channel through which rural land can be allocated to industrial, commercial, or other nonagricultural use is land taking by the state; the state, in turn, acts as a monopoly land supplier rather than permits direct negotiation between farmers and land consumers. Farmers are therefore legally excluded from the process of marketisation for rural land. The only reward that farmers can expect from land loss is compensation for land taking rather than value appreciation from land-use conversion.

As another major player in this game, local governments are motivated by a growth-oriented incentive system[212] to make full use of the resources that are under their control to pursue economic growth. Economic growth can be

---

[212] Under the cadre evaluation system that is used by the Party, which sets criteria for the performance and, hence, the remuneration and promotion prospects of local party cadres and government officials, the most heavily weighted performance criteria emphasise promoting economic growth (Clarke et al., 2008). For example, Li and Zhou (2005) show that provincial leaders' likelihood of promotion increases with their economic performance

promoted by accommodating as many manufacturing enterprises as possible; however, because of a special attribute of manufacturing enterprises, namely, their location nonspecificity, manufacturing enterprises can move to other areas and set up production facilities with relative ease, resulting in fierce competition among local governments in attracting manufacturing investment (Cao et al., 2008; Tao et al., 2010; Huang, 2011). Taking of rural land has therefore become a powerful weapon of competing local governments, who try to engage in this practice as much as possible, to minimise the compensation that they pay to farmers, and to offer the taken land to manufacturing enterprises at a discounted cost or even zero cost to attract them.

Law plays a role as accomplice in this land-taking process. While according to the Constitution, the Property Law, and the Land Administration Law, land should be taken only in the public interest and those who have been adversely affected by land taking should receive just compensation, no details have been offered regarding what constitutes "public interest". Even worse, as we have shown, under the present legal regime, a farmer has no power to negotiate or privately transfer his or her land rights for nonagricultural use. If a commercial developer is interested in converting a parcel of agricultural land for nonagricultural use, he or she must ask the local government to exercise its power of eminent domain so that the designated use of the land can be legally changed. Thus, the legal scope of land acquisition is inevitably expanded to the extent that "the operation of the LML (Land Management Law) is in effect an authorization of state expropriation of rural land for all purposes, including pure commercial purposes" (Zhu et al., 2006: 780).

Much rural land in China is taken by local governments for purely private or commercial purposes. For instance, in the province of Zhejiang, land has been acquired for a variety of projects. Although land acquired for basic infrastructure, such as transportation, energy, and water projects, represents the highest percentage of all acquisitions (52%), commercial projects accounted for 22% of all acquisitions in 2000–2001 (Ding, 2007). Similarly, in a survey conducted in 2008 on 1,773 rural households in 1,657 villages of the seventeen major agricultural provinces, Prosterman et al. (2009) show that 40% of the seizures can hardly be categorised as in the public interest (12.9% was for developmental zones or industrial parks, 9.1% for factories, 6.4% for urban housing, 0.9% for gas stations, and 10.7% for other uses).

The legal provisions regarding compensation also diminish the legitimacy of China's land-taking framework. According to article 47 of the Land Administration Law, compensation for rural land under requisition consists of three components: (1) compensation for the land itself (six to ten times the annual average output value for the three years preceding the taking of the land); (2)

(measured by GDP growth), while their likelihood of termination decreases with their economic performance.

compensation for resettlement (four to six times the annual average output value for the three years preceding the taking of the land); and (3) compensation for attachments to or green crops on the land. This law also stipulates that the maximum compensation for land acquisition cannot exceed 30 times the annual average output value for the three years preceding the taking of the land and that the maximum compensation can only be awarded under special circumstances and with approval from provincial authorities. In summary, the compensation owed to farmers is calculated only according to lost income from the original agricultural use of the land for a limited time period rather than according to a standard reflecting the expectation of continued land use for the lifetime of the adult who is presently involved in the agricultural use of the land; thus, farmer's compensation for taken land falls far short of the potential commercial or speculative gains that are associated with the land urbanisation process (Pils, 2005).

In practice, compensation for land taking is further reduced because of other factors, including artificially depressed agricultural prices (Ding, 2007) and the reluctance of village cadres that represent the collective to defend the interests of farmers against local officials (Cai, 2003). Compensation for the farmers' lost land is therefore very low. Cao et al. (2008) report that in the Yangtze River Delta, the price of the land leased in markets for commercial use is, per hectare, seven to ten times higher than the compensation that is offered to the owners of the taken rural land. This finding is supported by many other studies, which confirm that land-losing farmers typically receive only 10–20% of the market value of the land (Cai, 2003; Ding, 2007; Zhu et al., 2006). In some extreme cases, the amount of compensation was only RMB 16–21 per mu (one fifteenth of a hectare) (Zhu and Prosterman, 2007).

Following the land-taking process, local governments typically offer the taken land at a very low price to attract manufacturing enterprise; this discounted price is equivalent to a subsidy for these enterprises. For example, Huang (2011) reports that in Zhejiang province, approximately one-quarter of the land was leased to enterprises for less than half of the amount that it cost the local government to develop it for sale. Similarly, Cao et al. (2008) show that, in the province of Jiangsu, the 2005 average leasing price for industrial land was only one-third of that for residential land leasing and one-fifth of that for commercial land leasing; between 2000 and 2005, the average leasing price of industrial land increased only by 7%, whereas the prices for commercial and residential land increased by 42% and 68%, respectively.

When facing unfair compensation or a violation of the principle of public interest, farmers can, in principle, file a lawsuit in court. However, given the dependence of courts on local governments for funding and other political support, judges are not in a position to aggressively pursue allegations of legal violations on the part of local officials. In practice, local courts rarely take cases pertaining to land taking by local governments (Pils, 2005; Wilhelm, 2004).

Aggrieved farmers are therefore forced to appeal to the petition system or to engage in mass protests (Zhu and Prosterman, 2007).

In addition to land prices, the costs associated with other factors of production, including those related to labour, capital, energy, and the environment, are also distorted by laws, regulations, and policies. The major driver of the distortion of labour costs is China's notorious *hukou* (household registration) system. The *hukou* system was introduced in the late 1950s as a major instrument of migration control. According to the Regulation of the People's Republic of China on Household Registration issued in 1958, which even today represents the only national legislation on migration and residence and remains fully in force, *hukou* designates a person's legal place of residence and work at the time of his or her birth on the basis of the locality of his or her mother's registration. Possession of the appropriate *hukou* (agricultural versus nonagricultural) also determines one's access to various amenities and social services, such as health care, schooling, and, until recently, rationed or subsidised food products that were provided only to urban residents (Fleisher and Yang, 2006).

Although the harsh restrictions on rural-urban migration have gradually been eased, the *hukou* system remains a critical barrier[213] to the development of an integrated labour market in China. Compared with urban residents who have secure jobs, receive high salaries, and are entitled to many social benefits, rural migrants suffer from considerable discrimination and exploitation in the labour market (Knight and Song, 1999; Meng and Zhang, 2001).[214] The income gap between urban residents and rural migrants is therefore very large. For example, Huang (2010) reports that in Guangzhou, the capital city of Guangdong province and one of the major destinations of rural migrant workers, an employed urban *hukou* resident earned more than twice as much as a rural migrant worker. Moreover, migrants have almost no chance of obtaining a valuable pension, unemployment insurance, or health insurance benefits, and they must pay

---

[213]   In addition to the *hukou* system, local governments have pursued other active policies of regulating the inflow of migrants to protect their residents. See, for example, Knight and Song (1999).

[214]   On the basis of a survey of 2900 migrants employed in 118 enterprises located in four cities, Knight and Song (1999) show that the occupational composition of migrants and nonmigrants is sharply different: only 1% of the former but 19% of the latter are managerial and technical staff, whereas 68% of the former and 48% of the latter are production workers. Part of the observed difference in occupational distribution results from the greater human capital of urban workers. However, the lower human capital of migrant workers cannot explain much of their disadvantages. Meng and Zhang (2001)'s estimates show that if rural migrants had been treated equally to their urban counterparts, about 6% more migrants who are currently holding blue-collar jobs would have obtained white-collar jobs. If urban residents were treated equally to their migrant counterparts, 22% of the residents who are currently employed as white-collar workers would have been in blue-collar jobs. In addition, the average hourly earnings of rural migrants are 48% of those of urban resident. However, if the two groups had been treated equally, rural migrants would have earned 10.6% more, on average, than their urban counterparts.

significantly higher school fees for their children if they do not have a local *hukou*[215] (World Bank, 2009). Being excluded from benefits customarily associated with urban citizenship, rural migrant workers have much higher savings rates compared with their urban *hukou* counterparts. Huang (2010) finds that in 2007, the urban *hukou* household savings rate for Guangzhou was 15.6%, while that for Shenzhen was 27.5%. By contrast, rural migrant workers in Guangzhou in 2007 had a household savings rate of 41%, and those in Shenzhen had a household savings rate of 42%. The funds that are available to these workers for consumption are therefore very limited.

The interests of rural migrant workers are further impaired by various strategies that are adopted by their employers, who are equipped with extremely strong bargaining powers as a result of the *hukou* system. These strategies include illegal extensions of work hours and arrears of wages. For example, a report shows that of 142 factories surveyed, 133 had employees who worked longer than the legal limit, with the largest percentage of employees working more than 100 hours of overtime per month (Harney, 2009). On the basis of a survey of more than 8,000 rural migrant workers in eight provinces conducted in December 2003, the Beijing Youth Centre for Legal Aid and Research reports that 48% of these migrants had experienced nonpayment of wages that they had earned (Naughton, 2007). When the illegally long work hours and unpaid wages are taken into consideration, a sizeable proportion of rural migrants receive considerably less pay than their payrolls reflect.

The bargaining power of employers has been strengthened by another legal principle, i.e., the deprivation of collective rights, such as the rights of workers to organise, strike, and collectively bargain. According to the Trade Union Law, the right to organise must be exercised through the official union controlled by the Party, the All-China Federation of Trade Unions (ACFTU); independent union organisation remains illegal and can lead to suppression (Chen, 2007). However, the official union is generally viewed by workers to be irrelevant as a source of effective representation because, as a subordinate to the Party whose primary goal is to promote economic growth, the union has interests that are inevitably aligned with the interests of business owners and management (Zheng, 2009). Moreover, the right to strike was removed from the 1982 Constitution, and since then, strikes have been considered illegal. As a result, "unions in China lack the basic weapon to defend workers' rights from arbitrary and abusive management practices" (Zheng, 2009: 609). Finally, while unions have the legal power to

---

[215] According to the 2005 China Urban Labor Survey, which was conducted in twelve cities, the coverage rate for migrants was 8.3% for pensions, 6.8% for medical insurance, and 4.4% for unemployment insurance, compared with 61.7%, 52.3%, and 18.8%, respectively, for urban residents (World Bank, 2009: 184). According to the China Urban Labor Survey, which was conducted in four large cities in 2005, 70% of migrants with children in school reported facing higher schooling costs because they lacked local *hukou*; they estimated that the costs of schooling would decrease by 35% if they had local *hukou* (World Bank, 2009: 182).

negotiate collective contracts, collective contracts often result from the local government's direct intervention in the signing process, and such a contract thus becomes in effect "an agreement between the local party-state and the firm's management" (Gallagher, 2004: 23). Workers are seldom consulted before the negotiations or informed of the contents of the contracts afterward. Many workers are simply not aware of the existence of a collective contract in their enterprises. Collective contracts thus become "formalistic and ritualistic, having limited effects on labor relations" (Chen, 2007: 74).

Migrant rural workers can hardly resort to courts or regulatory agencies to challenge the illegal activities conducted by their employers. As Ho (2009: 39) clearly states, "China has earned a reputation for lax enforcement of its labour laws, and the gap between the law on the books and the law in practice has been wide indeed". On the one hand, public enforcement by labour authorities has proved to be too weak to be regarded by law-breaking factories as a serious threat to their operation. Administrative fines, the only meaningful legal enforcement tool that is available to labour inspectors, are charged at a very low level; for example, in one major manufacturing district in Guangzhou, the average fine was only RMB 3,000 (Ho, 2009). On the other hand, private enforcement of labour rights through litigation is not a very practical option for migrant workers, as they are "too poor to afford legal representation, too poorly educated to navigate the labyrinthine regulations of the legal system, too scared to challenge authority" (Harney, 2009: 75). Other factors such as shortages of qualified judges and lawyers, courts' lack of resources to enforce their judgments, and political influence from local governments who try to attract investment by limiting labour disputes further undermine the effectiveness of the judicial system as a protector of migrant workers' interests.

For the reasons cited above, the cost of labour in China has been depressed to an extremely low level. For example, Banister and Cook (2011) report that in 2008, the average hourly compensation for manufacturing workers in China was only $1.36, approximately 4% of that in the United States and approximately 3% of that in the eurozone. By 2007, China's manufacturing wage level was comparable to the levels in the Philippines and Thailand but still significantly below the levels in Brazil, Malaysia, Mexico, and the majority of other emerging economies (Ceglowski and Golub, 2011; Yang et al., 2010). By one estimate, Chinese labour costs are even lower than wages that handloom operators earned in the early Industrial Revolution in the UK and the wages that workers in a Chicago lumber yard received in the mid-nineteenth century (Harney, 2009).

The cost of capital in China has been artificially lowered by financial regulation and monetary policy,[216] particularly by the government's tight control

---

[216] China's fiscal policy should also be blamed for contributing to the unbalanced economy. On the one hand, for years, the growth rate of China's fiscal revenue has outpaced that of the overall economy as well as that of household incomes. The institutional foundation behind the rise in fiscal revenue can be traced back to the 1994 Fiscal Reform in China, which

over interest rates. The liberalisation of interest rates in China is placed relatively late in the sequence of economic reforms and follows a gradual approach. The sequencing of interest rate liberalisation was carefully crafted (Laurens and Maino, 2007). The process involved first lifting restrictions on wholesale transactions and then gradually liberalising retail transactions. The progression of liberalisation occurred as follows: deposit and lending interest rates on foreign currencies were liberalised before those on the local currency, loan rates were liberalised before deposits, and the liberalisation of long-term and large loans and deposits preceded short-term and small loans and deposits. The policy of the gradual liberalisation of interest rates on loans and deposits, however, was largely abandoned after 2004 (Lardy, 2012). No further reform has been implemented since, although in some critical respects, interest rate liberalisation is far from complete in China. For example, the central bank maintained the cap on deposit rates for all financial institutions and mandated that lending rates could not fall below 0.9 times its established benchmark rates.

More important, the central bank seems to adjust the benchmark interest rates in an asymmetric manner in response to inflation (Liu et al., 2009). In practice, the central bank adjusts deposit and lending rates downward faster than it adjusts them upward. When inflation increases, the rigidity of interest rates leads to lower or even negative real interest rates. This trend became more obvious after 2004. For example, Lardy (2012: 80) reports that "beginning in 2004, whenever inflation picked up, the central bank raised the nominal deposit rates with a lag, and the upward adjustment was substantially less than the

---

managed to reverse a declining trend in state revenues beginning in the mid-1980s. The reform was so successful that the proportion of the government's disposable income to the national income increased from 19% in 1992 to 24% in 2007. On the other hand, some institutional defects exist in China's public spending system. A report issued by the OECD concludes, "[c]apital spending and public administration take a large and, until recently, increasing share of China's overall public spending. In contrast, the portion devoted to certain human capital and other developmental needs, such as education, health, and science and technology, appear somewhat low, both in relation to international standards and China's own goals" (OECD, 2006: 45).

One important reason for the rise in the savings rate – and hence the decline in household consumption – is the reduction in social services provided by the government. In the past, state-owned enterprises (SOEs) employed the most workers and provided basic social services directly to their employees. However, a reform related to SOEs at the beginning of the 1990s shifted these obligations from SOEs to local governments. Given China's highly decentralised fiscal system, different local governments with different fiscal revenues provide different levels of public services, and local governments in many locations do not have adequate resources to fund basic social services (Dollar, 2007). The increased risk faced by households that incur significant health or education expenditures, therefore, has played a significant role in the rise in the savings rate. For example, Chamon and Prasad (2010) show that the increasing private burden of social expenditures has driven the increase in the household savings rate as younger families accumulate assets for future education spending and older families prepare for uncertain health expenses. Similarly, Qi and Prime (2009) find that local government expenditures on health and education are significant and have a relatively large effect on consumption.

increase in inflation. When inflation ebbed, the bank adjusted the nominal deposit rate downward rather quickly".

As a direct result of the way in which the central bank sets nominal interest rates, household interest earnings in China have been far less than they would have been in a more liberalised financial environment in which market forces play a major role in determining interest rates. While from 1997 to 2003 the real return on a one-year bank deposit was persistently positive and averaged 3.0%, since the beginning of 2004, the real return on a one-year deposit has been negative over approximately half of the time period and has averaged –0.5%.[217] By contrast, the corporate sector benefits greatly from such a monetary policy. A marked decline in real lending rates occurred after 2003. While the real rate on a one-year loan averaged 6.8% in 1997–2003, since the beginning of 2004, the real interest rate on a one-year loan has averaged only 1.7%, thus artificially lowering the cost of capital and encouraging investment in projects that have much lower returns[218] (Lardy, 2012).

The low cost of capital in China has made China an anomaly compared with other, developed or developing, countries. For example, on the basis of data for 30,000 firms across 53 economies, Geng and N'Diaye (2012) show that the real cost of capital – defined as a weighted average of the real cost of bank loans, bonds, and equity – faced by Chinese listed firms is below the global average. These authors further argue that compared with the high productivity of the Chinese economy, capital in China is particularly cheap. An estimate of the marginal product of reproducible capital (i.e., capital adjusted for land) shows that China's return to capital is well above its real loan rate, which makes China an outlier in international comparisons.

The low cost of financing, together with other factors, such as low dividend payment[219] and low labour compensation, has led to a significant increase in enterprises' profitability since the early 1990s. While nominal firm profits increased more than fifteen-fold from 1992 to 2007, the ratio of profits to industrial value added also increased remarkably from approximately 21% in the

---

[217] Households' interest income, which account for about 80% of households' investment income, has fallen as a share of GDP since the early 1990s. Although household deposits in the banking system as a share of GDP increased by about two-thirds between the early 1990s and 2003, the pretax interest earnings generated by these savings declined from an average of about 5% in 1992–1995 to only 2.5% of GDP in 2003 (Bergsten et al., 2008: 118). If interest earnings after the early 1990s had grown in line with the stock of household bank deposits, by 2003, the contribution of interest income to household disposable income would have been 8.9% of GDP, which is 6.4 percentage points greater than the actual contribution. According to Lardy (2008), owing to interest rate ceilings, the loss to savers in the first quarter of 2008 was RMB 255 billion ($36 billion), which is the equivalent of 4.1% of GDP.

[218] Ma and Wang (2010) find that net interest payments as a share of GDP by the nonfinancial corporate sector dropped by 50% between 1992 and 2007.

[219] Yang et al. (2011) report that the ratio of total dividend payment to the total value added of enterprises was less than 0.5% in 2007. One reason for this is that the Chinese government did not require SOEs to pay dividends until 2008.

late 1990s to close to 30% in 2007 (Yang et al., 2011). Because of the lack of attractive financial investments, firms will either choose to spend their retained earnings on investment projects to expand their capacity or place them into a low-yielding bank deposit. Thus, the implication of the distorted interest rate structure is that firms face a very low hurdle rate when deciding whether to pursue a given investment project. In summary, restricted bank lending rates and retained earnings have kept the cost of investment funds very low and, hence, helped China to achieve one of the highest ratios of investment to GDP in the world (Aziz, Dunaway, 2007).

While Chinese industry has indeed helped lift tens of millions of people out of poverty, it is also blamed for bringing about serious environmental harm.[220] As a response to the increasing number of environmental problems in China, China's State Environmental Protection Administration (SEPA) was established in 1998, and environmental laws and regulations began to appear after its establishment. The main regulatory framework to date is command and control, with SEPA issuing regulations, sending inspectors to check on compliance, and imposing fines for violations (Roumasset, Burnett, and Wang, 2008). These regulations include discharge limits based on both total emissions and ambient emissions concentrations. New manufacturing enterprises are required to receive certification before production can begin, and time limits are set for compliance by existing enterprises.

The effective implementation of environmental laws and regulations is largely the responsibility of local SEPA branches, given the decentralised nature of China's environmental protection system. For their funding, local SEPA branches depend on local governments, which also approve promotions and allocate resources and personnel. This dependence leaves local SEPA branches financially vulnerable and under intense pressure from growth-driven local officials (Bergsten, et al., 2008: 79). Enforcement is therefore inconsistent across regions and firms.[221] Even worse, lax enforcement has been the rule rather than the exception. For example, central government inspections in October 2006 revealed that local governments had checked only 30% of projects for compliance

---

[220] China's State Environmental Protection Administration (SEPA) estimates that in 1995, industrial pollution accounted for over 70% of national total pollution, including 70% of organic water pollution (COD, or chemical oxygen demand), 72% of SO^2 emissions, and 75% of flue dust (a major component of suspended particulates) (Wang, Wheeler, 2005).

[221] Wang and Wheeler (1996) show that the effective implementation of pollution levies at the provincial level is a function of provincial income and education: the higher the level of income and education is, the higher the effective levy is. Wang et al. (2003) analyse the determinants of the relative bargaining power that firms may have in their relationship with local environmental authorities pertaining to the enforcement of pollution levies, and they report that (1) firms from the private sector appear to have less bargaining power than SOEs; (2) firms facing an adverse financial situation have more bargaining power and are more likely to pay fewer pollution levies than what they should be paying; and (3) firms with emissions that have a higher social impact (as measured by the presence and number of complaints) have less bargaining power with local environmental authorities.

with environmental regulations before approval and that nearly half of the projects that were checked did not implement the required pollution controls (Bergsten, et al., 2008: 80). In some extreme cases, local officials prevent inspectors from completing their work, pay them to overlook violations, or evade orders to close down polluting plants (Roumasset, Burnett, and Wang, 2008). For example, when the three-year "zero-hour operation" to clean up the Huai river targeted small factories along the river beginning in 1998, local officials sought to keep plants running by amalgamating small mills into larger units or by stopping daytime production but operating plants at night.

Chinese prices for energy commodities, such as oil, natural gas, and electricity, are still controlled or directly set by the state. The domestic price that is set by the government, according to Yusuf and Nabeshima (2006: 102), is a mix of world market prices, a domestic shadow price of production, and markup for distribution. The resulting prices are lower than those of China's comparators. For example, at the end of April 2008, Chinese gasoline and diesel prices were 20 and 40% lower than those in the United States, which is the country with the lowest fuel prices in the industrial world (Bergsten, et al., 2008: 146). Low energy prices make it difficult to recover the opportunity cost of resource depletion as well as the cost of environmental damage[222] in both production and consumption. In addition, fuel taxation in China is very low compared with that in other industrial countries (particularly Japan and the Republic of Korea) that are large net oil importers; indeed, it appears to be close to zero on a net basis (Berrah et al., 2007: 137).

In general, a report issued by the World Bank concludes that "energy consumption is increasingly conditioned by very decentralized economic and lifestyle choices, while policy is still mostly based on command and control. The reform of energy markets and pricing has stalled. Prices of energy commodities are sending the wrong signals to consumers because they do not include the social costs of environmental externalities and because they favour increased supply over efficient-use measures" (Berrah et al., 2007: Executive Summary). Inefficient pricing of energy resources tends to artificially increase energy consumption, raise investment returns in manufacturing (particularly in the most energy-intensive industries), and hence lead to overinvestment in heavy industry.[223]

---

[222] Bergsten et al. (2008: 146) claim that energy prices in China have not historically reflected environmental costs. For example, over 80% of the country's electricity is generated from coal. At the end of 2006, less than 15% of coal power plants had installed flue gas desulphurisation (FGD) systems (which are used to remove SO_2 from emissions streams), and even fewer had such systems running. If all the power plants in China installed and operated FGD systems, average electricity tariffs would rise by 10–20%.

[223] Myers and Kent (2001: 76) estimate that China's energy subsidies in 1998 pushed prices to 11% below world market levels; in that year, the cost of reduced efficiency amounted to $4 billion. If the government were to eliminate energy subsidies entirely, this would reduce energy consumption by 9% and cut carbon dioxide emissions by 13%.

Table 5.1. Estimated factor market distortions in China, 2000–2008 (% GDP)

	Labor	Capital	Land	Energy	Environment	Total
2000	0.1	4.1	0.5	0.0	3.8	8.5
2001	0.2	3.9	0.5	0.0	3.5	8.1
2002	0.8	3.9	0.4	0.0	3.3	8.4
2003	1.0	3.8	1.1	0.0	3.3	9.2
2004	2.0	3.1	0.9	0.6	3.0	9.5
2005	2.4	3.0	1.3	1.7	3.0	11.4
2006	2.7	3.1	2.0	1.6	2.8	12.2
2007	3.2	3.6	1.2	1.6	2.4	12.0
2008	3.6	3.4	1.0	0.7	1.9	10.6

Source: Huang and Tao (2010).

A series of studies conducted by Huang and his colleagues provide crude estimates of the factor market distortions in China. For example, Huang (2010) shows that total cost distortions, including the labour market distortion (RMB 411 billion), the capital market distortion (RMB 607 billion), the land market distortion (RMB 120 billion), the energy price distortion (RMB 204 billion) and the environmental cost distortion (RMB 591 billion), were RMB 2,138 billion in 2008 or 7.2% of GDP. The estimated percentages obtained by Huang and Tao (2010), which extend the period to include the nine years from 2000 to 2008, are summarised in Table 5.1. While the estimates vary from year to year, the findings are clear: producers in China receive significant subsidies from the rest of the economy, and these subsidies range from 8.1% to 12.2% of GDP.

China's investment-driven growth has resulted in developments that are increasingly considered to be problematic by both scholars and policymakers. These developments include environmental degradation,[224] slower job creation,[225] urban-rural inequality,[226] and production capacity overexpansion

---

[224] Yusuf and Nabeshima (2006: 24) report that nearly 38% of river waters in China were considered to be severely polluted in 2000; among the seven major river basins, only 42% of the watercourses reached grade-three standards, while 28% failed to achieve even grade-five standards. In addition, China is now the second-largest emitter of greenhouse gases and contains 16 of the 20 cities with the worst air pollution in the world (Lardy, 2007). In 2001, two of three cities in China failed to meet the residential ambient air quality standards of the SEPA, and the air quality problem causes more than 400,000 premature deaths annually (Yusuf, Nabeshima, 2006: 25, 27). A report issued by the World Bank in 2007 indicates that the total cost of air and water pollution in China in 2003 was RMB 781 billion, or about 5.78% of GDP (World Bank, 2007).

[225] Between 1978 and 1993 employment expanded by 2.5% per annum, but between 1993 and 2004, when the investment share of GDP was much higher than that in the 1980s, employment growth slowed to only slightly over 1% (Kuijs, Wang, 2006).

[226] Urban employment growth decreased from 5.4% per year from 1978 to 1993 to 2.9% from 1993 to 2004, leading to a slower relocation of labour out of agriculture and the rural areas

(Pivot Capital Management, 2009). After all, the Solow model shows that without technological progress, an economy has a limited ability to raise its output per capita via capital accumulation. According to the principle of diminishing returns, the impact of capital accumulation on GDP growth will continuously decline. In fact, as Kuijs and Wang (2006) show, if China's current economic growth pattern continues, an unprecedented average investment-to-GDP ratio of 55% would be required for the period from 2014 to 2024 to maintain China's GDP growth at 8% per year. Financing such a high level of investment is impossible in the long run; thus, under these circumstances, the investment-driven economy will ultimately reach a dead end.

5.5. CONCLUSION

Scholars have long argued that China is an exception to the so-called "law matters" hypothesis. According to this hypothesis, an effective legal system that reliably protects property rights, enforces contracts, and, hence, sustains the operation of market mechanisms is indispensable in pursuing economic prosperity. Most scholars agree that China has realised an economic miracle despite its poor legal system, which features a legislative system that is in disarray and a weak judiciary. Thus, law has been relatively irrelevant to China's economic success. In this chapter, however, we show that law does matter for China's economic development – but in a more complicated way than has formerly been elucidated. Current Chinese law and regulations for factor markets are enacted and enforced in such a way that factor prices are low, production and investment are subsidised, and citizen welfare and growth sustainability are sacrificed. Therefore, China has become an unbalanced fast-growing economy.

China's leadership has realised the necessity and urgency of transforming from a growth pattern that is driven by investment to a growth path that relies more on expanding domestic consumption. During the past several years, Premier Wen and his government have adopted a wide range of policy measures, including administrative controls, monetary instruments, and fiscal tools, that are aimed at adjusting China's economic structure. However, rebalancing the sources of economic growth has proved to be a much greater challenge than expected. The policy efforts have failed to reverse the overall trend toward a worsening economic structure, and China's economic growth has become even more imbalanced since 2003. We believe that the most important reason for this failure is that the majority of the policy measures that have been implemented

where productivity and income are much lower. The persistent productivity gap between agriculture and the rest of the economy has exacerbated rural-urban income inequality and is an important reason underlying the increase in the rural-urban income gap from 2.2 in 1990 to 3.3 in 2006 (He, Kuijs, 2007).

thus far have not been directed toward the laws and regulations that cause serious factor market distortions, such as interest rate controls, the *hukou* system, and the land-taking system. Without systematic legal and institutional reform aimed at liberalising factor markets and, hence, setting factor market prices in accordance with relative scarcities and social preferences, China will likely not achieve a balanced economy.

It is difficult to predict whether such a systematic reform will be adopted and implemented before the opportunity window closes. On the one hand, as Huang (2010) states, history shows that Chinese policymakers can act decisively when they face crises. For example, confronting the significant risk of a reversal of the reform process, Deng Xiaoping took a famous "Southern Tour" and reemphasised the need for accelerated economic reform in 1992. His interventions reignited the economic reform and ultimately led to an official endorsement of a "socialist market economy" in the 14th Congress of the Party. On the other hand, as Pei (2006) argues, China's gradualist reform strategy allows the ruling elites to protect their rents in vital sectors (such as factor markets) and use retained rents to maintain political support among key constituencies. Any further reform that may reduce economic distortion (and hence economic rents) will therefore undermine the regime's survival and risk resistance or sabotage from the ruling elites. Thus, a rebalancing strategy is economically efficient but politically infeasible.

Political reform, a precondition for further economic reform, particularly factor market liberalisation, therefore becomes a task that can no longer be bypassed by the Party, which has intentionally neglected such reform since 1989. In recent years, numerous warnings have signalled the danger of stagnation in economic reform. For example, Pei (2006: 24) claims that "gradualism in economic reform may be more likely to fail when it is undertaken without accompanying reforms that restructure the key political institutions that define power relations and enforce the rules essential to the functioning of markets". Yang Yao, a famous Chinese economist and an enthusiastic supporter of the Party, recently admitted that "ultimately there is no alternative to greater democratisation if the CCP wishes to encourage economic growth and maintain social stability" (Yao, 2010b). A political transition to a more democratic regime is undoubtedly desirable, considering the role of such a regime in contributing to China's long-term economic prosperity and social welfare by transforming the government from a "grabbing hand" to a "helping hand", from a market participant to a market regulator and public goods provider, and from a patron of special interest groups to a protector of public interests. However, as Naughton (2008) cautions, given China's weakly institutionalised political system and a highly contingent and perhaps precarious set of circumstances, only time will tell whether such a political transition will materialise and, if so, what form and cost such measures will take.

CHAPTER 6

CONCLUSION

One of the most striking facts about the world today is the remarkable difference in living standards among countries. In 2011, GDP per capita in the world's richest country (Monaco) was more than six hundred times that of the world's poorest country (Democratic Republic of the Congo).[227] In 2012, more than one billion people lived in high-income countries and enjoyed 68% of the world's income.[228] Meanwhile, approximately 1.2 billion people survived in extreme poverty (living on less than $1.25 a day), which amounts to approximately 21% of the population in the developing world.[229] These massive differences in country incomes are largely the product of economic growth during the last two centuries. Thus, according to Snowdon and Vane (2005: 579), "sustained economic growth is the most important determinant of living standards".

Great efforts have been undertaken to understand the causes of economic growth, which has resulted in an explosion of literature since the 1990s. As part of this movement, there is growing interest in exploring the connection between legal rules and economic growth, which can be attributed to the influence of LLSV. Thanks to LLSV's groundbreaking studies, which are regarded as "one of the most important and influential ideas to emerge in the social sciences in the past decade" (Armour, Deakin, Mollica, and Siems, 2009), law has been empirically identified for the first time as playing an important role in the process of economic growth. This conclusion has been subsequently confirmed by numerous studies, and a consensus that "law matters" seems to be emerging.

LLSV's contributions have undoubtedly deepened our understanding of the relationship between law and economic growth. Their conclusions, however, face serious challenges that range from methodological weaknesses to contradictory historical evidence. Important bodies of law, such as property law, contract law, and tort law, are not covered by LLSV's studies, which indicates that pieces of the puzzle are missing. The credibility of LLSV's theory has been further damaged by certain anomalies, such as China, in which a rapidly growing economy coexists with a weak legal system. Therefore, it can hardly be argued that the

---

[227] http://data.worldbank.org/indicator/NY.GDP.PCAP.CD/countries/1W?display=default.
[228] http://data.worldbank.org/country.
[229] World Development Indicators 2012, available at http://data.worldbank.org/sites/default/files/wdi-2012-ebook.pdf.

mission of exploring law's role in economic growth has been definitively accomplished by LLSV. More work must be undertaken.

This study can be regarded as part of the academic efforts attempting to fill gaps in LLSV's studies. This study performs the following tasks: the contribution of and controversy over LLSV's studies are systematically reviewed; the relationship between law (both corporate and securities law) and stock market development, which has attracted the most attention from LLSV are further scrutinised; property law, which is a fundamental institution that has been overlooked by LLSV, is analysed with the help of the literature from economic history, development economics, transition economics, etc.; and, finally, China, an apparent anomaly to LLSV's proposition, is examined from a unique perspective.

The main findings of this study are as follows.

1. *The importance of legal origins should not be overestimated.* The core finding of LSSV is that common law is superior to civil law in supporting financial development, sustaining the operation of a market economy, and thus promoting economic growth. Therefore, "legal origins are central to understanding the varieties of capitalism". However, as showed in chapter 2, this conclusion does not hold under certain conditions, such as when the initial conditions in the colonies, culture, and political institutions are controlled for in the regressions; when legal rules are measured and codified more accurately; when countries are classified more cautiously; and when contrary historical evidence is taken into consideration.

The classification based on legal origins seems to bear little relevance to the study of a specific legal field. For example, in chapter 3, we found that the United States and the United Kingdom – the two leading common law systems and two economies that are characterised by developed stock markets and dispersed share ownership – have fundamentally different regulatory environments. Compared with American corporate law, which is considered more "board-centric", British corporate law is more consistent with continental civil law countries in which shareholders' interests are prioritised over those of directors and managers.

The alleged borders among legal origins become even more blurred when less-developed countries are investigated. As we demonstrated in chapter 4, African countries, whether common law or civil law in origin, show great similarities to one another in terms of the dysfunction of their factor markets, the complicated interactions between customary property systems and formal property law, and the failure of states as enforcers of property rights. Compared with these factors, the influence of legal origins seems negligible.

2. *The importance of informal institutions should not be underestimated.* There is general agreement that the role of legal rules dwarfs that of informal institutions, including norms, culture, religion, etc., in sustaining modern economic growth (Cross, 2002). LLSV's studies adhere to this position by paying exclusive attention to formal legal provisions, which, unfortunately, narrows the

applicability of their theory. For example, in chapter 3, we found that private ordering, market-based solutions, and self-regulation – as opposed to legal rules and regulatory instruments – played essential roles in the development of the stock market in the United Kingdom. Even in the United States, which has been used by LLSV as a tacit benchmark to evaluate financial development and judicial quality in other countries, self-regulatory institutions, such as investment banks and stock exchanges, have been found to be responsible for the prosperity of stock markets, at least in their early stages.

Informal institutions also matter for the definition, enforcement, and protection of property rights, as showed in chapter 4. In many developing countries, customary property regimes continue to be more important in governing land issues than formal property law. Before being undermined by the process of formalisation, customary property systems can be trusted not only to guarantee basic tenure security (which is enough to warrant land-related investments) but also to stabilise the community, such as by acting as a social safety net.

The importance of informal rules in economic development is further confirmed by China's growth experience. It has been argued that China's economic growth is supported mainly by informal institutions, such as governance mechanisms based on reputation and relationships (Allen et al., 2005). Clarke et al. (2008) reach a similar conclusion and show that informal contract enforcement institutions – such as negotiation, mediation, and self-enforcement through reputation and long-term relationships – are used extensively by Chinese businesses.

3. *The relationship between law and economic growth is bidirectional rather than unidirectional.* There is reciprocal causation, rather than a unidirectional causal sequence (as suggested by LLSV), between a legal system and the economy it serves. As showed in chapter 3, law is important for the development of stock markets; however, law will not emerge out of a void. The legislature will supply the legal protections demanded by investors only when stock markets have developed to such an extent that minority shareholders have become a powerful constituency whose concerns must be taken seriously. It is therefore not surprising to find that a prosperous stock market predates a sophisticated regulatory framework that is designed to ensure that investors receive a reasonable return on their investment. Of course, after they are enacted, these regulations will further influence the direction, speed, and size of future stock market development.[230]

An identical logic applies to the study of property rights. As chapter 4 showed, secure property rights may encourage investment; however, investment can also

---

[230]   In the words of Milhaupt and Pistor (2008: 5), "[g]overnance structures of all types, including law, must adapt and respond to changes in the economy. Rather than thinking of a legal system as a fixed endowment for the economy, it is more productive to view the relationship between law and markets as a highly iterative process of action and strategic reaction. We call this a 'rolling relationship' between law and markets".

be viewed as a commitment to the long-term productive use of the resource and may therefore be undertaken to increase the security of property rights. On a more general level, property rights will influence the speed of technological progress, the level of market development, and overall economic performance, which will in turn determine the costs and benefits related to defining and enforcing property rights and thus the direction in which property rights will evolve.

Similarly, in China, the economy prospered for an extended period of time in the absence of the market-oriented legal system that is supposed to protect property rights and enforce contracts. Only in the 1990s did the Chinese government attempt to establish a solid legal foundation for its rapidly growing economy. These legal changes helped achieve a new round of economic expansion, which broadened the size of the market, complicated the organisation of production, transaction, and transportation, and thus stimulated the need for further legal reform. The relationship between legal and economic development in China is, therefore, "bidirectional – a coevolutionary process" (Clarke et al., 2008: 376).

4. *Other factors, particularly political ones, should be taken into consideration.* Law is not a standardised product that is designed and manufactured by certain social engineers who are value-neutral, preference-free, and public-interest-oriented; by contrast, it is enacted by legislatures, enforced by courts and public agents, and used by ordinary citizens, all of whom have their own interests, incentives, and agendas. These interests, incentives, and agendas are shaped to a large extent by a nation's political factors, such as its level of democratisation, the characteristics of its electoral system, the extent to which it tolerates corruption and rent-seeking, the role of interest groups, its level of income inequality and the corresponding division of ideology, etc. The relationship between law and economic growth therefore should be examined in the context of a jurisdiction's political landscape, which, however, will vary substantially across countries and over time and lead to significant difficulties in establishing a universal and stable connection between law and economic growth.

Politics matter for stock market development, as chapter 3 demonstrated. Social ideology, political conflict and compromise, electoral systems, and rent-seeking efforts by interest groups are all important factors that can be used to explain the dynamic evolution of stock markets within an economy and differences in the performances of stock markets across economies. It is more likely that the successful development of capital markets in the common law countries, particularly in the United States and the United Kingdom, should be attributed more to favourable political conditions, such as weak social democratic traditions, strong liberal features, majoritarian electoral systems, etc., and less to their common law origin.

It is also futile to discuss the functioning of a property regime without accounting for political variables. Chapter 4 suggested that the alleged benefits of formal private ownership cannot be taken for granted when political factors –

particularly the effectiveness of the state – are considered. Formal private ownership will not emerge and function simply because it benefits the economy and society; private property rights must be supplied – defined, enforced, and protected – by the state in a cost-effective manner. States in the developing world, however, frequently fail to engage this task because of high transaction and information costs, incompetent and corrupt agents, lack of legitimacy, etc.

5. *Economic growth can be achieved with the help of a "bad" legal system, at least in the short term.* According to LLSV, there is only one type of law, i.e., the body of legal rules associated with common law countries, that is committed to protect private property rights against expropriation by the state and isolate markets from state over-regulation and that can thus be expected to promote economic growth. By contrast, laws that grant considerable power to the state, such as those found in French civil law countries, will be deemed to be inefficient, unproductive, detrimental to economic prosperity, and therefore "bad". The problem with such dichotomy is that there are many counterexamples in which a rapid-growth economy coexists with a "bad" legal system.

China stands out as the most notable among these counterexamples. As demonstrated in chapter 5, the legal system in China is too flawed to be relied upon to support the functioning of a market economy. The legislative process in China is intentionally designed to maximise the discretion of bureaucrats. In addition, Chinese courts, particularly courts of first instance, are susceptible to political pressures from (local) governments and therefore fail to enforce legal rules independently and impartially. This type of legal environment inevitably results in high transaction costs, destabilises expectations for the future, and harms prospects for economic growth. Despite such a weak legal framework, China has witnessed remarkable economic growth over the past three decades.

The secret to this development lies in the fact that such a legal environment can also lead to lower factor prices, subsidised investment and production, and, therefore, accelerated growth. The apparent enigma of China's "bad" legal system not slowing down its economic growth can be explained by the following: when the pro-growth effects of a legal system outweigh its anti-growth effects, the overall influence of even a "bad" legal system may enhance, rather than harm, economic growth. If China's success, however, is shown to be unsustainable, it may therefore challenge LLSV's conclusions only in the short run.

We believe that we will reach a deeper understanding of the relationship between law and economic growth by incorporating these findings into the existing literature. Specifically, these findings lead us to question the simple, static, and unidirectional causal chain suggested by LLSV, i.e., legal origin → legal rules → economic performance. The connections between law and economic growth in the real world, as we have shown, are more complicated, more dynamic, more interactive, more context-contingent, and more history- (path-) dependent. We therefore suggest a more cautious stance: whereas we agree on the importance of law in explaining economic performance, we also acknowledge that the role of law is defined and shaped by a broader context within which political, legal, economic, and social variables influence one another and evolve together over time. *Law matters, but it depends.*

In addition, as the experience of China shows, even when specific laws are shown to be beneficial for economic growth, it does not mean that these laws are necessarily desirable from a social welfare perspective. Law may be systematically distorted by the government to facilitate economic growth at the expense of ordinary citizens' welfare. For example, the government may lower the interest income of households, slow wage increases, and/or relax the standard of environmental quality to subsidise investment and production. In these cases, economic growth will diminish (rather than improve) the population's standard of living and is therefore questionable from the perspective of social policy.

Certainly, this study has limitations. First, given the breadth of the topic, we rely heavily on existing literature rather than first-hand data, which may endanger the originality and credibility of this study to some extent. More empirical work should and will be conducted in the future to test the main findings presented herein. In fact, we have partially examined and confirmed finding five above in a recently published paper, based on data from China (Xu and Gui, 2013).

Second, important bodies of law, such as contract law and tort law, which have been argued to be relevant to understanding the process of economic development (Trebilcock and Leng, 2006; Cross, 2011), are not covered in this study. Nor do we address certain interesting topics, such as the relative desirability of rules versus standards, the interaction between public regulation and judicial processes, the comparative advantage of banks versus stock markets in promoting economic growth, the convergence and divergence debate on corporate governance standards, etc. More new frontiers are waiting to be explored.

Finally, certain countries or regions are chosen or omitted from consideration because of the topic that we chose and because of the availability of relevant literature, which may lead to a selection bias. For example, we focused on stock market development in developed countries in chapter 3 and therefore overlook the situation in the developing world in which corporate governance practices and pathologies present marked differences from those in developed countries (Morck, Wolfenzon, and Yeung, 2005). By contrast, chapter 4 focused primarily on developing and transitional countries in exploring the role of property law and leaves no room for discussing property law problems faced by developed economies, such as the anti-commons tragedy and the resultant "gridlock economy" problem (Heller, 1998, 2008).

There is a long way to go before a consensus on the relationship between law and economic growth can be reached. In future studies, more empirical work must be undertaken. These studies, however, may not deepen our understanding of the role of law if they continue to follow the methodology and approach employed by LLSV, which have been shown by this book to be problematic. As we argued in chapter 2, legal rules should be measured and codified more accurately (perhaps with the help of lawyers), countries should be classified more cautiously, and the problems of reverse causality and omitted variable bias should be addressed more carefully. More generally, law should be treated endogenously rather than exogenously because law is not only the rule of the game in the society but also the equilibrium solution for the game.

Additionally, more legal fields must be explored. Current studies focus on commercial law and regulations, such as corporate law, bankruptcy law, and securities regulation, rather than on bodies of private law, such as property, contracts, and torts; however, the differences between common law and civil law can be identified more clearly in such bodies of private law and merit systematic investigations. In addition, bodies of public law – constitutional law, administrative law, and taxation law, among others – that define, regulate, and enforce aspects of relationships within government and those between governments and individuals are currently attracting less attention from scholars, which may impair our understanding of the law and growth nexus because government is playing an increasingly important role in modern society.

More special cases or even anomalies must be scrutinised. Case studies, as conducted in chapter 5, may reveal underlying information that is not able to be detected by cross-country regressions. After all, not all variables of interest can be quantifiable, and these unquantifiable variables will therefore be missed in purely quantitative studies, which may lead to a precise but not accurate measurement.[231] Qualitative case studies can serve as an important complement to quantitative statistical studies because they can address unquantifiable factors more effectively.

It may not be an exaggeration to say that LLSV's works have resulted in an academic revolution that not only urges mainstream economists to pay more attention to the role of law in the operations of economies but also shifts the focus of law and economics scholars from the micro-level to the macro-level. It is not surprising to find debates, controversies, and disagreements over their conclusions, given that the movement remains in its infancy. As an infant will grow and mature, a theory will do the same. With the increasing interests of scholars from different fields in LLSV propositions and the development of more literature, the movement may finally mature to an extent that a sub-discipline labelled "law and economic growth" is recognised as an independent academic subject, and the term "law and economic growth" becomes as popular as "law and economics".

---

[231]   In the various fields of statistics, accuracy is the degree of closeness of measurements of a quantity to that quantity's actual (true) value. The precision, also called reproducibility or repeatability, is the degree to which repeated measurements under unchanged conditions show identical results. For more details, see http://en.wikipedia.org/wiki/Accuracy_and_precision.

REFERENCES

Acemoglu, Daron, 2005. "Politics and Economics in Weak and Strong States", *Journal of Monetary Economics* 52: 1199–1226.

Acemoglu, Daron, 2009. *Introduction to Modern Economic Growth.* Princeton, NJ: Princeton University Press.

Acemoglu, Daron, and Simon Johnson, 2005. "Unbundling Institutions", *Journal of Political Economy* 113: 949–995.

Acemoglu, Daron, Johnson, Simon, and James A. Robinson, 2001. "The Colonial Origins of Comparative Development: An Empirical Investigation", *American Economic Review* 91: 1369–1401.

Acemoglu, Daron, Johnson, Simon, and James A. Robinson, 2002. "Reversal of Fortune: Geography and Institutions in the Making of the Modern World Income Distribution", *Quarterly Journal of Economics* 117: 1231–1294.

Acemoglu, Daron, Johnson, Simon, and James A. Robinson, 2005. "Institutions as a Fundamental Cause of Long-Run Growth", in Philippe Aghion and Steven N. Durlauf (eds.), *Handbook of Economic Growth.* Amsterdam: Elsevier B.V.

Agnello, Richard J., and Lawrence P. Donnelley, 1975. "Property Rights and Efficiency in the Oyster Industry", *Journal of Law and Economics* 18: 521–533.

Ahuja, Vinod, 1998. "Land Degradation, Agricultural Productivity and Common Property: Evidence from Côte d'Ivoire", *Environment and Development Economics* 3: 7–34.

Alchian, Armen A., 1965. "Some Economics of Property Rights", *Il Politico* 30: 816–829.

Alchian, Armen A., 1987. "Property Rights", in John Eatwell, Murray Milgate and Peter Newman (eds.), *The New Palgrave Dictionary of Economics* (First Edition), London: Palgrave Macmillan.

Alchian, Armen A., and Harold Demsetz, 1973. "The Property Rights Paradigm", *Journal of Economic History* 33: 16–27.

Alesina, Alberto, Ozler, Sule, Roubini, Nouriel, and Phillip Swagel, 1996. "Political Instability and Economic Growth", *Journal of Economic Growth* 1: 189–211.

Alesina, Alberto, and Roberto Perotti, 1996. "Income Distribution, Political Instability and Investment", *European Economic Review* 40: 1203–1228.

Alesina, Alberto, and Dani Rodrik, 1994. "Distributive Politics and Economic Growth", *Quarterly Journal of Economics* 109: 465–490.

Allen, Douglas W., 1999. "Transaction Costs", in Boudewijn Bouckaert and Gerrit De Geest (eds.), *The Encyclopedia of Law and Economics*, Cheltenham: Edward Elgar.

Allen, Franklin, Jun Qian, and Meijun Qian. 2005. "Law, Finance, and Economic Growth in China", *Journal of Financial Economics* 77: 57–116.

Alston, Lee J., Libecap, Gary D., and Robert Schneider, 1996. "The Determinants and Impact of Property Rights: Land Titles on the Brazilian Frontier", *Journal of Law. Economics, and Organization* 12: 25–61.

Alston, Lee J., Libecap, Gary D., and Bernardo Mueller, 1999. "A Model of Rural Conflict: Violence and Land Reform Policy in Brazil", *Environment and Development Economics* 4: 135–160.

Alston, Lee J., Libecap, Gary D., and Bernardo Mueller, 2000. "Land Reform Policies, the Sources of Violent Conflict, and Implications for Deforestation in the Brazilian Amazon", *Journal of Environmental Economics and Management* 39: 162–188.

Amihud, Yakov, and Baruch Lev, 1981. "Risk Reduction as a Managerial Motive for Conglomerate Mergers", *Bell Journal of Economics* 12: 605–617.

Amsden, Alice H. 1989. *Asia's Next Giant: South Korea and Late Industrialization*. New York: Oxford University Press.

Anabtawi, Iman, 2006. "Some Skepticism about Increasing Shareholder Power", *UCLA Law Review* 53: 561–599.

Anabtawi, Iman, and Lynn Stout, 2008. "Fiduciary Duties for Activist Shareholders", *Stanford Law Review 60: 1255–1308*.

Anderson, Terry L., and Dean Lueck, 1992. "Land Tenure and Agriculture Productivity on Indian Reservations", *Journal of Law and Economics* 35: 427–454.

Andrade, Gregor, Mitchell, Mark, and Erik Stafford, 2001. "New Evidence and Perspectives on Mergers", *Journal of Economic Perspectives* 15: 103–120.

André, Catherine, and Jean-Philippe Platteau, 1998. "Land Relations under Unbearable Stress: Rwanda Caught in the Malthusian Trap", *Journal of Economic Behavior and Organization* 34: 1–47.

Aoki, Masahiko, 2001. *Toward a Comparative Institutional Analysis*. Cambridge, MA: MIT Press.

Arestis, Philip, Demetriades, Panicos O., and Kul B. Luintel, 2001. "Financial Development and Economic Growth: The Role of Stock Markets", *Journal of Money, Credit and Banking* 33: 16–41.

Armour, John, 2008. "Enforcement Strategies in UK Corporate Governance: A Roadmap and Empirical Assessment", ECGI Working Paper No.106/2008, available at http://papers.ssrn.com/sol3/papers.cfm?abstract_id=1133542.

Armour, John, Black, Bernard, Cheffins, Brian, and Richard Nolan, 2009. "Private Enforcement of Corporate Law: An Empirical Comparison of the United Kingdom and the United States", *Journal of Empirical Legal Studies* 6: 687–722.

Armour, John, Deakin, Simon, Mollica, Viviana, and Mathias Siems, 2009. "Law and Financial Development: What We Are Learning from Time-Series Evidence", *Brigham Young University Law Review* 2009: 1435–1500.

Armour, John, Deakin, Simon, Sarkar, Prabirjit, Siems, Mathias, and Ajit Singh, 2009. "Shareholder Protection and Stock Market Development: An Empirical Test of the Legal Origins Hypothesis", *Journal of Empirical Legal Studies* 6 (2): 343–380.

Armour, John, Hansmann, Henry, and Reinier Kraakman, 2009. "Agency Problems and Legal Strategies", in Reinier Kraakman et al., *The Anatomy of Corporate Law: A Comparative and Functional Approach (Second Edition)*. New York: Oxford University Press.

Armour, John, and David A. Skeel, Jr., 2007. "Who Writes the Rules for Hostile Takeovers, and Why? The Peculiar Divergence of U.S. and U.K. Takeover Regulation", *Georgetown Law Journal* 95: 1727–1794.

Arnold, J.E.M., and J. Gabriel Campbell, 1986. "Collective Management of Hill Forests in Nepal: The Community Forestry Development Project", in *Proceedings of the Conference on Common Property Resource Management* (April 21–26, 1985). Washington D.C.: National Academy Press.

Arruñada, Benito, 2003. "Property Enforcement as Organized Consent", *Journal of Law, Economics, and Organization* 19 (2): 401–444.

Arruñada, Benito, and Nuno Garoupa, 2005. "The Choice of Titling System in Land", *Journal of Law and Economics* 48: 709–727.

Atwood, David A., 1990. "Land Registration in Africa: The Impact on Agricultural Production", *World Development* 18: 659–671.

Aziz, Jahangir, and Steven Dunaway, 2007. "China's Rebalancing Act", *Finance and Development* 44 (3): 27–31.

Bailey, Martin J., 1992. "The Approximate Optimality of Aboriginal Property Rights", *Journal of Law and Economics* 35: 183–198.

Bailey, Martin J., 1998. "Property Rights in Aboriginal Societies", in Peter Newman (ed.), *The New Palgrave Dictionary of Economics and Law*, London: Macmillan Reference Ltd.

Bainbridge, Stephen M., 1999. "Insider Trading", in B. Bouckaert and G. De Geest (eds.), *The Encyclopedia of Law and Economics*, Cheltenham: Edward Elgar.

Bainbridge, Stephen M., 2002. "Director Primacy in Corporate Takeovers: Preliminary Reflections", *Stanford Law Review* 55: 791–818.

Bainbridge, Stephen M., 2006. "The Case for Limited Shareholder Voting Rights", *UCLA Law Review* 53: 601–636.

Bainbridge, Stephen M., 2008. *The New Corporate Governance in Theory and Practice.* New York: Oxford University Press.

Baland, Jean-Marie, and Jean-Philippe Platteau, 1996. *Halting Degradation of Natural Resources: Is There a Role for Rural Communities.* Oxford: FAO and Clarendon Press.

Bandiera, Oriana, 2003. "Land Reform, the Market for Protection, and the Origins of the Sicilian Mafia: Theory and Evidence", *Journal of Law, Economics and Organization* 19: 218–244.

Banister, Judith, and George Cook, 2011. "China's Employment and Compensation Costs in Manufacturing through 2008", *Monthly Labor Review* (March 2011): 39–52.

Barnes, Grenville, and Charisse Griffith-Charles, 2007. "Assessing the Formal Land Market and Deformalization of Property in St. Lucia", *Land Use Policy* 24: 494–501.

Barnes, Grenville, Stanfield, David, and Kevin Barthel, 2000. "Land Registration Modernization in Developing Economies: A Discussion of the Main Problems in Central/Eastern Europe, Latin America, and the Caribbean", *URISA Journal* 12 (4): 33–42.

Barro, Robert J., 1991. "Economic Growth in a Cross Section of Countries", *Quarterly Journal of Economics* 106: 407–443.

Barro, Robert J., 1996. "Democracy and Growth", *Journal of Economic Growth* 1: 1–27.

Barro, Robert J., 2000. "Inequality and Growth in a Panel of Countries", *Journal of Economic Growth* 5: 5–32.

Barro, Robert J., and Xavier Sala-i-Martin, 2003. *Economic Growth.* Cambridge, MA: MIT Press.

Barrows, Richard, and Michael Roth, 1990. "Land Tenure and Investment in African Agriculture: Theory and Evidence", *Journal of Modern African Studies* 28: 265–297.

Barth, James R., Caprio, Gerard Jr., and Ross Levine, 2004. "Bank Regulation and Supervision: What Works Best", *Journal of Financial Intermediation* 13: 205–248.

Barzel, Yoram, 1997. *Economic Analysis of Property Rights*. Cambridge: Cambridge University Press.

Barzel, Yoram, 2002. *A Theory of the State: Economic Rights, Legal Rights, and the Scope of the State*. New York: Cambridge University Press.

Baskin, Jonathan Barron, and Paul J. Miranti, Jr., 1997. *A History of Corporate Finance*. New York: Cambridge University Press.

Battalio, Robert, Hatch, Brian, and Tim Loughran, 2011. "Who Benefited from the Disclosure Mandates of the 1964 Securities Acts Amendments?" *Journal of Corporate Finance* 17: 1047–1063.

Baumol, William J., 1990. "Entrepreneurship: Productive, Unproductive, and Destructive", *Journal of Political Economy* 98: 893–921.

Baumol, William J., 2002. *The Free-Market Innovation Machine: Analyzing the Growth Miracle of Capitalism*. Princeton, NJ: Princeton University Press.

Baumol, William J., Litan, Robert E., and Carl J. Schramm, 2007. *Good Capitalism, Bad Capitalism, and the Economics of Growth and Prosperity*. New Haven: Yale University Press.

Bebchuk, Lucian A., 2005. "The Case for Increasing Shareholder Power", *Harvard Law Review* 118: 833–913.

Bebchuk, Lucian A., 2007. "The Myth of the Shareholder Franchise", *Virginia Law Review* 93: 675–732.

Bebchuk, Lucian A., Coates, IV, John C., and Guhan Subramanian, 2002. "The Powerful Antitakeover Force of Staggered Boards: Theory, Evidence, and Policy", *Stanford Law Review* 54: 887–952.

Bebchuk, Lucian A., and Alma Cohen, 2003. "Firms' Decisions Where to Incorporate", *Journal of Law and Economics* 46: 383–425.

Bebchuk, Lucian A., Cohen, Alma, and Allen Ferrell, 2009. "What Matters in Corporate Governance", *Review of Financial Studies* 22: 783–827.

Bebchuk, Lucian A., and Allen Ferrell, 1999. "Federalism and Corporate Law: The Race to Protect Managers from Takeovers", *Columbia Law Review* 99: 1168–1199.

Bebchuk, Lucian A., and Chaim Fershtman, 1994. "Insider Trading and the Managerial Choice among Risky Projects", *Journal of Financial and Quantitative Analysis* 29 (1): 1–14.

Bebchuk, Lucian A., and Jesse M. Fried, 2003. "Executive Compensation as an Agency Problem", *Journal of Economic Perspectives* 17: 71–92.

Bebchuk, Lucian A., and Jesse M. Fried, 2004. *Pay Without Performance: The Unfulfilled Promise of Executive Compensation*. Cambridge, MA: Harvard University Press.

Bebchuk, Lucian A., and Assaf Hamdani, 2006. "Federal Corporate Law: Lessons from History", *Columbia Law Review* 106: 1793–1838.

Becht, Marco, Bolton, Patrick, and Ailsa Röell, 2007. "Corporate Law and Governance", in A. Mitchell Polinsky and Steven Shavell (eds.), *Handbook of Law and Economics*. Amsterdam: Elsevier B.V.

Becht, Marco, Franks, Julian, Mayer, Colin, and Stefano Rossi, 2009. "Returns to Shareholder Activism: Evidence from a Clinical Study of the Hermes UK Focus Fund", *Review of Financial Studies* 22 (8): 3093–3129.

Beck, Thorsten, 2008. "The Econometrics of Finance and Growth", *World Bank Policy Research Working Paper* 4608.

Beck, Thorsten, Demirgüç-Kunt, Asli, and Patrick Honohan, 2009. "Access to Financial Services: Measurement, Impact, and Policies", *World Bank Research Observer* 24 (1): 119–145.

Beck, Thorsten, Demirgüç-Kunt, Asli, Laeven, Luc, and Ross Levine, 2008. "Finance, Firm Size, and Growth", *Journal of Money, Credit and Banking* 40: 1379–1405.

Beck, Thorsten, Demirgüç-Kunt, Asli, and Ross Levine, 2003a. "Law, Endowments, and Finance", *Journal of Financial Economics* 70: 137–181.

Beck, Thorsten, Demirgüç-Kunt, Asli, and Ross Levine, 2003b. "Law and Finance: Why Does Legal Origin Matter", *Journal of Comparative Economics* 31: 653–675.

Beck, Thorsten, Demirgüç-Kunt, Asli, and Ross Levine, 2005. "Law and Firms' Access to Finance", *American Law and Economics Review* 7: 211–252.

Beck, Thorsten, Demirgüç-Kunt, Asli, and Vojislav Maksimovic, 2006. "The Influence of Financial and Legal Institutions on Firm Size", *Journal of Banking and Finance* 30: 2995–3015.

Beck, Thorsten, and Ross Levine, 2002. "Industry Growth and Capital Allocation: Does Having a Market- or Bank-Based System Matter", *Journal of Financial Economics* 64: 147–180.

Beck, Thorsten, and Ross Levine, 2004. "Stock Markets, Banks, and Growth: Panel Evidence", *Journal of Banking and Finance* 28: 423–442.

Beck, Thorsten, and Ross Levine, 2005. "Legal Institutions and Financial Development", in Claude Menard and Mary M. Shirley (eds.), *Handbook of New Institutional Economics*. Dordrecht, Netherlands: Springer.

Becker, Gary S., 1968. "Crime and Punishment: An Economic Approach", *Journal of Political Economy* 76: 169–217.

Becker, Gary S., 1976. *The Economic Approach to Human Behavior.* Chicago: University of Chicago Press.

Becker, Gary, and Gregg Lewis, 1973. "On the Interaction between the Quantity and Quality of Children", *Journal of Political Economy* 81: 279–288.

Bell, Abraham, and Gideon Parchomovsky, 2005. "A Theory of Property", *Cornell Law Review* 90: 531–615.

Belloc, Marianna, and Ugo Pagano, 2009. "Co-evolution of Politics and Corporate Governance", *International Review of Law and Economics* 29: 106–114.

Bencivenga, Valerie R., Smith, Bruce D., and Ross M. Starr, 1996. "Equity Markets, Transactions Costs, and Capital Accumulation: An Illustration", *World Bank Economic Review* 10: 241–265.

Benjaminsen, Tor A., and Espen Sjaastad, 2002. "Race for the Prize: Land Transactions and Rent Appropriation in the Malian Cotton Zone", *European Journal of Development Research* 14: 129–152.

Benston, George J., 1973. "Required Disclosure and the Stock Market: An Evaluation of the Securities Exchange Act of 1934", *American Economic Review* 63: 132–155.

Beny, Laura Nyantung, 2005. "Does Insider Trading Law Matter? Some Preliminary Comparative Evidence", *American Law and Economics Review* 7: 144–183.

Beny, Laura Nyantung, 2007. "Insider Trading Laws and Stock Markets Around the World: An Empirical Contribution to the Theoretical Law and Economics Debate", *Journal of Corporation Law* 32: 237–300.

Beny, Laura Nyantung, 2008. "Do Investors in Controlled Firms Value Insider Trading Laws? International Evidence", *Journal of Law, Economics and Policy* 4: 267–310.

Berger, Philip G, and Eli Ofek, 1996. "Bustup Takeovers of Value-Destroying Diversified Firms", *Journal of Finance* 51: 1175–1200.

Bergsten, C. Fred, Freeman, Charles, Lardy, Nicholas R., and Derek J. Mitchell, 2008. *China's Rise: Challenges and Opportunities*. Washington, D.C.: The Center for Strategic and International Studies and the Peterson Institute for International Economics.

Berkes, Fikret, 1992. "Success and Failure in Marine Coastal Fisheries of Turkey", in Daniel W. Bromley (ed.), *Making the Commons Work: Theory, Practice, and Policy*. San Francisco, CA: ICS Press.

Berkowitz, Daniel, Pistor, Katharina, and Jean-Francois Richard, 2003. "Economic Development, Legality, and the Transplant Effect", *European Economic Review* 47: 165–195.

Berkowitz, Daniel, and Karen Clay, 2006. "The Effect of Judicial Independence on Courts: Evidence from the American States", *Journal of Legal Studies* 35: 399–440.

Berle, Adolf, and Gardiner Means, 1932. *The Modern Corporation and Private Property*. New Brunswick, N.J.: Transaction Publishers.

Bernstein, William J., 2004. *The Birth of Plenty: How the Prosperity of the Modern World Was Created*. New York: McGraw-Hill.

Berrah, Noureddine, Feng, Fei, Priddle, Roland, and Leiping Wang, 2007. *Sustainable Energy in China: The Closing Window of Opportunity*. Washington, D.C.: World Bank.

Berry, Sara, 1997. "Tomatoes, Land and Hearsay: Property and History in Asante in the Time of Structural Adjustment", *World Development* 25: 1225–1241.

Bertrand, Marianne and Sendhil Mullainathan, 1999. "Is There Discretion in Wage Setting? A Test Using Takeover Legislation", *Rand Journal of Economics* 30: 535–554.

Besley, Timothy, 1995. "Property Rights and Investment Incentives: Theory and Evidence from Ghana", *Journal of Political Economy* 103: 903–937.

Besley, Timothy, 1998. "Investment Incentives and Property Rights", in Peter Newman (ed.), *The New Palgrave Dictionary of Economics and the Law*, London: Macmillan Reference Ltd.

Bhagat, Sanjai, and Bernard Black, 2002. "The Non-Correlation Between Board Independence and Long-Term Firm Performance", *Journal of Corporate Law* 27: 231–273.

Bhagat, Sanjai, Bolton, Brian, and Roberta Romano, 2008. "The Promise and Peril of Corporate Governance Indices", *Columbia Law Review* 108: 1803–1882.

Bhattacharya, Utpal, and Hazem Daouk, 2002. "The World Price of Insider Trading", *Journal of Finance* 57: 75–108.

Black, Bernard S., 1990. "Shareholder Passivity Reexamined", *Michigan Law Review* 89: 520–608.

Black, Bernard S., 1992. "Agents Watching Agents: The Promise of Institutional Investor Voice", *UCLA Law Review* 39: 811–893.

Black, Bernard S., 2001. "The Legal and Institutional Preconditions for Strong Securities Markets", *UCLA Law Review* 48: 781–855.

Black, Bernard, Cheffins, Brian, and Michael Klausner, 2006. "Outside Director Liability", *Stanford Law Review* 58: 1055–1159.

Black, Bernard S., and John Coffee, 1994. "Hail Britannia? Institutional Investor Behavior under Limited Regulation", *Michigan Law Review* 92: 1997–2087.

Blair, Margaret M., and Lynn A. Stout, 1999. "A Team Production Theory of Corporate Law", *Virginia Law Review* 85: 247–328.

Blarel, Benoit, 1994. "Tenure Security and Agricultural Production under Land Scarcity: The Case of Rwanda", in John Bruce and Shem Migot-Adholla (eds.), *Searching for Land Tenure Security in Africa*. Dubuque, IA: Kendall/Hunt.

Blaug, Mark, 1992. *The Methodology of Economics: Or, How Economists explain*. Cambridge: Cambridge University Press.

Bloom, David E., and Jeffery Sachs, 1998. "Geography, Demography, and Economic Growth in Africa", *Brookings Papers on Economic Activity* 2: 207–295.

Bodie, Zvi, and Robert C Merton, 1999. *Finance*. Upper Saddle River, N.J.: Prentice-Hall.

Bordo, Michael D., and Peter L. Rousseau, 2006. "Legal-Political Factors and the Historical Evolution of the Finance-Growth Link", *European Review of Economic History* 10: 412–444.

Borokhovich, Kenneth A., Brunarski, Kelly R., and Robert Parrino, 1997. "CEO Contracting and Antitakeover Amendments", *Journal of Finance* 52: 1495–1517.

Borstadt, Lisa F., and Thomas J. Zwirlein, 1992. "The Efficient Monitoring Role of Proxy Contests: An Empirical Analysis of Post-Contest Control Changes and Firm Performance", *Financial Management* 21: 22–34.

Bosworth, Barry P., and Susan M. Collins, 2003. "The Empirics of Growth: An Update", *Brookings Papers on Economic Activity* 2: 113–206.

Botero, Juan C., Djankov, Simeon, La Porta, Rafael, Lopez-de-Silanes, Florencio, and Andrei Shleifer, 2004. "The Regulation of Labor", *Quarterly Journal of Economics* 119: 1339–1382.

Bottomley, Anthony, 1963. "The Effect of the Common Ownership of Land Upon Resource Allocation in TripoliTania", *Land Economics* 39: 91–95.

Bradley, Michael, Desai, Anand, and E. Han Kim, 1988. "Synergistic Gains from Corporate Acquisitions and Their Division between the Stockholders of Target and Acquiring Firms", *Journal of Financial Economics* 21: 3–40.

Braguinsky, Serguey, 1999. "Enforcement of Property Rights during the Russian Transition: Problems and Some Approaches to a New Liberal Solution", *Journal of Legal Studies* 28: 515–544.

Brasselle, Anne-Sophie, Gaspart, Frédéric, and Jean-Philippe Platteau, 2002. "Land Tenure Security and Investment Incentives: Puzzling Evidence from Burkina Faso", *Journal of Development Economics* 67: 373–418.

Bromley, Daniel W., and Jean-Paul Chavas, 1989. "On Risk, Transactions and Economic Development in the Semiarid Tropics", *Economic Development and Cultural Change* 37: 719–736.

Brunner, Christopher M., 2009. "Power and Purpose in the 'Anglo-American' Corporation", *Virginia Journal of International Law* 50: 579–653.

Burkart, Mike, 1999. "Economics of Takeover Regulation", *Working Paper*, Stockholm School of Economics.

Burns, Natasha, and Simi Kedia, 2006. "The Impact of Performance-based Compensation on Misreporting", *Journal of Financial Economics* 79: 35–67.

Bushee, Brian J., and Christian Leuz, 2005. "Economic Consequences of SEC Disclosure Regulation: Evidence from the OTC Bulletin Board", *Journal of Accounting and Economics* 39: 233–264.

Cai, Yongshun, 2003. "Collective Ownership or Cadres' Ownership? The Non-agricultural Use of Farmland in China", *The China Quarterly* 175: 662–680.

Calabresi, Guido, 1961. "Some Thoughts on Risk Distribution and the Law of Torts", *Yale Law Journal* 70: 499–553.

Callaghan, Helen, 2009. "Insiders, Outsiders, and the Politics of Corporate Governance: How Ownership Structure Shapes Party Positions in Britain, Germany, and France", *Comparative Political Studies* 42: 733–762.

Campbell, Gareth, and John D. Turner, 2011. "Substitutes for Legal Protection: Corporate Governance and Dividends in Victorian Britain", *Economic History Review* 64 (2): 571–597.

Cao, Guangzhong, Changchun Feng, and Ran Tao, 2008. "Local 'Land Finance' in China's Urban Expansion: Challenges and Solutions", *China & World Economy* 16 (2): 19–30.

Caprio, Gerard, Laeven, Luc, and Ross Levine, 2007. "Governance and Bank Valuation", *Journal of Financial Intermediation*16: 584–617.

Carlton, Dennis W., and Daniel R. Fischel, 1983. "The Regulation of Insider Trading", *Stanford Law Review* 35: 857–895.

Carter, Michael R., and Pedro Olinto, 2003. "Getting Institutions 'Right' for Whom? Credit Constraints and the Impact of Property Rights on the Quality and Composition of Investment", *American Journal of Agricultural Economics* 85: 173–186.

Cary, William, 1974. "Federalism and Corporate Law: Reflections upon Delaware", *Yale Law Journal* 83: 663–705.

Cavendish, William, 2000. "Empirical Regularities in the Poverty-Environment Relationship of Rural Households: Evidence from Zimbabwe", *World Development* 28: 1979–2003.

Ceglowski, Janet, and Stephen Golub, 2011. *Does China Still Have a Labor Cost Advantage?* CESifo Working Paper, No 3579. Munich: CESifo Group.

Chamon, Marcos D., and Eswar S. Prasad, 2010. "Why Are Saving Rates of Urban Households in China Rising", *American Economic Journal: Macroeconomics* 2 (1): 93–130.

Cheffins, Brian R., 2001. "Does Law Matter? The Separation of Ownership and Control in the United Kingdom", *Journal of Legal Studies* 30: 459–484.

Cheffins, Brian R., 2003. "Law as Bedrock: The Foundations of an Economy Dominated by Widely Held Public Companies", *Oxford Journal of Legal Studies* 23 (1): 1–23.

Cheffins, Brian R., 2008. *Corporate Ownership and Control: British Business Transformed.* New York: Oxford University Press.

Cheffins, Brian R., and Steven A. Bank, 2009. "Is Berle and Means Really a Myth?" *Business History Review* 83: 443–474.

Cheffins, Brian R., Bank, Steven A., and Harwell Wells, 2013. "Questioning 'Law and Finance': US Stock Market Development, 1930–70", *Business History* 55: 601–619.

Chen, Feng, 2007. "Individual Rights and Collective Rights: Labor's Predicament in China", *Communist and Post-Communist Studies* 40: 59–79.

Cheung, Steven N.S., 1970. "The Structure of a Contract and the Theory of a Non-Exclusive Resource", *Journal of Law and Economics* 13: 49–70.

Cheung, Steven N.S., 1987. "Common Property Rights", in John Eatwell, Murray Milgate, and Peter Newman (eds.), *The New Palgrave: A Dictionary of Economics*. London: Macmillan.

China Law and Governance Review, 2004. *Enforcement of Civil Judgments: Harder than Reaching the Sky*. www.chinareview.info/issue2/pages/legal.htm (accessed December 16, 2011).

Choi, Stephen, 2000. "Regulating Investors Not Issuers: A Market-Based Proposal", *California Law Review* 88: 279–334.

Choi, Stephen J., and Jill E. Fisch, 2003. "How to Fix Wall Street: A Voucher Financing Proposal for Securities Intermediaries", *Yale Law Journal* 113: 269–345.

Cioffi, John W., and Martin Hopner, 2006. "The Political Paradox of Finance Capitalism: Interests, Preferences, and Center-Left Party Politics in Corporate Governance Reform", *Politics and Society* 34: 463–502.

Clague, Christopher, Keefer, Philip, Knack, Stephen, and Mancur Olson, 1999. "Contract-Intensive Money: Contract Enforcement, Property Rights, and Economic Performance", *Journal of Economic Growth* 4: 185–211.

Clark, Gregory, 1996. "The Political Foundations of Modern Economic Growth: England, 1540–1800", *Journal of Interdisciplinary History* 26: 563–588.

Clark, Robert C., 1986. *Corporate Law*. Boston, MA: Little, Brown & Company.

Clarke, Donald, 1996. "Power and Politics in the Chinese Court System: The Enforcement of Civil Judgments", *Columbia Journal of Asian Law* 10 (1): 1–92.

Clarke, Donald, 2005. "How Do We Know When an Enterprise Exists? Unanswerable Questions and Legal Polycentricity in China", *Columbia Journal of Asian Law* 19 (1): 50–71.

Clarke, Donald, 2007. "Legislating for a Market Economy in China", *The China Quarterly* 191: 567–585.

Clarke, Donald, Peter Murrell, and Susan Whiting, 2008. "The Role of Law in China's Economic Development", in Loren Brandt and Thomas G. Rawski (eds.), *China's Great Economic Transformation*. Cambridge: Cambridge University Press.

Clay, Karen, 2006. "Squatters, Production, and Violence", Working Paper, Carnegie Mellon University.

Coase, Ronald H, 1937. "The Nature of the Firm", *Economica* 4: 386–405.

Coase, Ronald H. 1960. "The Problem of Social Cost", *Journal of Law and Economics* 3: 1–44.

Coase, Ronald H., 1993. "Coase on Posner on Coase", *Journal of Institutional and Theoretical Economics* 149: 96–98.

Coates, John C., IV, 2000. "Empirical Evidence on Structural Takeover Defenses: Where Do We Stand", *University of Miami Law Review* 54: 783–797.

Coffee, John C., Jr., 1984. "Market Failure and the Economic Case for a Mandatory Disclosure System", *Virginia Law Review* 70: 717–753.

Coffee, John C., Jr., 2001. "The Rise of Dispersed Ownership: The Roles of Law and the State in the Separation of Ownership and Control", *Yale Law Journal* 111: 1–82.

Coffee, John C., Jr., 2006. *Gatekeepers: The Professions and Corporate Governance.* Oxford: Oxford University Press.

Coffee, John C., Jr., 2007. "Law and Markets: The Impact of Enforcement", *University of Pennsylvania Law Review* 156: 229–311.

Coffee, John C., Jr., 2012. "Dispersed Ownership: The Theories, the Evidence, and the Enduring Tension between 'Lumpers' and 'Splitters'", in Dennis C. Mueller (ed.), *The Oxford Handbook of Capitalism.* New York: Oxford University Press.

Coffee, John C., Jr., and Hillary A. Sale, 2009. "Redesigning the SEC: Does the Treasury Have a Better Idea", *Virginia Law Review* 95: 707–783.

Cole, Daniel H., 2002. *Pollution and Property, Comparing Ownership Institutions for Environmental Protection.* Cambridge: Cambridge University Press.

Cole, Daniel H., and Peter Z., Grossman, 2002. "The Meaning of Property Rights: Law versus Economics", *Land Economics* 78: 317–330.

Comment, Robert, and G. William Schwert, 1995. "Poison or Placebo? Evidence on the Deterrence and Wealth Effects of Modern Antitakeover Measures", *Journal of Financial Economics* 39: 3–43.

Cools, Sofie, 2005. "The Real Difference in Corporate Law between the United States and Continental Europe: Distribution of Powers", *Delaware Journal of Corporate Law* 30: 697–766.

Core, John E., Guay, Wayne R., and David F. Larcker, 2003. "Executive Equity Compensation and Incentives: A Survey", *FRBNY Economic Policy Review* 9: 27–50.

Corne, Peter, 1996. *Foreign Investment in China: The Administrative Legal System.* Hong Kong: Hong Kong University Press.

Cox, James D., 1986. "Insider Trading and Contracting: A Critical Response to the 'Chicago School'", *Duke Law Journal* 1986: 628–659.

Crafts, Nicholas, 1999. "Implications of Financial Crisis for East Asian Trend Growth", *Oxford Review of Economic Policy* 15 (3): 110–130.

Cross, Frank B., 2002. "Law and Economic Growth", *Texas Law Review* 80: 1737–1775.

Cross, Frank B., 2011. "Tort Law and the American Economy", *Minnesota Law Review* 96: 28–89.

Cross, Frank B., and Robert A. Prentice, 2006. "The Economic Value of Securities Regulation", *Cardozo Law Review* 28: 333–389.

Cross, Frank B., and Robert A. Prentice, 2007. *Law and Corporate Finance.* Cheltenham, UK; Northampton, MA, USA: Edward Elgar.

Cusack, Thomas, Iversen, Torben, and David Soskice, 2007. "Economic Interests and the Origins of Electoral Systems", *American Political Science Review* 101: 373–391.

Cusack, Thomas, Iversen, Torben, and David Soskice, 2010. "Coevolution of Capitalism and Political Representation: The Choice of Electoral Systems", *American Political Science Review* 104: 393–403.

Dahya, Jay, Dimitrov, Orlin, and John J. McConnell, 2008. "Dominant Shareholders, Corporate Boards, and Corporate Value: A Cross-Country Analysis", *Journal of Financial Economics* 87: 73–100.

Dam, Kenneth W., 2006. *The Law-Growth Nexus: The Rule of Law and Economic Development*. Washington, D.C.: Brookings Institution Press.

Damaška, Mirjan R. 1986. *The Faces of Justices and State Authority: A Comparative Approach to the Legal Process*. New Haven and London: Yale University Press.

Daouk, Hazem, Lee, Charles M.C., and David Ng, 2006. "Capital Market Governance: How do Security Laws Affect Market Performance?" *Journal of Corporate Finance* 12: 560–593.

Davydenko, Sergei A., and Julian R. Franks, 2008. "Do Bankruptcy Codes Matter? A Study of Defaults in France, Germany, and the U.K.", *Journal of Finance* 63: 565–608.

De Alessi, Louis, 1980. "The Economics of Property Rights: A Review of the Evidence", *Research in Law and Economics* 2: 1–47.

de Soto Hernando, 2000. *The Mystery of Capital: Why Capitalism Triumphs in the West and Fails Everywhere Else*. New York: Basic Books.

De Vany, Arthur, and Nicolas Sanchez, 1979. "Land Tenure Structures and Fertility in Mexico", *Review of Economics and Statistics* 61: 67–72.

DeAngelo, Harry, and Linda DeAngelo, 1989. "Proxy Contests and the Governance of Publicly Held Corporations", *Journal of Financial Economics* 23: 29–59.

Deininger, Klaus, 2003. *Land Policies for Growth and Poverty Reduction*. Washington, D.C.: The World Bank.

Deininger, Klaus, and Hans Binswanger, 1999. "The Evolution of the World Bank's Land Policy: Principles, Experience, and Future Challenges", *World Bank Research Observer* 14: 247–276.

Deininger, Klaus, and Juan Sebastian Chamorro, 2004. "Investment and Equity Effects of Land Regularisation: The Case of Nicaragua", *Agricultural Economics* 30: 101–116.

Deininger, Klaus, and Gershon Feder, 2009. "Land Registration, Governance, and Development: Evidence and Implications for Policy", *World Bank Research Observer* 24: 233–266.

Deininger, Klaus, and Songqing Jin, 2006. "Tenure Security and Land-Related Investment: Evidence from Ethiopia", *European Economic Review* 50: 1245–1277.

Delong, J. Bradford, and Andrei Shleifer, 1989. "Princes and Merchants: European City Growth before the Industrial Revolution", *Journal of Law and Economics* 36: 671–702.

Demirgüç-Kunt, Asli, and Ross Levine, 2001. "Bank-Based and Market-Based Financial Systems: Cross-Country Comparisons", in Asli Demirgüç-Kunt and Ross Levine (eds.), *Financial Structure and Economic Growth: A Cross-Country Comparison of Banks, Markets and Development*. Cambridge, MA: MIT Press.

Demirgüç-Kunt, Asli, and Vojislav Maksimovic, 1998. "Law, Finance, and Firm Growth", *Journal of Finance* 53: 2107–37.

Demirgüç-Kunt, Asli, and Vojislav Maksimovic, 2002. "Funding Growth in Bank-Based and Market-Based Financial Systems: Evidence from Firm-Level Data", *Journal of Financial Economics* 65: 337–363.

Demsetz, Harold, 1967. "Toward a Theory of Property Rights", *American Economic Review* 57: 347–359.

Demsetz, Harold, 1996. "A Framework for the Study of Ownership", in George Yarrow and Piotr Jasinski (eds.), *Privatization: Critical Perspectives on the World Economy*, London: Routledge.

Demsetz, Harold, 1998. "Property Rights", in Peter Newman (ed.), *The New Palgrave Dictionary of Economics and Law*, London: Macmillan Reference LTD.

Demsetz, Harold, 2002. "Toward a Theory of Property Rights II: The Competition between Private and Collective Ownership", *Journal of Legal Studies* 31: S653–S672.

Denis, David J., Hanouna, Paul, and Atulya Sarin, 2006. "Is There a Dark Side to Incentive Compensation", *Journal of Corporate Finance* 12: 467–488.

Diamond, Jared, 1997. *Guns, Germs, and Steel: The Fates of Human Societies*. New York: W.W Norton & Company.

Diermeier, Daniel, Ericson, Joel M., Frye, Timothy, and Steven Lewis, 1997. "Credible Commitment and Property Rights: The Role of Strategic Interaction between Political and Economic Actors", in David L. Weimer (ed.), *The Political Economy of Property Rights: Institutional Change and Credibility in the Reform of Centrally Planned Economies*. New York: Cambridge University Press.

Ding, Chengri, 2007. "Policy and Praxis of Land Acquisition in China", *Land Use Policy* 24: 1–13.

Djankov, Simeon, Glaeser, Edward, La Porta, Rafael, Lopez-de-Silanes, Florencio, and Andrei Shleifer, 2003. "The New Comparative Economics", *Journal of Comparative Economics* 31: 595–619.

Djankov, Simeon, La Porta, Rafael, Lopez-de-Silanes, Florencio, and Andrei Shleifer, 2002. "The Regulation of Entry", *Quarterly Journal of Economics* 117: 1–37.

Djankov, Simeon, La Porta, Rafael, Lopez-de-Silanes, Florencio, and Andrei Shleifer, 2003. "Courts", *Quarterly Journal of economics* 118: 453–517.

Djankov, Simeon, La Porta, Rafael, Lopez-de-Silanes, Florencio, and Andrei Shleifer, 2008. "The Law and Economics of Self-Dealing", *Journal of Financial Economics* 88: 430–465.

Djankov, Simeon, McLiesh, Caralee, and Andrei Shleifer, 2007. "Private Credit in 129 Countries", *Journal of Financial Economics* 84: 209–329.

Do, Quy-Toan, and Lakshmi Iyer, 2003. "Land Rights and Economic Development: Evidence from Vietnam", *World Bank Policy Research Working Paper* No. 3120.

Dodd, Peter, and Jerold B. Warner, 1983. "On Corporate Governance: A Study of Proxy Contests", *Journal of Financial Economics* 11: 401–438.

Doidge, Craig, Karolyi, G. Andrew, and Rene M. Stulz, 2007. "Why Do Countries Matter So Much for Corporate Governance", *Journal of Financial Economics* 86: 1–39.

Dollar, David, 1992. "Outward-Oriented Developing Economies Really Do Grow More Rapidly: Evidence from 95 LDCs, 1976–85", *Economic Development and Cultural Change* 40 (3): 523–544.

Dollar, David, 2007. "Poverty, Inequality and Social Disparities during China's Economic Reform", World Bank Policy Research Working Paper 4253.

Domar, Evsey D., 1946. "Capital Expansion, Rate of Growth and Employment", *Econometrica* 14: 137–147.

Dowall, David E., and Michael Leaf, 1991. "The Price of Land for Housing in Jakarta", *Urban Studies* 28: 707–722.

Durham, J. Benson, 1999. "Economic Growth and Political Regimes", *Journal of Economic Growth* 4: 81–111.

Durnev, Art, and E. Han Kim, 2005. "To Steal or Not to Steal: Firm Attributes, Legal Environment, and Valuation", *Journal of Finance* 60: 1461–1493.

Dyck, Alexander, Morse, Adair, and Luigi Zingales, 2010. "Who Blows the Whistle on Corporate Fraud", *Journal of Finance* 65: 2213–2253.

Dyck, Alexander, and Luigi Zingales, 2004. "Private Benefits of Control: An International Comparison", *Journal of Finance* 59: 537–600.

Easterbrook, Frank H., and Daniel R. Fischel, 1983. "Voting in Corporate Law", *Journal of Law and Economics* 26: 395–427.

Easterbrook, Frank H., and Daniel R. Fischel, 1984. "Mandatory Disclosure and the Protection of Investors", *Virginia Law Review* 70: 669–715.

Easterbrook, Frank H., and Daniel R. Fischel, 1989. "The Corporate Contract", *Columbia Law Review* 89: 1416–1448.

Easterbrook, Frank H., and Daniel R. Fischel, 1991. *The Economic Structure of Corporate Law.* Cambridge, MA: Harvard University Press.

Easterly, William, 2002. *The Elusive Quest for Growth: Economist's Adventures and Misadventures in the Tropics.* Cambridge, MA: MIT Press.

Easterly, William, 2006. *The White Man's Burden: Why the West's Efforts to Aid the Rest Have Done So Much Ill and So Little Good.* New York: The Penguin Press.

Edwards, Sebastian, 1993. "Openness, Trade Liberalization, and Growth in Developing Countries", *Journal of Economic Literature* 31: 1358–1393.

Eggertsson, Thrainn, 1990. *Economic Behavior and Institutions.* Cambridge: Cambridge University Press.

Eggertsson, Thrainn, 2003. "Open Access versus Common Property", in Terry L. Anderson and Fred S. McChesney (eds.), *Property Rights: Cooperation, Conflict, and Law.* Princeton, NJ: Princeton University Press.

Eizenstat, Stuart E., Porter, John Edwards, and Jeremy M. Weinstein, 2005. "Rebuilding Weak State", *Foreign Affairs* 84: 134–146.

Elisofon, Howard R., 2008. "Crossing Our Borders: Insider Trading, A Global Perspective", *Securities Regulation & Law Report* 40 (23): 897–900.

Ellickson, Robert C., 1991. *Order without Law: How Neighbors Settle Disputes.* Cambridge, MA: Harvard University Press.

Ellickson, Robert C., 1993. "Property in Land", *Yale Law Journal* 102: 1315–1400.

Engerman, Stanley L., and Kenneth L. Sokoloff, 1997. "Factor Endowments, Institutions, and Differential Paths of Growth among New World Economies", in Stephen Haber (ed.), *How Latin America Fell Behind.* Stanford: Stanford University Press.

Enriques, Luca, Hansmann, Henry, and Reinier Kraakman, 2009. "The Basic Governance Structure: The Interests of Shareholders as a Class", in Reinier Kraakman et al., *The Anatomy of Corporate Law: A Comparative and Functional Approach (Second Edition).* New York: Oxford University Press.

Faccio, Mara, 2006. "Politically Connected Firms", *American Economic Review* 96 (1): 369–386.

Fama, Eugene F., 1980. "Agency Problems and the Theory of the Firm", *Journal of Political Economy* 88: 288–307.

Fama, Eugene F., and Michael C. Jensen, 1983. "Separation of Ownership and Control", *Journal of Law and Economics* 26: 301–325.

Faysse, Nicolas, 2005. "Coping with the Tragedy of the Commons: Game Structure and Design of Rules", *Journal of Economic Surveys* 19 (2): 239–261.

Feder, Gershon, and David Feeny, 1991. "Land Tenure and Property Rights: Theory and Implications for Development Policy", *World Bank Economic Review* 5: 135–153.

Feder, Gershon, and Akihiko Nishio, 1999. "The Benefits of Land Registration and Titling: Economic and Social Perspectives", *Land Use Policy* 15 (1): 25–43.

Feder, Gershon, and Tongroj Onchan, 1987. "Land Ownership Security and Farm Investment in Thailand", *American Journal of Agricultural Economics* 69: 311–320.

Fernandes, Nuno, and Miguel A. Ferreira, 2009. "Insider Trading Laws and Stock Price Informativeness", *Review of Financial Studies* 22 (5): 1845–1887.

Ferran, Eilis, 2003. "Examining the United Kingdom's Experience in Adopting the Single Financial Regulator Model". *Brooklyn Journal of International Law* 28: 258–307.

Ferrell, Allen, 2007a. "The Case for Mandatory Disclosure in Securities Regulation Around the World", *Brooklyn Journal of Corporate, Financial & Commercial Law* 2: 81–132.

Ferrell, Allen, 2007b. "Mandatory Disclosure and Stock Returns: Evidence from the Over-the-Counter Market", *Journal of Legal Studies* 36: 213–251.

Field, Erica, 2005. "Property Rights and Investment in Urban Slums", *Journal of the European Economic Association* 3 (2–3): 279–290.

Field, Erica, 2007. "Entitled to Work: Urban Property Rights and Labor Supply in Peru", *Quarterly Journal of Economics* 122: 1561–1602.

Field, Erica, and Maximo Torero, 2004. "Do Property Titles Increase Credit Access Among the Urban Poor? Evidence from a Nationwide Titling Program", *Working Paper*, Harvard University.

Fisch, Jill E., 2000. "The Peculiar Role of the Delaware Courts in the Competition for Corporate Charters", *University of Cincinnati Law Review* 68: 1061–1100.

Fisch, Jill E., 2006. "Measuring Efficiency in Corporate Law: The Role of Shareholder Primacy", *Journal of Corporation Law* 31: 637–674.

Fisman, Raymond, and Inessa Love, 2007. "Financial Dependence and Growth Revisited", *Journal of the European Economic Association* 5: 470–479.

Fitzpatrick, Daniel, 2006. "Evolution and Chaos in Property Rights Systems: The Third World Tragedy of Contested Access", *Yale Law Journal* 115: 996–1048.

Fleisher, Belton M., and Dennis Tao Yang, 2006. "Problems of China's Rural Labor Markets and Rural-Urban Migration", *Chinese Economy* 39 (3): 6–25.

Fox, Merritt, 1999. "Retaining Mandatory Securities Disclosure: Why Issuer Choice is Not Investor Empowerment?" *Virginia Law Review* 85: 1335–1419.

Franco, Joseph A., 2002. "Why Antifraud Prohibitions are Not Enough: The Significance of Opportunism, Candor and Signaling in the Economic Case for Mandatory Securities Disclosure", *Columbia Business Law Review* 2002: 223–362.

Frankel, Richard M., Johnson, Marilyn F., and Karen K. Nelson, 2002. "The Relation between Auditors' Fees for Nonaudit Services and Earnings Management", *Accounting Review* (Supplement) 77: 71–105.

Frankel, Tamar, 1998. "Fiduciary Duties", in Peter Newman (ed.), *The New Palgrave Dictionary of Economics and the Law*, London: Macmillan Reference LTD.

Franks, Julian, Mayer, Colin, and Stefano Rossi, 2009. "Ownership: Evolution and Regulation", *Review of Financial Studies* 22 (10): 4009–4056.

Fred-Mensah, Ben K., 1999. "Capturing Ambiguities: Communal Conflict Management Alternative in Ghana", *World Development* 27: 951–965.

Frey, Bruno S., and Alois Stutzer, 2001. *Happiness and Economics: How the Economy and Institutions Affect Human Well-Being*. Princeton, NJ: Princeton University Press.

Friedman, David D., 2001. *Law's Order: What Economics Has to Do with Law and Why It Matters*. Princeton, NJ: Princeton University Press.

Friedman, Milton, 1953. "The Methodology of Positive Economics", in *Essays in Positive Economics*. Chicago: University of Chicago Press.

Frye, Timothy, and Ekaterina Zhuravskaya, 2000. "Rackets, Regulation, and the Rule of Law", *Journal of Law, Economics and Organization* 16: 478–502.

Fukuyama, Francis, 1995. *Trust: The Social Virtues and the Creation of Prosperity*. New York: Free Press.

Fukuyama, Francis, 2004. *State-Building: Governance and World Order in the 21st Century*. Ithaca: Cornell University Press.

Furubotn, Eirik G., and Svetozar Pejovich, 1972. "Property Rights and Economic Theory: A Survey of Recent Literature", *Journal of Economic Literature* 10: 1137–1162.

Gadinis, Stavros, and Howell E. Jackson, 2007. "Markets as Regulators: A Survey", *Southern California Law Review* 80: 1239–1382.

Galiani, Sebastian, and Ernesto Schargrodsky, 2006. "Property Rights for the Poor: Effects of Land Titling", *Working Paper*, Universidad Torcuato Di Tella.

Gallagher, Mary E., 2004. "'Time is Money, Efficiency is Life': The Transformation of Labor Relations in China", *Studies in Comparative International Development* 39 (2): 11–44.

Gambetta, Diego, 1993. *The Sicilian Mafia: the Business of Private Protection*. Cambridge, MA: Harvard University Press.

Gavian, Sarah, and Marcel Fafchamps, 1996. "Land Tenure and Allocative Efficiency in Niger", *American Journal of Agricultural Economics* 78: 460–471.

Gechlik, Mei Ying, 2005. "Judicial Reforms in China: Lessons from Shanghai", *Columbia Journal of Asian Law* 19 (1): 97–137.

Gehlbach, Scott, and Philip Keefer, 2011. "Investment Without Democracy: Ruling-party Institutionalization and Credible Commitment in Autocracies", *Journal of Comparative Economics* 39: 123–139.

Gelter, Martin, 2009. "The Dark Side of Shareholder Influence: Managerial Autonomy and Stakeholder Orientation in Comparative Corporate Governance", *Harvard International Law Journal* 50: 129–194.

Geng, Nan, and Papa N'Diaye, 2012. *Determinants of Corporate Investment in China: Evidence from Cross-Country Firm Level Data*. IMF Working Paper, WP/12/80. Washington, D.C.: International Monetary Fund.

Giannetti, Mariassunta, 2003. "Do Better Institutions Mitigate Agency Problems? Evidence from Corporate Finance Choices", *Journal of Financial and Quantitative Analysis* 38: 185–213.

Glaeser, Edward L., La Porta, Rafael, Lopez-de-Silanes, Florencio, and Andrei, Shleifer, 2004. "Do Institutions Cause Growth", *Journal of Economic Growth* 9: 271–303.

Glaeser, Edward, Scheinkman, Jose, and Andrei Shleifer, 2003. "The Injustice of Inequality", *Journal of Monetary Economics* 50: 199–222.

Glaeser, Edward, and Andrei Shleifer, 2002. "Legal Origins", *Quarterly Journal of Economics* 117: 1193–1230.

Glaeser, Edward, and Andrei Shleifer, 2003. "The Rise of the Regulatory State", *Journal of Economic Literature* 41: 401–425.

Goldsmith, Raymond W., 1969 *Financial Structure and Development*. New Haven, CT: Yale University Press.

Gompers, Paul, Ishii, Joy, and Andrew Metrick, 2003. "Corporate Governance and Equity Prices", *Quarterly Journal of Economics* 118: 107–155.

Gompers, Paul A., Ishii, Joy, and Andrew Metrick, 2010. "Extreme Governance: An Analysis of Dual-Class Firms in the United States", *Review of Financial Studies* 23 (3): 1051–1088.

Goshen, Zohar, and Gideon Parchomovsky, 2006. "The Essential Role of Securities Regulation", *Duke Law Journal* 55: 711–782.

Gourevitch, Peter A., 2003. "The Politics of Corporate Governance", *Yale Law Journal* 112: 1829–1880.

Gourevitch, Peter A., and James Shinn, 2005. *Political Power and Corporate Control: The New Global Politics of Corporate Governance*. Princeton, NJ: Princeton University Press.

Gradstein, Mark, 2007. "Inequality, Democracy and the Protection of Property Rights", *Economic Journal* 117: 252–269.

Graff, Michael, 2005. "Socio-Economic Factors and the Finance-Growth Nexus", *European Journal of Finance* 11 (3): 183–205.

Grafton, R. Quentin, Squires, Dale, and Kevin J. Fox, 2000. "Private Property and Economic Efficiency: A Study of a Common-Pool Resource", *Journal of Law and Economics* 43: 679–713.

Gray, Leslie C., and Michael Kevane, 2001. "Evolving Tenure Rights and Agricultural Intensification in Southwestern Burkina Faso", *World Development* 29: 573–587.

Greenstone, Michael, Oyer, Paul, and Annette Vissing-Jorgensen, 2006. "Mandated Disclosure, Stock Returns, and the 1964 Securities Act Amendments", *Quarterly Journal of Economics* 121: 399–460.

Greenwood, Jeremy, and Bruce D. Smith, 1997. "Financial Markets in Development, and the Development of Financial Markets", *Journal of Economic Dynamics and Control* 21: 145–181.

Greif, Avner, 1993. "Contract Enforceability and Economic Institutions in Early Trade: the Maghribi Trader's Coalition", *American Economic Review* 83: 525–548.

Greif, Avner, 1994. "Cultural Beliefs and the Organization of Society: A Historical Theoretical Reflection on Collectivist and Individualist Societies", *Journal of Political Economy* 102: 912–950.

Grossman, Herschel, I., and Minseong Kim, 1995. "Swords or Plowshares? A Theory of the Security of Claims to Property", *Journal of Political Economy* 103: 1275–1288.

Grossman, Stanford J., and Joseph E. Stiglitz, 1980. "On the Impossibility of Informationally Efficient Markets", *American Economic Review* 70: 393–408.

Guiso, Luigi, Sapienza, Paola, and Luigi Zingales, 2003. "People's Opium? Religion and Economic Attitudes", *Journal of Monetary Economics* 50: 225–282.

Guiso, Luigi, Sapienza, Paola, and Luigi Zingales, 2006. "Does Culture Affect Economic Outcomes", *Journal of Economic Perspectives* 20 (2): 23–48.

Haber, Stephen H., 1991. "Industrial Concentration and the Capital Markets: A Comparative Study of Brazil, Mexico, and the United States, 1830–1930", *Journal of Economic History* 51: 559–580.

Haber, Stephen, Maurer, Noel, and Armando Razo, 2003. "When the Law Does Not Matter: The Rise and Decline of the Mexican Oil Industry", *Journal of Economic History* 63: 1–32.

Haggard, Stephan, 1999. "Governance and Growth: Lessons from the Asian Economic Crisis", *Asian Pacific Economic Literature* 13: 30–42.

Hall, Peter A., and Daniel W. Gingerich, 2009. "Varieties of Capitalism and Institutional Complementarities in the Political Economy: An Empirical Analysis", *British Journal of Political Science* 39: 449–482.

Hall, Peter A., and David Soskice, 2001. *Varieties of Capitalism: The Institutional Foundations of Comparative Advantage*. New York: Oxford University Press.

Hall, Robert E., and Charles I. Jones, 1999. "Why Do Some Countries Produce So Much More Output Per Works than Others", *Quarterly Journal of Economics* 114: 83–116.

Hamermesh, Lawrence A., 2006. "The Policy Foundations of Delaware Corporate Law", *Columbia Law Review* 106: 1749–1792.

Hanstad, Tim, 1998. "Designing Land Registration Systems for Developing Countries", *American University International Law Review* 13: 647–703.

Hardin, Garrett, 1968. "The Tragedy of the Commons", *Science* 162: 1243–1248.

Harney, Alexandra, 2009. *The China Price: The True Cost of Chinese Competitive Advantage*. New York: Penguin Press.

Harrod, Roy, 1939. "An Essay in Dynamic Theory", *Economic Journal* 49: 14–33.

Hart, Oliver, Shleifer, Andrei, and Robert Vishny, 1997. "The Proper Scope of Government: Theory and an Application to Prisons", *Quarterly Journal of Economics*112: 1127–1161.

Haselmann, Rainer, Pistor, Katharina, and Vikrant Vig, 2009. "How Law Affects Lending", *Review of Financial Studies* 23: 549–580.

Hausman, Daniel M., and Michael S. McPherson, 2006. *Economic Analysis, Moral Philosophy, and Public Policy*. New York: Cambridge University Press.

Hayami, Yujiro, and Yoshihisa Godo, 2005. *Development Economics: From the Poverty to the Wealth of Nations*. New York: Oxford University Press.

Hayek, Friedrich A., 1945. "The Use of Knowledge in Society", *American Economic Review* 35: 519–530.

He, Jianwu, and Louis Kuijs, 2007. *Rebalancing China's Economy-Modeling a Policy Package*. World Bank China Research Paper, No.7. Beijing: World Bank Beijing Office.

He, Xin, 2009. "Enforcing Commercial Judgments in the Pearl River Delta of China", *American Journal of Comparative Law* 57: 419–456.

Heller, Michael A., 1998. "The Tragedy of the Anticommons: Property in the Transition from Marx to Markets", *Harvard Law Review* 111: 621–688.

Heller, Michael A., 1999. "The Boundaries of Private Property", *Yale Law Journal* 108: 1163–1223.

Heller, Michael A., 2008. *The Gridlock Economy: How Too Much Ownership Wrecks Markets, Stops Innovation, and Costs Lives*. New York: Basic Books.

Hellman, Joel S., Jones, Geraint, and Daniel Kaufmann, 2003. "Seize the State, Seize the Day: State Capture and Influence in Transition Economies", *Journal of Comparative Economics* 31: 751–773.

Helpman, Elhanan, 2004, *The Mystery of Economic Growth*. Cambridge, MA: Harvard University Press.

Heltberg, Rasmus, 2001. "Determinants and Impact of Local Institutions for Common Resource Management", *Environmental and Development Economics* 6: 183–208.

Heltberg, Rasmus, 2002. "Property Rights and Natural Resource Management in Developing Countries", *Journal of Economic Surveys* 16 (2): 189–214.

Hermalin, Benjamin E., and Michael S. Weisbach, 1991. "The Effects of Board Composition and Direct Incentives on Firm Performance", *Financial Management* 20: 101–112.

Hermalin, Benjamin E., and Michael S. Weisbach, 2003. "Boards of Directors as an Endogenously Determined Institution: A Survey of the Economic Literature", *FRBNY Economic Policy Review* 9 (April): 7–26.

Hertig, Gerard, Kraakman, Reinier, and Edward Rock, 2004. "Issuers and Investor Protection", in Reinier Kraakman et al. (eds.), *The Anatomy of Corporate Law: A Comparative and Functional Approach*. New York: Oxford University Press.

Hertig, Gerard, Kraakman, Reinier, and Edward Rock, 2009. "Issuers and Investor Protection", in Reinier Kraakman et al. (eds.), *The Anatomy of Corporate Law: A Comparative and Functional Approach (Second Edition)*. New York: Oxford University Press.

Hicks, John, 1969. *A Theory of Economic History*. New York: Oxford University Press.

Hilt, Eric, 2008. "When Did Ownership Separate from Control? Corporate Governance in the Early Nineteenth Century", *Journal of Economic History* 68 (3): 645–685.

Ho, Peter, 2005. *Institutions in Transition: Land Ownership, Property Rights, and Social Conflict in China*. New York: Oxford University Press.

Ho, Virginia E. Harper, 2009. "From Contracts to Compliance? An Early Look at Implementation under China's New Labor Legislation", *Columbia Journal of Asian Law* 23: 35–107.

Holmstrom, Bengt, and Steven N. Kaplan, 2001. "Corporate Governance and Merger Activity in the United States: Making Sense of the 1980s and 1990s", *Journal of Economic Perspectives* 15: 121–144.

Holmstrom, Bengt, and Jean Tirole, 1993. "Market Liquidity and Performance Monitoring", *Journal of Political Economy* 101: 678–709.

Honohan, Patrick, 2004. "Financial Development, Growth, and Poverty: How Close are the Links", *World Bank Policy Research Working Paper* 3203.

Huang, Philip C.C., 2011. "The Theoretical and Practical Implications of China's Development Experience: The Role of Informal Economic Practices", *Modern China* 37 (1): 3–43.

Huang, Yasheng, 2010. *Urbanization, Hukou System and Government Land Ownership: Effects on Rural Migrant Workers and on Rural and Urban Hukou Residents.* (Background Paper for the Global Development Outlook 2010). www.oecd.org/dataoecd/30/13/44772487.pdf (accessed July 4, 2012).

Huang, Yiping, 2010. "China's Great Ascendancy and Structural Risks: Consequences of Asymmetric Market Liberalization", *Asian-Pacific Economic Literature* 24 (1): 65–85.

Huang, Yiping, and Kunyu Tao, 2010. "Factor Market Distortion and the Current Account Surplus in China", *Asian Economic Papers* 9 (3): 1–36.

Hung, Veron Mei-Ying, 2004. "China's WTO Commitment on Independent Judicial Review: Impact on Legal and Political Reform", *American Journal of Comparative Law* 52: 77–132.

Iversen, Torben, and David Soskice, 2009. "Distribution and Redistribution: The Shadow of the Nineteenth Century", *World Politics* 61: 438–486.

Jackson, Howell E., 2007. "Variation in the Intensity of Financial Regulation: Preliminary Evidence and Potential Implications", *Yale Journal on Regulation* 24: 253–291.

Jackson, Howell E., and Mark J. Roe, 2009. "Public and Private Enforcement of Securities Laws: Resource-Based Evidence", *Journal of Financial Economics* 93: 207–238.

Jacoby, Hanan G., Li, Guo, and Scott Rozelle, 2002. "Hazards of Expropriation: Tenure Insecurity and Investment in Rural China", *American Economic Review* 92: 1420–1447.

Jacoby, Hanan G., and Bart Minten, 2007. "Is Land Titling in Sub-Saharan Africa Cost-Effective? Evidence from Madagascar", *World Bank Economic Review* 21: 461–485.

Jancyzk, Joseph T., 1977. "An Economic Analysis of the Land Title Systems for Transferring Real Property", *Journal of Legal Studies* 6: 213–233.

Jarrell, Gregg A., Brickley, James A., and Jeffry M. Netter, 1988. "The Market for Corporate Control: The Empirical Evidence since 1980", *Journal of Economic Perspectives* 2: 49–68.

Jensen, Michael C., 1986. "The Takeover Controversy: Analysis and Evidence", *Midland Corporate Finance Journal* 4: 6–32.

Jensen, Michael C., 1993. "The Modern Industrial Revolution, Exit, and the Failure of Internal Control Systems", *Journal of Finance* 48: 831–880.

Jensen, Michael, and William Meckling, 1976. "Theory of the Firm: Managerial Behavior, Agency Costs, and Capital Structure", *Journal of Financial Economics* 3: 305–360.

Jensen, Michael, and Richard S. Ruback, 1983. "The Market for Corporate Control: The Scientific Evidence", *Journal of Financial Economics* 11: 5–50.

Jimenez, Emmanuel, 1984. "Tenure Security and Urban Squatting", *Review of Economics and Statistics* 66: 556–567.

Jodha, N.S., 1992. "Common Property Resources: A Missing Dimension of Development Strategies", *World Bank Discussion Paper*, No. 169.

Johnson, Omotunde E.G., 1972. "Economic Analysis, the Legal Framework and Land Tenure Systems", *Journal of Law and Economics* 15: 259–276.

Johnson, Shane A., Ryan, Harley E. Jr., and Yisong S. Tian, 2009. "Managerial Incentives and Corporate Fraud: The Sources of Incentives Matter", *Review of Finance* 13: 115–145.

Johnson, Simon, La Porta, Rafael, Lopez-de-Silanes, Florencio, and Andrei Shleifer, 2000. "Tunneling", *American Economic Review* 90 (2): 22–27.

Jolls, Christine, Sunstein, Cass R., and Richard Thaler, 1998. "A Behavioral Approach to Law and Economics", *Stanford Law Review* 50: 1471–1550.

Jones, Charles I., 1998. *Introduction to Economic Growth*. New York: W.W. Norton & Company.

Jones, Eric L., 1981. *The European Miracle: Environments, Economies, and Geopolitics in the History of Europe and Asia*. Cambridge: Cambridge University Press.

Kahan, Marcel, 1997. "Some Problems with Stock Exchange-Based Securities Regulation", *Virginia Law Review* 83: 1509–1519.

Kaplow, Louis, and Steven Shavell, 2002. *Fairness Versus Welfare*. Cambridge, MA: Harvard University Press.

Karpoff, Jonathan M., Lee, D. Scott, and Gerald S. Martin, 2008a. "The Consequences to Managers for Financial Misrepresentation", *Journal of Financial Economics* 88: 193–215.

Karpoff, Jonathan M., Lee, D. Scott, and Gerald S. Martin, 2008b. "The Cost to Firms of Cooking the Books", *Journal of Financial and Quantitative Analysis* 43: 581–611.

Kim, Annette M., 2004. "A Market without the 'Right' Property Rights: Ho Chi Minh City, Vietnam's Newly-Emerged Private Real Estate Market", *Economics of Transition* 12 (2): 275–305.

Kim, Jong-Il, and Lawrence J. Lau, 1994. "The Sources of Economic Growth of the East Asian Newly Industrialized Countries", *Journal of the Japanese and International Economies* 8: 235–271.

Kim, Jong-Il, and Lawrence J. Lau, 1995. "The Role of Human Capital in the Economic Growth of the East Asian Newly Industrialized Countries", *Asia-Pacific Economic Review* 1 (3): 3–22.

Kim, Jong-Il, and Lawrence J. Lau, 1996. "The Sources of Asian Pacific Economic Growth", *Canadian Journal of Economics* 29: S448-S454.

King, Robert G., and Charles Plosser, 1986. "Money as the Mechanism of Exchange", *Journal of Monetary Economics* 17: 93–115.

Kini, Omesh, Kracaw, William, and Shehzad Mian, 2004. "The Nature of Discipline by Corporate Takeovers", *Journal of Finance* 59: 1511–1552.

Klapper, Leora F., and Inessa Love, 2004. "Corporate Governance, Investor Protection, and Performance in Emerging Markets", *Journal of Corporate Finance* 10: 703–728.

Klerman, Daniel M., and Paul G. Mahoney, 2005. "The Value of Judicial Independence: Evidence from Eighteenth Century England", *American Law and Economics Review* 7: 1–27.

Klerman, Daniel, and Paul G. Mahoney, 2007. "Legal Origins?" *Journal of Comparative Economics* 35: 278–293.

Klenow, Peter J., and Andrés Rodríguez-Clare, 1997. "The Neoclassical Revival in Growth Economics: Has It Gone Too Far?" In Ben S. Bernanke and Julio J. Rotemberg (eds.), *NBER Macroeconomics Annual 1997*. Cambridge, MA: MIT Press.

Knack, Stephen, and Philip Keefer, 1995. "Institutions and Economic Performance: Cross-Country Tests Using Alternative Institutional Measures", *Economics and Politics* 7: 207–227.

Knack, Stephen, and Philip Keefer, 1997. "Does Social Capital Have an Economic Payoff? A Cross Country Investigation", *Quarterly Journal of Economics* 112: 1251–1288.

Knight, John, and Lina Song, 1999. "Employment Constraints and Sub-Optimality in Chinese Enterprises", *Oxford Economic Papers* 51: 284–299.

Korobkin, Russell B., and Thomas S. Ulen, 2000. "Law and Behavioral Science: Removing the Rationality Assumption from Law and Economics", *California Law Review* 88: 1051–1144.

Kraakman, Reinier, 1991. "The Legal Theory of Insider Trading Regulation in the United States", in Klaus J. Hopt and Eddy Wymeersch (eds.), *European Insider Dealing: Law and Practice*. London: Butterworths.

Kronman, Anthony T., 1995. "The Second Driker Forum for Excellence in the Law", *Wayne Law Review* 42: 115–160.

Kuijs, Louis, and Tao Wang, 2006. "China's Pattern of Growth: Moving to Sustainability and Reducing Inequality", *China and World Economy* 14 (1): 1–14.

Kung, James K.S., 1995. "Equal Entitlement versus Tenure Security under a Regime of Collective Property Rights: Peasants' Preference for Institutions in Post-Reform Chinese Agriculture", *Journal of Comparative Economics* 21: 82–111.

Kuznets, Simon, 1966. *Modern Economic Growth*. New Haven: Yale University Press.

La Porta, Rafael, Lopez-de-Silanes, Florencio, Pop-Eleches, Cristian, and Andrei Shleifer, 2004. "Judicial Checks and Balances", *Journal of Political Economy* 112: 445–470.

La Porta, Rafael, Lopez-de-Silanes, Florencio, and Andrei Shleifer, 1999. "Corporate Ownership Around the World", *Journal of Finance* 54: 471–517.

La Porta, Rafael, Lopez-de-Silanes, Florencio, and Andrei Shleifer, 2002. "Government Ownership of Banks", *Journal of Finance* 57: 265–301.

La Porta, Rafael, Lopez-de-Silanes, Florencio, and Andrei Shleifer, 2006. "What Works in Securities Law", *Journal of Finance* 61: 1–31.

La Porta, Rafael, Lopez-de-Silanes, Florencio, and Andrei Shleifer, 2008. "The Economic Consequences of Legal Origins", *Journal of Economic Literature* 46 (2): 285–332.

La Porta, Rafael, Lopez-de-Silanes, Florencio, Shleifer, Andrei, and Robert Vishny, 1997. "Legal Determinants of External Finance", *Journal of Finance* 52: 1131–1150.

La Porta, Rafael, Lopez-de-Silanes, Florencio, Shleifer, Andrei, and Robert Vishny, 1998. "Law and Finance", *Journal of Political Economy* 106: 1113–1155.

La Porta, Rafael, Lopez-de-Silanes, Florencio, Shleifer, Andrei, and Robert Vishny, 1999. "The Quality of Government", *Journal of Law, Economics, and Organization* 15: 222–279.

La Porta, Rafael, Lopez-de-Silanes, Florencio, Shleifer, Andrei, and Robert Vishny, 2000. "Agency Problem and Dividend Policies around the World", *Journal of Finance* 55: 1–33.

La Porta, Rafael, Lopez-de-Silanes, Florencio, Shleifer, Andrei, and Robert Vishny, 2002. "Investor Protection and Corporate Valuation", *Journal of Finance* 57: 1147–1170.

Lakatos, Imre, 1970. "Falsification and the Methodology of Scientific Research Programs", in Imre Lakatos and Alan Musgrave (eds.), *Criticism and the Growth of Knowledge*. Cambridge: Cambridge University Press.

Lamoreaux, Naomi R., and Jean-Laurent Rosenthal, 2005. "Legal Regime and Contractual Flexibility: A Comparison of Business's Organizational Choices in France and the United States during the Era of Industrialization", *American Law and Economics Review* 7 (1): 28–61.

Landau, David H., 1987. "SEC Proposals to Facilitate Multinational Securities Offerings: Disclosure Requirements in the United States and the United Kingdom", *N.Y.U. Journal of International Law and Politics* 19: 457–478.

Landes, David S., 1998. *The Wealth and Poverty of Nations: Why Some Are So Rich and Some Are So Poor*. New York: W.W. Norton & Company.

Lange, Oscar, 1936. "On the Economic Theory of Socialism: Part One", *Review of Economic Studies* 4: 53–71.

Lange, Oscar, 1937. "On the Economic Theory of Socialism: Part Two", *Review of Economic Studies* 4: 123–142.

Langevoort, Donald C., 2009. "The SEC, Retail Investors, and the Institutionalization of the Securities Markets", *Virginia Law Review* 95: 1025–1083.

Lanjouw, Jean O, and Philip I. Levy, 2002. "Untitled: A Study of Formal and Informal Property Rights in Urban Ecuador", *Economic Journal* 112: 986–1019.

Lanjouw, Jean O, and Philip I. Levy, 2004. "A Difficult Question in Deed: A Cost-Benefit Framework for Titling Programs", *William and Mary Law Review* 45: 889–952.

Lardy, Nicholas R., 2007. "China: Rebalancing Economic Growth", in C. Fred Bergsten, Bates Gill, Nicholas R. Lardy, and Derek J. Mitchell (eds.), *The China Balance Sheet in 2007 and Beyond*. Washington, D.C.: The Center for Strategic and International Studies and the Peterson Institute for International Economics.

Lardy, Nicholas R., 2008. "Financial Repression in China", The Peterson Institute for International Economics, *Policy Brief* 08–8.

Lardy, Nicholas R., 2012. *Sustaining China's Economic Growth After the Global Financial Crisis*. Washington, D.C.: Peterson Institute for International Economics.

Laurens, Bernard J., and Rodolfo Maino, 2007. *China: Strengthening Monetary Policy Implementation*. IMF Working Paper, WP/07/14. Washington, D.C.: International Monetary Fund.

Leeson, Peter T., 2007. "Better Off Stateless: Somalia Before and After Government Collapse", *Journal of Comparative Economics* 35: 689–710.

Leeson, Peter T., and Claudia R. Williamson, 2009. "Anarchy and Development: An Application of the Theory of Second Best", *Law and Development Review* 2 (1): 76–96.

Lele, Priya P., and Mathias M. Siems, 2007. "Shareholder Protection: A Leximetric Approach", *Journal of Corporate Law Studies* 7: 17–50.

Lerner, Abba, 1944. *The Economics of Control*. New York: The Macmillan Company.

Lerner, Josh, and Antoinette Schoar, 2005. "Does Legal Enforcement Affect Financial Transactions? The Contractual Channel in Private Equity", *Quarterly Journal of Economics* 120: 223–246.

Leuz, Christian, and Peter Wysocki, 2008. "Economic Consequences of Financial Reporting and Disclosure Regulation: A Review and Suggestion for Future Research", Working Paper, available at http://papers.ssrn.com/sol3/papers. cfm?abstract_id=1105398.

Levine, Ross, 1991. "Stock Markets, Growth, and Tax Policy", *Journal of Finance* 46: 1445–1465.

Levine, Ross, 1997. "Financial Development and Economic Growth: Views and Agenda", *Journal of Economic Literature* 35: 688–726.

Levine, Ross, 1998. "The Legal Environment, Banks, and Long-run Economic Growth", *Journal of Money, Credit, and Banking* 30: 596–620.

Levine, Ross, 1999. "Law, Finance, and Economic Growth", *Journal of Financial Intermediation* 8: 8–35.

Levine, Ross, 2002. "Bank-Based or Market-Based Financial Systems: Which Is Better", *Journal of Financial Intermediation* 11: 398–428.

Levine, Ross, 2005. "Finance and Growth: Theory and Evidence", in Philippe Aghion and Steven N. Durlauf (eds.), *Handbook of Economic Growth*. Amsterdam: Elsevier B.V.

Levine, Ross, Loayza, Norman, and Thorsten Beck, 2000. "Financial Intermediation and Growth: Causality and Causes", *Journal of Monetary Economics* 46: 31–77.

Levine, Ross, and Sara Zervos, 1998. "Stock Markets, Banks, and Economic Growth", *American Economic Review* 88: 537–558.

Li, Guo, Rozelle, Scott, and Loren Brandt, 1998. "Tenure, Land Rights, and Farmer Investment Incentives in China", *Agricultural Economics* 19: 63–71.

Li, Hongbin, and Li-An Zhou, 2005. "Political Turnover and Economic Performance: The Incentive Role of Personnel Control in China", *Journal of Public Economics* 89: 1743–1762.

Libecap, Gary D., 1989. *Contracting for Property Rights*. New York: Cambridge University Press.

Libecap, Gary D. 1998. "Common Property", in Peter Newman (ed.), *The New Palgrave Dictionary of Economics and Law*, London: Macmillan Reference LTD.

Liebman, Benjamin L., 2007. "China's Courts: Restricted Reform", *Columbia Journal of Asian Law* 21 (1): 1–44.

Liu, M.-H., D. Margaritis, and A. Tourani-Rad, 2009. "Monetary Policy and Interest Rate Rigidity in China", *Applied Financial Economics* 19: 647–657.

López, Ramón, 1997. "Environmental Externalities in Traditional Agriculture and the Impact of Trade Liberalization: The Case of Ghana", *Journal of Development Economics* 53: 17–39.

Lubman, Stanley, 1999. *Bird in a Cage: Legal Reform in China after Mao*. Stanford, CA: Stanford University Press.

Lubman, Stanley, 2000. "Bird in a Cage: Chinese Law Reform After Twenty Years", *Northwestern Journal of International Law and Business* 20: 383–423.

Lubman, Stanley, 2006. "Looking for Law in China", *Columbia Journal of Asian Law* 20 (1): 1–92.

Lucas, Robert Jr., 1988. "On the Mechanics of Economic Development", *Journal of Monetary Economics* 22: 3–42.

Lueck, Dean, 1994. "Common Property as an Egalitarian Share Contract", *Journal of Economic Behavior and Organization* 25: 93–108.

Lueck, Dean, and Thomas Miceli, 2007. "Property Law", in A. Mitchell Polinsky and Steven Shavell (eds.), *Handbook of Law and Economics*, Amsterdam: Elsevier B.V.

Ma, Guonan, and Wang Yi, 2010. *China's High Saving Rate: Myth and Reality*. Bank for International Settlements Working Paper, No. 312. Basel: Bank for International Settlements.

Mackaay, Ejan, 1999. "History of Law and Economics", in Boudewijn Bouckaert and Gerrit De Geest (eds.), *The Encyclopedia of Law and Economics*. Cheltenham: Edward Elgar.

Maddison, Angus, 2003. *The World Economy: A Millennial Perspective*. Paris: OECD Development Centre Studies.

Mahoney, Paul, 1995. "Mandatory Disclosure as a Solution to Agency Problems", *University of Chicago Law Review* 62: 1047–1112.

Mahoney, Paul, 2001. "The Common Law and Economic Growth: Hayek Might Be Right", *Journal of Legal Studies* 30: 503–525.

Mahoney, Paul, and Jianping Mei, 2008. "Mandatory vs. Contractual Disclosure in Securities Markets: Evidence from the 1930s", Working Paper, available at http://business.nd.edu/uploadedFiles/Academic_Centers/Study_of_Financial_Regulation/pdf_and_documents/MahoneyMei2008.pdf.

Mankiw, N. Gregory, Romer, David, and David N. Weil, 1992. "A Contribution to the Empirics of Economic Growth", *Quarterly Journal of Economics* 107: 407–437.

Manne, Henry G., 1965. "Mergers and the Market for Corporate Control", *Journal of Political Economy* 73: 110–120.

Manne, Henry G., 1966. *Insider Trading and the Stock Market*. New York: Free Press.

Matlon, Peter, 1994. "Indigenous Land Use Systems and Investment in Soil Fertility in Burkina Faso", in John Bruce and Shem Migot-Adholla (eds.), *Searching for Land Tenure Security in Africa*. Dubuque, IA: Kendall/Hunt.

Mattei, Ugo, 1997. *Comparative Law and Economics*. Ann Arbor: The University of Michigan Press.

McChesney, Fred S., 2003. "Government as Definer of Property Rights: Tragedy Exiting the Commons", in Terry L. Anderson and Fred S. McChesney (eds.), *Property Rights: Cooperation, Conflict, and Law*, Princeton: Princeton University Press.

McCloskey, Donald N., 1994. "1780–1860: A Survey", in Roderick Floud and Donald N. McCloskey (eds.), *The Economic History of Britain Since 1700*, Vol. I. Cambridge: Cambridge University Press.

McGregor, Richard, 2010. *The Party: The Secret World of China's Communist Rulers*. New York: HarperCollins Publishers.

McGuire, Martin C., and Mancur Olson, 1996. "The Economics of Autocracy and Majority Rule: The Invisible Hand and the Use of Force", *Journal of Economic Literature* 34: 72–96.

Mckean, Margaret A., 1982. "The Japanese Experience with Scarcity: Management of Traditional Common Lands", *Environmental Review* 6: 63–88.

Meinzen-Dick, Ruth, and Esther Mwangi, 2008. "Cutting the Web of Interests: Pitfalls of Formalizing Property Rights", *Land Use Policy* 26: 36–43.

Meng, Xin, and Junsen Zhang, 2001. "The Two-Tier Labor Market in Urban China: Occupational Segregation and Wage Differentials between Urban Residents and Rural Migrants in Shanghai", *Journal of Comparative Economics* 29: 485–504.

Mercuro, Nicholas, and Steven G. Medema, 1997. *Economics and the Law: From Posner to Post-Modernism*. Princeton, NJ: Princeton University Press.

Merrill, Thomas W., and Henry Smith, 2000. "Optimal Standardization in the Law of Property: The Numerus Clausus Principle", *Yale Law Journal* 110: 1–70.

Metrick, Andrew, 2008. "Insider Trading", in Steven N. Durlauf and Lawrence E. Blume (eds.), *The New Palgrave Dictionary of Economics* (Second Edition). London: Palgrave Macmillan.

Miceli, Thomas J., 1998. "Land Title Systems", in Peter Newman (ed.), *The New Palgrave Dictionary of Economics and Law*, London: Macmillan Reference Ltd.

Miceli, Thomas J., and C. F. Sirmans, 1995. "The Economics of Land Transfer and Title Insurance", *Journal of Real Estate Finance and Economics* 10: 81–88.

Miceli, Thomas J., Sirmans, C.F., and Geoffrey K. Turnbull, 1998. "Title Assurance and Incentives for Efficient Land Use", *European Journal of Law and Economics* 6: 305–323.

Miceli, Thomas J., Sirmans, C.F., and Geoffrey K. Turnbull, 2000. "The Dynamic Effects of Land Title Systems", *Journal of Urban Economics* 47: 370–389.

Migot-Adholla, Shem, Hazell, Peter, Blarel, Benoît, and Frank Place, 1991. "Indigenous Land Rights Systems in Sub-Saharan Africa: A Constraint on Productivity", *World Bank Economic Review* 5: 155–175.

Mikkelson, Wayne H., and M. Megan Partch, 1997. "The Decline of Takeovers and Disciplinary Managerial Turnover", *Journal of Financial Economics* 44: 205–228.

Milgrom, Paul R., North, Douglass C., and Barry R. Weingast, 1990. "The Role of Institutions in the Revival of Trade: the Law Merchant, Private Judges, and the Champagne Fairs", *Economics and Politics* 2: 1–23.

Milgrom, Paul R., and John Roberts, 1992. *Economics, Organization, and Management.* Englewood Cliffs, NJ: Prentice-Hall.

Milhaupt, Curtis J., and Katharina Pistor, 2008. *Law and Capitalism: What Corporate Crises Reveal about Legal Systems and Economic Development around the World.* Chicago: University of Chicago Press.

Milhaupt, Curtis J., and Mark D. West, 2000. "The Dark Side of Private Ordering: An Institutional and Empirical Analysis of Organized Crime", *University of Chicago Law Review* 67: 41–98.

Millstein, Ira M., and Paul W. MacAvoy, 1998. "The Active Board of Directors and Performance of the Large Actively Traded Corporation", *Columbia Law Review* 98: 1283–1321.

Minier, Jenny A., 1998. "Democracy and Growth: Alternative Approaches", *Journal of Economic Growth* 3: 241–266.

Mishkin, Frederic S., 2004. *The Economics of Money, Banking, and Financial Markets* (Seventh Edition). Upper Saddle River, NJ: Pearson Addison Wesley.

Mishkin, Frederic S., 2006. *The Next Great Globalization: How Disadvantaged Nations Can Harness Their Financial Systems to Get Rich.* Princeton, NJ: Princeton University Press.

Mitchell, Gregory, 2002. "Taking Behavioralism Too Seriously? The Unwarranted Pessimism of the New Behavioral Analysis of Law", *William and Mary Law Review* 43: 1907–2021.

Mitchell, Mark L., and Kenneth Lehn, 1990. "Do Bad Bidders Become Good Targets", *Journal of Political Economy* 98: 372–398.

Mokyr, Joel, 1990. *The Lever of Richs: Technological Creativity and Economic Progress.* New York: Oxford University Press.

Mokyr, Joel, 2008. "The Institutional Origins of the Industrial Revolution", in Elhanan Helpman (ed.), *Institutions and Economic Performance.* Cambridge, MA: Harvard University Press.

Mokyr, Joel, 2009. "Intellectual Property Rights, the Industrial Revolution, and the Beginnings of Modern Economic Growth", *American Economic Review* 99: 349–355.

Morck, Randall K., and Lloyd Steier, 2005. "The Global History of Corporate Governance: An Introduction", in Randall K. Morck (ed.), *A History of Corporate Governance around the World: Family Business Groups to Professional Managers.* Chicago: University of Chicago Press.

Morck, Randall, Wolfenzon, Daniel, and Bernard Yeung, 2005. "Corporate Governance, Economic Entrenchment, and Growth", *Journal of Economic Literature* 43: 655–720.

Morck, Randall K., and Bernard Yeung, 2010. "Corporatism and the Ghost of the Third Way", *Capitalism and Society* 5 (3): 1–59.

Morck, Randall, Yeung, Bernard, and Wayne Yu, 2000. "The Information Content of Stock Markets: Why Do Emerging Markets Have Synchronous Stock Price Movements", *Journal of Financial Economics* 58: 215–260.

Moselle, Boaz, and Benjamin Polak, 2001. "A Model of a Predatory State", *Journal of Law, Economics and Organization* 17: 1–33.

Mulherin, J. Harold, and Annette B. Poulsen, 1998. "Proxy Contests and Corporate Change: Implications for Shareholder Wealth", *Journal of Financial Economics* 47: 279–313.

Murphy, Kevin J., 1999. "Executive Compensation", in Orley Ashenfelter and David Card (eds.), *Handbook of Labor Economics*, Vol.3. Amsterdam: Elsevier Science B.V.

Murphy, Kevin M., Shleifer, Andrei, and Robert W. Vishny, 1991. "The Allocation of Talent: Implications for Growth", *Quarterly Journal of Economics* 106: 503–530.

Murphy, Kevin M., Shleifer, Andrei, and Robert W. Vishny, 1993. "Why is Rent-Seeking So Costly to Growth", *American Economic Review* 83: 409–414.

Musacchio, Aldo, 2008. "Can Civil Law Countries Get Good Institutions? Lessons from the History of Creditor Rights and Bond Markets in Brazil", *Journal of Economic History* 68: 80–108.

Musacchio, Aldo, 2010. "Law and Finance c. 1900", NBER Working Paper No.16216, available at www.nber.org/papers/w16216.

Myers, Norman, and Jennifer Kent, 2001. *Perverse Subsidies: How Tax Dollars Can Undercut the Environment and the Economy.* Washington, D.C.: Island Press.

Naughton, Barry, 2007. *The Chinese Economy: Transitions and Growth.* Cambridge, MA: MIT Press.

Naughton, Barry, 2008. "A Political Economy of China's Economic Transition", in Loren Brandt and Thomas G. Rawski (eds.), *China's Great Economic Transformation.* Cambridge: Cambridge University Press.

Nenova, Tatiana, 2003. "The Value of Corporate Voting Rights and Control: A Cross-Country Analysis", *Journal of Financial Economics* 68: 325–351.

Newkirk, Thomas C., and Melissa A. Robertson, 1998. "Insider Trading: A U.S. Perspective", Speech by SEC Stuff at the 16th International symposium on Economic Crime, available at www.sec.gov/news/speech/speecharchive/1998/spch221.htm.

North, Douglass C., 1981. *Structure and Change in Economic History.* New York: W.W. Norton & Company.

North, Douglass C., 1990. *Institutions, Institutional Change and Economic Performance.* New York: Cambridge University Press.

North, Douglass C., 1993. "Institutions and Credible Commitment", *Journal of Institutional and Theoretical Economics* 149: 11–23.

North, Douglass C., and Robert Paul Thomas, 1973. *The Rise of the Western World: A New Economic History.* New York: Cambridge University Press.

North, Douglass C., and Barry R. Weingast, 1989. "Constitutions and Commitment: The Evolution of Institutions Governing Public Choice in Seventeenth-Century England", *Journal of Economic History* 49: 803–832.

Obstfeld, Maurice, 1994. "Risk Taking, Global Diversification, and Growth", *American Economic Review* 84: 1310–1329.

OECD, 2006. *Challenges for China's Public Spending: Toward Greater Effectiveness and Equity*. Paris: OECD Publishing.

Ohnesorge, John K.M., 2003. "China's Economic Transition and the New Legal Origins Literature", *China Economic Review* 14: 485–493.

Olson, Mancur, 1993. "Dictatorship, Democracy, and Development", *American Political Science Review* 87: 567–576.

Olson, Mancur, 1996. "Big Bills Left on the Sidewalk: Why Some Nations are Rich, and Others Poor", *Journal of Economic Perspective* 10 (2): 3–24.

Olson, Mancur, 2000. *Power and Prosperity: Outgrowing Communist and Capitalist Dictatorships*. New York: Basic Books.

Ostrom, Elinor, 1990. *Governing the Commons: The Evolution of Institutions for Collective Action*. New York: Cambridge University Press.

Ostrom, Elinor, 1999. "Private and Common Property Rights", in B. Bouckaert and G. De Geest (eds.), *The Encyclopedia of Law and Economics*, Cheltenham: Edward Elgar.

Ostroy, Joseph M., and Ross M. Starr, 1990. "The Transactions Role of Money", in Benjamin M. Friedman and Frank H. Hahn (eds.), *Handbook of Monetary Economics*, Vol. 1. Amsterdam: Elsevier Science B.V.

O'Sullivan, Mary, 2007. "The Expansion of the U.S. Stock Market: 1885–1930: Historical Facts and Theoretical Fashions", *Enterprise and Society* 8 (3): 489–542.

Pacces, Alessio M., 2012. *Rethinking Corporate Governance: The Law and Economics of Control Powers*. New York: Routledge.

Pagano, Marco, and Paolo F. Volpin, 2005. "The Political Economy of Corporate Governance", *American Economic Review* 95: 1005–1030.

Pande, Rohini, and Christopher Udry, 2006. "Institutions and Development: A View from Below", in Richard Blundell, Whitney K. Newey, and Torsten Persson (eds.), *Advances in Economics and Econometrics: Theory and Applications* (Ninth World Congress). New York: Cambridge University Press.

Parisi, Francesco, and Jonathan Klick, 2003. "Functional Law and Economics: The Search of Value-Neutral Principles of Lawmaking", *Chicago-Kent Law Review* 79: 431–450.

Pattanayak, Subhrendu K., and Erin O. Sills, 2001. "Do Tropical Forests Provide Natural Insurance? The Microeconomics of Non-Timber Forest Product Collection in the Brazilian Amazon", *Land Economics* 77: 595–612.

Peerenboom, Randall, 2002. *China's Long March toward Rule of Law*. Cambridge: Cambridge University Press.

Pei, Minxin, 2001. "Does Legal Reform Protect Economic Transactions? Commercial Disputes in China", in Peter Murrell (ed.), *Assessing the Value of Law in Transition Economies*. Ann Arbor: University of Michigan Press.

Pei, Minxin, 2006. *China's Trapped Transition: The Limits of Developmental Autocracy*. Cambridge, MA: Harvard University Press.

Pejovich, Svetozar, 1990. *The Economics of Property Rights: Towards a Theory of Comparative Systems*. Dordrecht: Kluwer Academic Publishers.

Pender, John L., and John M. Kerr, 1998. "Determinants of Farmers' Indigenous Soil and Water Conservation Investments in Semi-Arid India", *Agricultural Economics* 19: 113–125.

Pender, John L., Nkonya, Ephraim, Jagger, Pamela, Sserunkuuma, Dick, and Henry Ssali, 2004. "Strategies to Increase Agricultural Productivity and Reduce Land Degradation: Evidence from Uganda", *Agricultural Economics* 31: 181–195.

Peng, Lin, and Ailsa Röell, 2008. "Executive Pay and Shareholder Litigation", *Review of Finance* 12: 141–184.

Perotti, Enrico C., and Ernst-Ludwig von Thadden, 2006. "The Political Economy of Corporate Control and Labor Rents", *Journal of Political Economy* 114: 145–174.

Persson, Torsten and Guido Tabellini, 1994. "Is Inequality Harmful for Growth", *American Economic Review* 84: 600–621.

Peters, Pauline E., 2004. "Inequality and Social Conflict over Land in Africa", *Journal of Agrarian Change* 4 (3): 269–314.

Pils, Eva, 2005. "Land Disputes, Rights Assertion, and Social Unrest in China: A Case from Sichuan", *Columbia Journal of Asian Law* 19: 235–292.

Pinckney, Thomas C., and Peter K. Kimuyu, 1994. "Land Tenure Reform in East Africa: Good, Bad, or Unimportant", *Journal of African Economics* 3 (1): 1–28.

Pipes, Richard, 1999. *Property and Freedom*. London: The Harvill Press.

Pirrong, Stephen C., 1995. "The Self-Regulation of Commodity Exchanges: The Case of Market Manipulation", *Journal of Law and Economics* 38: 141–206.

Pistor, Katharina, 2009. "Rethinking the 'Law and Finance' Paradigm", *Brigham Young University Law Review* 2009: 1647–1670.

Pistor, Katharina, and Chenggang Xu, 2003. "Fiduciary Duty in Transitional Civil Law Jurisdictions: Lessons from the Incomplete Law", in Curtis J. Milhaupt (ed.), *Global Markets, Domestic Institutions: Corporate Law and Governance in a New Era of Cross-Border Deals*. New York: Columbia University Press.

Pistor, Katharina, and Philip A. Wellons. 1999. *The Role of Law and Legal Institutions in Asian Economic Development: 1960–1995*. New York: Oxford University Press.

Pivot Capital Management, 2009. *China's Investment Boom: The Great Leap into the Unknown*. www.pivotcapital.com (accessed September 16, 2009).

Place, Frank, 2009. "Land Tenure and Agricultural Productivity in Africa: A Comparative Analysis of the Economics Literature and Recent Policy Strategies and Reforms", *World Development* 37: 1326–1336.

Place, Frank, and Peter Hazell, 1993. "Productivity Effects of Indigenous Land Tenure Systems in Sub-Saharan Africa", *American Journal of Agricultural Economics* 75: 10–19.

Place, Frank, and Keijiro Otsuka, 2001. "Tenure, Agricultural Investment, and Productivity in the Customary Tenure Sector of Malawi", *Economic Development and Cultural Change* 50 (1): 77–99.

Place, Frank, and Keijiro Otsuka, 2002. "Land Tenure Systems and Their impacts on Agricultural Investments and Productivity in Uganda", *Journal Development Studies* 38: 105–128.

Platteau, Jean-Philippe, 2000. *Institutions, Social Norms, and Economic Development*. Amsterdam: Harwood Academic Publishers.

Platteau, Jean-Philippe, and Patrick Francois, 2005. "Commons as Insurance and the Welfare Impact of Privatization", *Journal of Public Economics* 89: 211–231.

Polinsky, A. Mitchell, and Steven Shavell, 2007. *Handbook of Law and Economics.* Amsterdam: Elsevier B.V.

Polishchuk, Leonid, and Alexei Savvateev, 2004. "Spontaneous (Non)Emergence of Property Rights", *Economics of Transition* 12: 103–127.

Pomeranz, Kenneth, 2000. *The Great Divergence: China, Europe and the Making of the Modern World Economy.* Princeton, NJ: Princeton University Press.

Posner, Richard A., 1973. "An Economic Approach to Legal Procedure and Judicial Administration", *Journal of Legal Studies* 2: 399–458.

Posner, Richard A., 1995. *Overcoming Law.* Cambridge, MA: Harvard University Press.

Posner, Richard, 1998. "Rational Choice, Behavioral Economics, and the Law", *Stanford Law Review* 50: 1551–1575.

Posner, Richard A., 2002. *Economic Analysis of Law*, New York: Aspen Publishers.

Powell,Benjamin, Ford, Ryan, and Alex Nowrasteh, 2008. "Somalia after State Collapse: Chaos or Improvement", *Journal of Economic Behavior and Organization* 67: 657–670.

Prasad, Eswar S., and Raghuram G. Rajan, 2006. "Modernizing China's Growth Paradigm", *American Economic Review* 96 (2): 331–336.

Prentice, Robert A., 2006. "The Inevitability of a Strong SEC", *Cornell Law Review* 91: 775–839.

Pritchard, A.C., 1999. "Markets as Monitors: A Proposal to Replace Class Actions with Exchanges as Securities Fraud Enforcers", *Virginia Law Review* 85: 925–1020.

Pritchett, Lant, 2001. "Where Has All the Education Gone", *World Bank Economic Review* 15: 367–391.

Prosterman, Roy, Keliang Zhu, Jianping Ye, Jeffrey Riedinger, Ping Li, and Vandana Yadav, 2009. *Secure Land Rights as a Foundation for Broad-Based Rural Development in China: Results and Recommendations from a Seventeen-Province Survey.* National Bureau of Asian Research Special Report, No. 18. Seattle: National Bureau of Asian Research.

Putnam, Robert D., 1993. *Making Democracy Work: Civic Traditions in Modern Italy.* Princeton, NJ: Princeton University Press.

Qi, Li, and Penelope B. Prime, 2009. "Market Reforms and Consumption Puzzles in China", *China Economic Review* 20: 388–401.

Qian, Jun, and Philip E. Strahan, 2007. "How Laws and Institutions Shape Financial Contracts: The Case of Bank Loans", *Journal of Finance* 62: 2803–2834.

Qian, Yingyi, 2003. "How Reform Worked in China", in Dani Rodrik (ed.), *In Search of Prosperity: Analytical Narratives of Economic Growth.* Princeton, NJ: Princeton University Press.

Quinn, Stephen, 2001. "The Glorious Revolution's Effect on English Private Finance: A Microhistory, 1680–1705", *Journal of Economic History* 61: 593–615.

Quisumbing, Agnes R., Payongayong, Ellen, Aidoo, J.B., and Keijiro Otsuka, 2001. "Women's Land Rights in the Transition to Individualized Ownership: Implications for Tree-Resource Management in Western Ghana", *Economic Development and Cultural Change* 50: 157–182.

Rajan, Raghuram G., and Luigi Zingales, 1998. "Financial Dependence and Growth", *American Economic Review* 88: 559–586.

Rajan, Raghuram G., and Luigi Zingales, 2003a. "The Great Reversals: The Politics of Financial Development in the 20th Century", *Journal of Financial Economics* 69: 5–50.

Rajan, Raghuram G., and Luigi Zingales, 2003b. *Saving Capitalism from the Capitalists: Unleashing the Power of Financial Markets to Create Wealth and Spread Opportunity.* New York: Crown Business.

Robinson, Joan,1952. *The Rate of Interest and Other Essays.* London: MacMillan.

Rock, Edward B., 1991. "The Logic and (Uncertain) Significance of Institutional Shareholder Activism", *Georgetown Law Journal* 79: 445–506.

Rock, Edward, 2002. "Securities Regulation as Lobster Trap: A Credible Commitment Theory of Mandatory Disclosure", *Cardozo Law Review* 23: 675–704.

Rock, Edward B., and Michael L. Wachter, 2001. "Islands of Conscious Power: Law, Norms, and the Self-Governing Corporation", *University of Pennsylvania Law Review* 149: 1619–1700.

Rodriguez, Francisco, and Dani Rodrik, 2000. "Trade Policy and Economic Growth: A Skeptic's Guide to the Cross-National Evidence", *NBER Macroeconomics Annual* 15: 261–325.

Rodrik, Dani, 2003. "What Do We Learn from Country Narratives", in Dani Rodrik (ed.), *In Search of Prosperity: Analytic Narratives on Economic Growth.* Princeton, NJ: Princeton University Press.

Rodrik, Dani, 2005. "Growth Strategies", in Philippe Aghion and Steven N. Durlauf (eds.), *Handbook of Economic Growth*, Volume 1A. Amsterdam: Elsevier B.V.

Rodrik, Dani, 2007. *One Economics, Many Recipes: Globalization, Institutions, and Economic Growth.* Princeton, NJ: Princeton University Press.

Roe, Mark J., 2002. "Corporate Law's Limits", *Journal of Legal Studies* 31: 233–271.

Roe, Mark. J. 2003. *Political Determinants of Corporate Governance: Political Context, Corporate Impact.* New York: Oxford University Press.

Roe, Mark J., 2006. "Legal Origins, Politics, and Modern Stock Markets", *Harvard Law Review* 120: 460–527.

Roland, Gerard, 2000. *Transition and Economics: Politics, Markets, and Firms.* Cambridge, MA: MIT Press.

Roll, Richard, 1986. "The Hubris Hypothesis on Corporate Takeovers", *Journal of Business* 59: 176–216.

Romano, Roberta, 1991. "The Shareholder Suit: Litigation Without Foundation", *Journal of Law, Economics, and Organization* 7: 55–87.

Romano, Roberta, 1998. "Empowering Investors: A Market Approach to Securities Regulation", *Yale Law Journal* 107: 2359–2430.

Romano, Roberta, 2001. "The Need for Competition in International Securities Regulation", *Theoretical Inquiries in Law* 2: 387–501.

Romer, Paul, 1986. "Increasing Returns and Long-Run Growth", *Journal of Political Economy* 94: 1002–1037.

Root, Hilton, 1989. "Tying the King's Hands: Credible Commitments and Royal Fiscal Policy During the Old Regime", *Rationality and Society* 1: 240–258.

Rose, Amanda M., 2010. "The Multienforcer Approach to Securities Fraud Deterrence: An Critical Analysis", *University of Pennsylvania Law Review* 158: 2173–2231.

Rosenberg, Nathan, and L.E. Birdzell Jr., 1986. *How the West Grew Rich: The Economic Transformation of the Industrial World.* New York: Basic Books.

Roth, Michael, Cochrane, Jeff, and Wilberforce Kisamba-Mugerwa, 1994. "Tenure Security, Credit Use, and Farm Investment in the Rujumbura Pilot Land Registration Scheme, Uganda", in John Bruce and Shem Migot-Adholla (eds.), *Searching for Land Tenure Security in Africa*. Dubuque, IA: Kendall/Hunt.

Roumasset, James, Burnett, Kimberly, and Hua Wang, 2008. "Environmental Resources and Economic Growth", in Loren Brandt and Thomas G. Rawski (eds.), *China's Great Economic Transformation*. New York: Cambridge University Press.

Rousseau, Peter L., and Richard Sylla. 2003. "Financial Systems, Economic Growth, and Globalization", in Michael D. Bordo, Alan M. Taylor and Jeffrey G. Williamson (eds.), *Globalization in Historical Perspective*. Chicago: University of Chicago Press.

Rousseau, Peter L., and Richard Sylla. 2005. "Emerging Financial Markets and Early US Growth", *Explorations in Economic History* 42: 1–26.

Rousseau, Peter L., and Richard Sylla. 2006. "Financial Revolutions and Economic Growth: Introducing this EEH Symposium", *Explorations in Economic History* 43: 1–12.

Rousseau, Peter L., and Paul Wachtel, 2000. "Equity Markets and Growth: Cross-Country Evidence on Timing and Outcomes, 1980–1995", *Journal of Banking and Finance* 24: 1933–1957.

Rutherford, Malcolm, 1994. *Institutions in Economics: The Old and the New Institutionalism*. Cambridge: Cambridge University Press.

Ruttan, Lore M., 2008. "Economic Heterogeneity and the Commons: Effects on Collective Action and Collective Goods Provisioning", *World Development* 36 (5): 969–985.

Sachs, Jeffrey, and Andrew Warner, 1995. "Economic Reform and the Process of Global Integration", *Brookings Papers on Economic Activity* 1: 1–118.

Saint-Paul, Gilles, 1992. "Technological Choice, Financial Markets, and Economic Development", *European Economic Review* 36: 763–781.

Sarkar, Prabirjit, and Ajit Singh, 2010. "Law, Finance and Development: Further Analyses of Longitudinal Data", *Cambridge Journal of Economics* 34: 325–346.

Schauer, Frederick, 2004. "The Failure of the Common Law", *Arizona State Law Journal* 36: 765–782.

Schnyder, Gerhard, 2010. "Revisiting the Party Paradox of Finance Capitalism: Social Democratic Preferences and Corporate Governance Reforms in Switzerland, Sweden, and the Netherlands", *Comparative Political Studies* 44: 184–210.

Schotter, Andrew, 1981. *The Economic Theory of Social Institutions*. Cambridge, UK: Cambridge University Press.

Schumpeter, Joseph A. 1961 (original published in German, 1912). *The Theory of Economic Development: An Inquiry into Profits, Capital, Credit, Interest, and the Business Cycle*. New York: Oxford University Press.

Schweigert, Thomas, 2006. "Land Title, Tenure Security, Investment and Farm Output: Evidence from Guatemala", *Journal of Developing Areas* 40: 115–126.

Schwert, G. William, 2000. "Hostility in Takeovers: In the Eyes of the Beholder", *Journal of Finance* 55: 2599–2640.

Seligman, Joel, 2003. *The Transformation of Wall Street: A History of the Securities and Exchange Commission and Modern Corporate Finance.* New York: Aspen Publishers.

Sgard, Jérôme, 2006. "Do Legal Origins Matter? The Case of Bankruptcy Laws in Europe 1808–1914", *European Review of Economic History* 10: 389–419.

Shavell, Steven, 2004. *Foundations of Economic Analysis of Law.* Cambridge, MA: Belknap Press of Harvard University Press.

Shleifer, Andrei, 1998. "State versus Private Ownership", *Journal of Economic Perspectives* 12 (4): 133–150.

Shleifer, Andrei, and Lawrence Summers, 1988. "Breach of Trust in Hostile Takeovers", in Alan J. Auerbach (ed.), *Corporate Takeovers: Causes and Consequences.* Chicago: University of Chicago Press.

Shleifer, Andrei, and Robert W. Vishny, 1997. "A Survey of Corporate Governance", *Journal of Finance* 52: 737–783.

Siems, Mathias M., 2007. "Legal Origins: Reconciling Law & Finance and Comparative Law", *McGill Law Journal* 52: 55–81.

Siems, Mathias, and Simon Deakin, 2010. "Comparative Law and Finance: Past, Present, and Future Research", *Journal of Institutional and Theoretical Economics* 166: 120–140.

Sirri, Eric R., and Peter Tufano, 1995. "The Economics of Pooling", in Dwight B. Crane et al. (eds.), *The Global Financial System: A Functional Perspective.* Boston, MA: Harvard Business School Press.

Sjaastad, Espen, and Daniel W. Bromley, 1997. "Indigenous Land Rights in Sub-Saharan Africa: Appropriation, Security, and Investment Demand", *World Development* 25: 549–562.

Skaperdas, Stergios, 1992. "Cooperation, Conflict, and Power in the Absence of Property Rights", *American Economic Review* 82: 720–739.

Smith, Adam, [1776] 1976. *An Inquiry into the Nature and Causes of the Wealth of Nations.* Chicago: University of Chicago Press.

Smith, Henry E., 2000. "Semicommon Property Rights and Scattering in the Open Fields", *Journal of Legal Studies* 29: 131–169.

Snowdon, Brian, and Howard R. Vane, 2005. *Modern Macroeconomics: Its Origins, Development and Current States.* Cheltenham, UK; Northampton, MA, USA: Edward Elgar.

Sokoloff, Kenneth L., and Stanley L. Engerman, 2000. "History Lessons: Institutions, Factor Endowments, and Paths of Development in the New World Economies", *Journal of Economic Perspectives* 14 (3): 217–232.

Solow, Robert M., 1956. "A Contribution to the Theory of Economic Growth", *Quarterly Journal of Economics* 70: 65–94.

Solow, Robert M., 1957. "Technical Change and the Aggregate Production Function", *Review of Economics and Statistics* 39: 312–320.

Sonin, Konstantin, 2003. "Why the Rich May Favor Poor Protection of Property Rights", *Journal of Comparative Economics* 31: 715–731.

Spamann, Holger, 2008. "'Law and Finance' Revisited", *Harvard John M. Olin Fellow's Discussion Paper,* No. 12.

Spamann, Holger, 2010. "The 'Antidirector Rights Index' Revisited", *Review of Financial Studies* 23 (2): 467–486.

Stasavage, David, 2003. *Public Debt and the Birth of the Democratic State: France and Great Brittan, 1688–1789.* New York: Cambridge University Press.

Stasavage, David, 2007. "Partisan Politics and Public Debt: The Importance of the 'Whig Supremacy' for Britain's Financial Revolution", *European Review of Economic History* 11: 123–153.

Stewart, G. Bennett, 1990. "Remaking the Corporation from Within", *Harvard Business Review* 68 (4): 126–137.

Stigler, George J., 1964. "Public Regulation of the Securities Markets", *Journal of Business* 37: 117–142.

Stigler, George J., 1970. "The Optimum Enforcement of Laws", *Journal of Political Economy* 78: 526–536.

Stokes, Shannon, Schutjer, Wayne A., and Rodolfo A. Bulatao, 1986. "Is the Relationship between Landholding and Fertility Spurious? A Response to Cain", *Population Studies* 40: 305–311.

Stout, Lynn A., 2003. "The Shareholder as Ulysses: Some Empirical Evidence on Why Investors in Public Corporations Tolerate Board Governance", *University of Pennsylvania Law Review* 152: 667–712.

Stout, Lynn A., 2007. "The Mythical Benefits of Shareholder Control", *Virginia Law Review* 93: 789–809.

Stulz, Rene M., Walkling, Ralph A., and Moon H. Song, 1990. "The Distribution of Target Ownership and the Division of Gains in Successful Takeovers", *Journal of Finance* 45: 817–833.

Stulz, Rene M., and Rohan Williamson, 2003. "Culture, Openness, and Finance", *Journal of Financial Economics* 70: 313–349.

Sussman, Nathan, and Yishay Yafeh, 2006. "Institutional Reforms, Financial Development and Sovereign Debt: Britain 1690–1790", *Journal of Economic History* 66: 906–935.

Sylla, Richard, 2006. "Schumpeter Redux: A Review of Raghuram G. Rajan and Luigi Zingales's *Saving Capitalism from the Capitalists*", *Journal of Economic Literature* 44: 391–404.

Tao, Ran, Fubing Su, Mingxing Liu, and Guangzhong Cao, 2010. "Land Leasing and Local Public Finance in China's Regional Development: Evidence from Prefecture-level Cities", *Urban Studies* 47 (10): 2217–2236.

Thompson, Robert B., 2003. "Collaborative Corporate Governance: Listing Standards, State Law, and Federal Regulation", *Wake Forest Law Review* 38: 961–982.

Thompson, Robert B., and Hillary A. Sale, 2003. "Securities Fraud as Corporate Governance: Reflections upon Federalism", *Vanderbilt Law Review* 56: 859–910.

Tirole, Jean, 2006. *The Theory of Corporate Finance.* Princeton, NJ: Princeton University Press.

Travlos, Nickolaos G., 1987. "Corporate Takeover Bids, Methods of Payment, and Bidding Firms' Stock Return", *Journal of Finance* 42: 943–963.

Trebilcock, Michael, and Jing Leng, 2006. "The Role of Formal Contract Law and Enforcement in Economic Development", *Virginia Law Review* 92: 1517–1580.

Trebilcock, Michael, and Paul-Erik Veel, 2008. "Property Rights and Development: The Contingent Case for Formalization", *University of Pennsylvania Journal of International Law* 30: 397–481.

Umbeck, John, 1981. "Might Makes Rights: A Theory of the Formation and Initial Distribution of Property Rights", *Economic Inquiry* 19: 38–59.

Varian, Hal R., 2005. *Intermediate Microeconomics: A Modern Approach.* New York: W.W. Norton & Company.

Veasey, E. Norman, 2007. "The Stockholder Franchise Is Not a Myth: A Response to Professor Bebchuk", *Virginia Law Review* 93: 811–825.

Velasco, Julian, 2010. "How Many Fiduciary Duties Are There in Corporate Law", *Southern California Law Review* 83: 1231–1318.

Verspoor, Adriaan, 1990. "Educational Development: Priorities for the Nineties", *Finance and Development* 27: 20–23.

Wade, Robert. 1990. *Governing the Market: Economic Theory and the Role of Government in East Asian Industrialization.* Princeton, NJ: Princeton University Press.

Wade, Robert, 1994. *Village Republics: Economic Conditions for Collective Action in South India.* San Francisco, CA: ICS Press.

Wang, Hua, Mamingi, Nlandu, Laplante, Benoit, and Susmita Dasgupta, 2003. "Incomplete Enforcement of Pollution Regulation: Bargaining Power of Chinese Factories", *Environmental and Resource Economics* 24: 245–262.

Wang, Hua, and David Wheeler, 1996. "Pricing Industrial Pollution in China: An Econometric Analysis of the Levy System", World Bank Policy Research Working Paper 1644.

Wang, Hua, and David Wheeler, 2005. "Financial Incentives and Endogenous Enforcement in China's Pollution Levy System", *Journal of Environmental Economics and Management* 49: 174–196.

Weber, Max, 1930. *The Protestant Ethic and the Spirit of Capitalism.* London: Allen and Unwin.

Weil, David N., 2005. *Economic Growth.* Boston: Addison-Wesley.

Wen, Guanzhong James, 1995. "The Land Tenure System and Its Saving and Investment Mechanism: The Case of Modern China", *Asian Economic Journal* 9: 223–259.

Wilhelm, Katherine, 2004. "Rethinking Property Rights in Urban China", *UCLA Journal of International Law and Foreign Affairs* 9: 227–299.

Winter, Ralph, 1977. "State Law, Shareholder Protection, and the Theory of the Corporation", *Journal of Legal Studies* 6: 251–292.

World Bank, 1993. *The East Asian Miracle: Economic Growth and Public Policy.* New York: Oxford University Press.

World Bank, 2001. *Finance for Growth: Policy Choices in a Volatile World.* New York: Oxford University Press.

World Bank, 2002. *Building Institutions for Markets.* Oxford: Oxford University Press.

World Bank, 2007. *Cost of Pollution in China: Economic Estimates of Physical Damages.* Washington, D.C.: World Bank.

World Bank, 2009. *China-From Poor Areas to Poor People: China's Evolving Poverty Reduction Agenda -An Assessment of Poverty and Inequality in China.* Washington, D.C.: World Bank.

World Bank, 2012a. *China – Land Transfer and Registration Technical Assistance: Report on Survey of Rural Households and Other Stakeholders in Anhui and Shandong Provinces.* http://documents.shihang.org/curated/zh/2012/01/16418165/china-land-transfer-registration-technical-assistance-report-survey-rural-households-other-stakeholders-anhui-shandong-provinces (accessed June 10, 2012).

World Bank, 2012b. *Doing Business 2012: Doing Business in a More Transparent World.* www.doingbusiness.org/~/media/FPDKM/Doing%20Business/Documents/Annual-Reports/English/DB12-FullReport.pdf (accessed October 19, 2013).

Wright, Robert E., 2002. *The Wealth of Nations Rediscovered: Integration and Expansion in American Financial Markets, 1780–1850.* Cambridge: Cambridge University Press.

Wurgler, Jeffery, 2000. "Financial Markets and the Allocation of Capital", *Journal of Financial Economics* 58: 187–214.

Xu, Guangdong, 2011. "The Role of Law in Economic Growth: A Literature Review", *Journal of Economic Surveys* 25 (5): 833–871.

Xu, Guangdong, 2013. "Property Rights, Law, and Economic Development", *Law and Development Review* 6 (1): 117–142.

Xu, Guangdong, 2014 (forthcoming). "Is China an Anomaly for the 'Law Matters' Hypothesis?" *Asian Journal of Law and Society.*

Xu, Guangdong, and Binwei Gui, 2013. "The Connection between Financial Repression and Economic Growth: The Case of China", *Journal of Comparative Asian Development* 12 (3): 385–410.

Xu, Guangdong, and Tianshu Zhou, 2013. "Is Implementing Fiduciary Duties in a Civil Law Country Feasible? The Case of China", *Company and Securities Law Journal* 31 (6): 378–398.

Yang, Dennis Tao, Vivian Weijia Chen, and Ryan Monarch, 2010. "Rising Wages: Has China Lost Its Global Labor Advantage?" *Pacific Economic Review* 15 (4): 482–504.

Yang, Dennis Tao, Zhang, Junsen, and Shaojie Zhou, 2011. "Why Are Saving Rates so High in China", NBER Working Paper 16771.

Yao, Yang. 2010a. "China Model and Its Future", in Ross Garnaut, Jane Golley, and Ligang Song (eds.), *China: The Next Twenty Years of Reform and Development.* Canberra: ANU E Press.

Yao, Yang, 2010b. "The End of the Beijing Consensus: Can China's Model of Authoritarian Growth Survive", *Foreign Affairs* (Online), 2 February. www.foreignaffairs.com/articles/65947/the-end-of-the-beijing-consensus.

Young, Alwyn, 1994. "Lessons From the East Asian NICs: A Contrarian View", *European Economic Review* 38: 964–973.

Young, Alwyn, 1995. "The Tyranny of Numbers: Confronting the Statistical Realities of the East Asian Growth Experience", *Quarterly Journal of Economics* 110: 641–680.

Yu, Guanghua, and Hao Zhang, 2008. "Adaptive Efficiency and Financial Development in China: The Role of Contracts and Contractual Enforcement", *Journal of International Economic Law* 11: 459–494.

Yu, Yongding, 2010. "A Different Road Forward", *China Daily*, December 23, 2010.

Yusuf, Shahid, and Kaoru Nabeshima, 2006. *China's Development Priorities.* Washington, D.C.: World Bank.

Zagorchev, Andrey, Vasconcellos, Geraldo, and Youngsoo Bae, 2011. "The Long-run Relation among Financial Development, Technology and GDP: A Panel Cointegration Study", *Applied Financial Economics* 21: 1021–1034.

Zak, Paul J., and Stephen Knack, 2001. "Trust and Growth", *Economic Journal* 111: 295–321.

Zerbe Jr., Richard O., 2001. *Economic Efficiency in Law and Economics*. Northampton, MA: Edward Elgar.

Zhang, Xiaobo, 2007. "Asymmetric Property Rights in China's Economic Growth", *William Mitchell Law Review* 33: 567–589.

Zheng, Yin Lily, 2009. "It's Not What Is on Paper, but What Is in Practice: China's New Labor Contract Law and the Enforcement Problem", *Washington University Global Studies Law Review* 8: 595–617.

Zhu, Keliang, Roy Prosterman, Jianping Ye, Ping Li, Jeffrey Riedinger, and Yiwen Ouyang, 2006. "The Rural Land Question in China: Analysis and Recommendations Based on a Seventeen-Province Survey", *New York University Journal of International Law and Politics* 38: 761–839.

Zhu, Keliang, and Roy Prosterman, 2007. *Securing Land Rights for Chinese Farmers: A Leap Forward for Stability and Growth*. Center for Global Liberty & Prosperity Development Policy Analysis, No. 3. Washington, D.C.: Center for Global Liberty & Prosperity.

Zingales, Luigi, 1995. "What Determines the Value of Corporate Votes?" *Quarterly Journal of Economics* 110: 1047–1073.

Zweigert, Konrad, and Hein Kötz, 1998. *An Introduction to Comparative Law*. New York: Oxford University Press.

About the author

Guangdong Xu obtained a Bachelor in Economics from the Renmin University of China (People's University of China) (1994) and a PhD in Economics from the Graduate School of The Chinese Academy of Social Science (2004). Since 2009 he has been an Associate Professor of Law and Economics at China University of Political Science and Law.